About Island Press

Since 1984, the nonprofit organization Island Press has been stimulating, shaping, and communicating ideas that are essential for solving environmental problems worldwide. With more than 1,000 titles in print and some 30 new releases each year, we are the nation's leading publisher on environmental issues. We identify innovative thinkers and emerging trends in the environmental field. We work with world-renowned experts and authors to develop cross-disciplinary solutions to environmental challenges.

Island Press designs and executes educational campaigns, in conjunction with our authors, to communicate their critical messages in print, in person, and online using the latest technologies, innovative programs, and the media. Our goal is to reach targeted audiences—scientists, policy makers, environmental advocates, urban planners, the media, and concerned citizens—with information that can be used to create the framework for long-term ecological health and human well-being.

Island Press gratefully acknowledges major support from The Bobolink Foundation, Caldera Foundation, The Curtis and Edith Munson Foundation, The Forrest C. and Frances H. Lattner Foundation, The JPB Foundation, The Kresge Foundation, The Summit Charitable Foundation, Inc., and many other generous organizations and individuals.

The opinions expressed in this book are those of the author(s) and do not necessarily reflect the views of our supporters.

Barons

Barons

MONEY, POWER, AND THE CORRUPTION OF AMERICA'S FOOD INDUSTRY

Austin Frerick

ISLANDPRESS | Washington | Covelo

Library of Congress Control Number: 2023945763

All Island Press books are printed on environmentally responsible materials.

Manufactured in the United States of America
10 9 8 7 6 5 4 3 2

This book builds on the following publications:

- Austin Frerick, "Big Meat, Small Towns: The Meatpacking Industry's Shift to Rural America and the Reemergence of Company Towns" (Grinnell College thesis, May 2012)
- Charlie Mitchell and Austin Frerick, "The Hog Barons," Vox and Food & Environment Reporting Network, April 19, 2021
- Austin Frerick and Charlie Mitchell, "Multinational Meat Farms Could Be Making Us Sick," *American Conservative*, April 21, 2020
- Austin Frerick, "The Outsourcing of America's Food," *American Conservative*, June 2, 2021
- Austin Frerick, "Rise of Majority-Minority Districts in Rural Iowa: How Changes in Meatpacking Impacted Rural Schooling" (Grinnell College thesis, August 2011)
- Austin Frerick, "To Revive Rural America, We Must Fix Our Broken Food System," *American Conservative*, February 27, 2019

Keywords: agricultural checkoffs; antitrust; Joesley Batista; Wesley Batista; Robert Bork; Louis Brandeis; CAFO (concentrated animal feeding operation); Cargill; commodity crops; company towns; confinement shed; contract farming; corporate consolidation; dairy farmers; Driscoll's; ethanol; family farm; Farm Bill; food system; Iowa; Iowa Select Farms; JAB Holding Company; JBS; Jeff and Deb Hansen; local food; locally owned; Mike and Sue McCloskey; monopoly; obesity; offshore produce; regional food supply chains; J. Miles Reiter; Garland Reiter; Robinson-Patman Act; sharecropping; slaughterhouse workers; small business; sustainable agriculture; USDA; Tom Vilsack; Walmart; Sam Walton

I dedicate this book to my husband, Daniel Honberg.

Contents

Foreword

ADAM SMITH DIDN'T LIKE MONOPOLIES. The great theorist and champion of capitalism believed that free markets were essential for the creation of an ideal society, one that would be guided by "a liberal plan of equality, liberty, and justice."[1] His most influential book, *The Wealth of Nations* (1776), offered a savage critique of mercantilism and "the wretched spirit of monopoly" that guided economic policies during the eighteenth century.[2] The book was partly inspired by the predatory behavior of the East India Company, which dominated Great Britain's colonial trade. While celebrating entrepreneurial risk-taking, Smith warned that merchants and manufacturers were "an order of men, whose interest is never exactly the same with that of the public, who have generally an interest to deceive and even to oppress the public."[3] They would always try to limit competition, gain excessive profits, and "levy, for their own benefit, an absurd tax upon the rest of their fellow-citizens."[4] Any new laws or government regulations proposed by merchants and manufacturers should be regarded with suspicion—and never adopted without careful scrutiny, Smith argued. Unchecked market power was antithetical to individual rights and "a system of natural liberty."[5]

The Founding Fathers of the United States shared Adam Smith's views of monopoly power. The Boston Tea Party, a pivotal event in the years leading to the American Revolution, was provoked not only by the tax policies of the British government but also by the monopoly on tea imports granted to the East India Company. Years later, Thomas Jefferson's principal critique of the Constitution of the United States was that it lacked a "bill of rights" guaranteeing basic freedoms. "By a declaration of rights I mean one which shall stipulate freedom of religion, freedom of the press, freedom of commerce against monopolies, trial by juries in all cases, no suspension of the habeas corpus, no standing armies," Jefferson wrote to a friend. "These are fetters against doing evil which no honest government should decline."[6] When the Bill of Rights was finally adopted, it didn't include a restriction on monopolies. But economic freedom was widely assumed to be an absolute necessity. In a letter to Jefferson, the rationale for that freedom was made clear by James Madison: "Monopolies are sacrifices of the many to the few."[7]

Roughly two hundred fifty years later, almost every sector of the American economy is dominated by a handful of corporations. Ever since the administration of President Ronald Reagan in the 1980s, the rhetoric of the free market has been cleverly used to thwart government oversight of corporate power, block antitrust enforcement—and eliminate free markets. When four firms control 40 percent or more of a market for products or services, true competition no longer exists. Instead you have monopolies, monopsonies (too few buyers), and oligopolies (too few sellers). Today, three firms control 61 percent of the American market for eyeglasses and contact lenses, three firms control 67 percent of the drugstore market, four firms control 76 percent of the market for air travel, and on and on. From birth until death, Americans must now confront markets that are anything but free. Two firms now control 64 percent of the market for disposable diapers—and two firms control 82 percent of the market for coffins.

Unchecked market power allows corporations to charge unfair prices, stifle innovation, set the prices paid to independent producers, break labor unions, and cut wages. It is the central driving force of inequality. During the past three decades, adjusted for inflation, the annual compensation of American workers has increased by about 18 percent—and the annual compensation of chief executive officers at the largest American corporations has increased by about 1,300 percent. In 1978, the compensation of the average CEO was about 30 times larger than that of the typical worker. By 2020, it was about 350 times larger. Meanwhile, the inflation-adjusted value of the federal minimum wage has declined from $12.54 to $7.50 since the early 1970s. As a result, the poorest workers in the United States have had their wages cut by about 40 percent.

All of these trends have come together to transform the most important sector of the American economy: the food system. And that is why *Barons* is such an urgently important book. The way in which the United States produces and distributes its food has a profound effect on worker rights, animal welfare, air quality, water quality, the landscape, rural communities, public health, international trade, and the global climate. Even the DNA of sentient creatures is now owned, manipulated, and sold to American farmers by a handful of corporations. Four companies control 66 percent of hog genetics; three companies control 95 percent of broiler chicken genetics; two companies control 99 percent of turkey genetics.

Austin Frerick is an ideal author to tell this story. He possesses a deep understanding of antitrust policy and agricultural economics. He has learned the names and faces behind these supposedly rational and impartial corporations. More important, he has a personal stake in the outcome. He's seen firsthand the impact of our industrial food system upon his home state of Iowa. He's witnessed the hollowing out of rural towns in the Midwest, the sickening pollution from factory farms, the inchoate anger and political extremism that stem from growing inequality. He knows that nothing less than our democracy is now at stake.

More than a century ago, when monopoly power posed similar threats to American society, Henry Demarest Lloyd warned about the danger in his classic book *Wealth against Commonwealth* (1894). "Monopoly cannot be content with controlling its own business," Lloyd wrote.[8] "Its lobbyists force the nomination of judges who will construe the laws as Power desires, and of senators who will get passed such laws as it wants for its judges to construe. . . . The press, too, must be controlled by Power."[9] *Barons* is a work in that great tradition of muckraking, an effort to expose corruption and misrule. I share Frerick's belief that the system we have now was not inevitable, that a better one is still possible, that the battle against unchecked corporate power is still worth fighting and can be won, that you could hardly find a set of ideals more relevant today, more necessary, more deserving of being finally lived and fulfilled than "equality, liberty, and justice."

Eric Schlosser
August 22, 2023

Introduction

WHEN I WAS YOUNG, MY FAMILY AND I would visit relatives in a corner of northeast Iowa known as the Driftless region. As we drove through green rolling hills, I'd stare out the window at pastures dotted with dairy cows and hogs. Corn was common, of course, but so were apple orchards and other crops. The landscape was alive.

I still go up to the Driftless; my parents park their camper up there to this day. But the land is now brown and barren, except during the few months of the year when corn and soybeans grow. These two commodities have spread like a prairie fire, and the apples and other crops that used to be grown all over the state are now sourced from well beyond its borders.

The road to the Driftless used to pass through vibrant small towns, but they've since been bypassed by multimillion-dollar highways that were built only so these commodities can leave the state a few minutes quicker. The local businesses have closed, replaced by national chains on the outskirts of town. A state that was once referred to as the "Middle Land"—both because of its geographic location right in the heart of the continental United States and because of its moderate politics and strong middle class—is now defined by its reactionary political land-scape and decaying towns.

The most jarring change is that the animals have disappeared from view. At some point, they started vanishing: first pigs, then cows. The red barns that used to house them sit abandoned or have been knocked down to plant more corn or beans. But even though you no longer see them, the hogs aren't gone. When you get a few miles outside town, you begin to sense—first smell, then see—clusters of massive windowless sheds. You would never guess that each one of them holds almost 2,500 pigs, until the thick stench of manure wafts in your direction. At this point, the countryside is so industrial that it no longer feels like coun-tryside at all.

I initially set out to write this book as a way to figure out why my home state has changed so dramatically since my childhood. Agriculture is to Iowa what motion pictures are to Hollywood, the cornerstone of the state's economy and the root of its identity. The state is blessed with some of the world's best soil: "black gold," which, coupled with con-sistently good rainfall, makes for ideal farming conditions. I wanted to understand how this blessing has, over the past forty years, turned into a curse.

But as I dug into that question, it became clear to me that these impacts go far beyond the state's borders. Researching and writing this book has taken me across the country, from the Pajaro Valley in Califor-nia to the remnants of the Grand Kankakee Marsh in Indiana and from the deserts of New Mexico to the booming towns of Northwest Arkan-sas. Though it's an American story at its heart, it's one that involves places as far-flung as Mexico, Germany, and Brazil.

The same forces that devastated my home state were unleashed by a series of fundamental changes to the American food system that have had profound consequences across the country and beyond. A set of legal and policy changes driven by a radical laissez-faire ideology has resulted in a dramatic concentration of power in the American food industry.

This book is about how that transformation occurred and what it has meant for workers, families, and communities. I decided to tell this story through the rise of a series of powerful actors in the industry who have benefited from, and in some cases helped bring about, this shift. I refer to these people as "barons" to hearken back to Gilded Age robber barons such as John D. Rockefeller and J. P. Morgan because I believe that we are living in a parallel moment when a few titans have the power to shape industries.

Although monopolies are common across the economy, there are few sectors more consolidated than the American food system. The following profiles of seven food industry barons show how each one built an empire by taking advantage of deregulation to amass extreme wealth at the expense of everyone else.

I start the book close to my home in Iowa, where a couple named Jeff and Deb Hansen have built an empire of hog confinements in the face of public opposition by capturing the state's government. This relatively new model of production tends to destroy surrounding communities and environments, which is a big reason why 61 percent of Iowa's rivers and streams and 67 percent of its lakes and reservoirs do not meet basic water quality standards.

I then profile the Cargill-MacMillan family, the owners of Cargill, the largest private company in America. The fortunes of the family mirror the history of the American Farm Bill. In particular, Cargill has benefited from a new approach to the Farm Bill that functions to subsidize corn and soy above almost everything else, which has dramatically reshaped our diets.

In the third chapter, I spotlight the mysterious Reimanns, a reclusive German family with historical ties to the Third Reich. The Reimann family, through a venture called JAB Holding Company, first entered the coffee industry in 2012 but now trails only Nestlé in the global market. The family accumulated this power through an aggressive acquisition spree that may have been permitted only because of a shift in antitrust and competition policy.

From there, I move to Northwest Indiana, where Mike and Sue McCloskey run a massive dairy operation that pumps more than four million school milk cartons' worth of milk per day. The rise of their empire, which came at a time when many family dairy farms were being run out of business, illustrates the importance of powerful agricultural entities called "checkoffs" that were established to help family farmers but now seemingly undermine them.

I then head west and dive into the rise of Driscoll's, the berry company built by the brothers J. Miles and Garland Reiter. Although their operation now employs over one hundred thousand people across every continent except Antarctica and the name has become synonymous with berries in American grocery stores, Driscoll's itself doesn't actually grow any berries. Rather, the company has accrued power through a production model that abdicates responsibility for labor and environmental issues by outsourcing the farming of its berries to independent contractors and, increasingly, out of the country entirely.

Next, I tell the story of Joesley and Wesley Batista. Their company, JBS Foods, butchers almost enough meat daily to give a four-ounce portion to every citizen of Australia, Canada, Poland, Spain, and Italy combined. Although they rose to power by skirting the law, they've faced minimal repercussions for their actions. Their ability to grow unchecked has come at the expense of workers, who often toil in conditions that give the slaughterhouses in Upton Sinclair's *The Jungle* a run for their money.

And finally, I dig into the Walton family and Walmart's grocery business. You might think you know all about Walmart's power, but the story frequently told about the company and its impacts is just the tip of the iceberg. Although it sells a bit of everything in its physical stores and online, Walmart is, at its core, a grocery company. In fact, it dominates the American grocery market so thoroughly that it has about the same market share as the number two, three, four, five, six, seven, and eight grocery store companies *combined*. As Walmart has grown, its power has compounded, reshaping not just the grocery industry but the entire food system.

The purpose of this book isn't to gawk at these barons or to suggest that they are uniquely responsible for the corruption of the American food system. In fact, I have a whole series of "B-side barons" that unfortunately just missed the cut but could have been included to illustrate many of the same points.

Rather, I want to use the barons to facilitate an honest conversation about what we eat and how it gets to our plate. In that way, this book is less about the specific barons themselves than it is about the conditions that facilitated their rise to power. I hope these stories give you a better sense of how the American food system was corrupted and why it matters for all of us.

Our food system may not get a lot of attention in political debates, but it has a profound impact on who we are and the way we live. Millions of Americans work in the food industry—as waiters, cooks, grocery store clerks, and cashiers; as farmers and farmworkers; as beer salesmen and small business owners and slaughterhouse workers.

In fact, the food system accounts for more than one-tenth of all jobs in the United States, and agriculture is one piece of a bigger puzzle: only 12 percent of food workers are farmers.[1] These jobs have traditionally been one of the most direct pathways to the middle class. Generations of Americans, including many immigrants, have looked to the sector as a launching pad for upward mobility.

Whether you work in the food system or not, it unquestionably affects your life, often in unseen ways. The food we consume and the way it is produced has enormous implications for our health and our environment. It affects the strength of our cities and towns, the cleanliness of our air and our water, and, in the face of global climate change, the livability of our planet.

On a more fundamental level, everyone eats. Food is incredibly important to our sense of identity and culture. It has a way of bringing people together and building community. As Anthony Bourdain once put it, "Food is everything we are. It's an extension of nationalist feeling, ethnic feeling, your personal history, your province, your region, your tribe, your grandma. It's inseparable from those from the get-go."[2] Local businesses in the food industry are an integral part of what makes a place a *place*.

As I wrote this book, it became clear to me how much the food system has influenced me and my family. I grew up helping my grandpa farm his plot and working with my mom in her bakery. My dad spent his entire career working in the food system, first as a beer truck driver and then at a corn processing plant. I've seen firsthand what the concentration of power in the American food system means for Iowa and for my hometown, Cedar Rapids. These experiences, and the institutions around me, shaped how I view food and local businesses.

But this story isn't specific to me; it could be told about any state and thousands of cities and towns across the country. I hope that reading this book will lead you to take a step back and realize just how much the corruption of the American food system has affected your family and community.

And though the issues raised here might seem overwhelming, I find them invigorating because history provides a road map for how to deal with unchecked concentrated power. In writing this book, I've had the honor of meeting so many people who are fighting to build a better food system. I'm confident that a bipartisan coalition can be mobilized to usher in what Alice Waters calls a "delicious revolution."

But to do so, we must first understand how we arrived where we are today. One point that's clear from the stories of these barons and from the history of the American food system is that power does not disperse organically. We have an opportunity to turn the corner and build a more balanced food system, but only if we challenge power directly.

CHAPTER 1

The Hog Barons

JULIE DUHN REMEMBERS HER FIRST TIME KAYAKING mostly for its after-math. When Duhn retired from her office job, she decided to start experimenting with the sport at Pine Lake State Park, near her home in Eldorado, Iowa. The collection of campgrounds and trails rings two small lakes that trickle into the Iowa River and is surrounded by rolling farmland. It was a hot afternoon in mid-August, just a few weeks after her first outing, when Duhn's arms began to itch, then grow red and raw. She consulted a doctor, who, after learning about her kayaking trip, blamed the rash on the lake water.

Indeed, the Iowa Department of Natural Resources has considered Pine Lake unsafe for human contact since 2012. It keeps a sign posted on the beach to discourage visitors from wading in. The problem is an overgrowth of algae, which feed on the phosphorus that continually flows into the lake from nearby farm fields spread with fertilizer and manure. A state report concluded that one clear contributor is the waste produced by the ten thousand hogs in the lake's watershed.[1]

Iowa has long been known for hog farming and was once dotted with idyllic barns to house the animals. But today, most of the state's hogs spend their lives in massive metal sheds known as "confinements": warehouses that allow operators to breed thousands of pigs in one building. The sheds are long and thin, with huge exhaust fans on either end, and each group of buildings includes several silos for storing feed, as well as a dumpster to dispose of the roughly 10 percent of hogs that don't survive until slaughtering time.[2] After being weaned in these industrial facilities, the pigs are transferred to a finishing operation to fatten up and then to the slaughterhouse. These two trips in a packed semitrailer are the only times the pigs will see daylight.

Jeff Hansen and his wife, Deb, built an empire out of these confinement sheds. The Hansens' company, Iowa Select Farms, employs more than 7,400 people, including contractors, and brings about five million pigs to market annually.[3] As the owners of Iowa's largest hog operation, the Hansens have constructed hundreds of confinement sheds in more than fifty of Iowa's ninety-nine counties.[4]

The sheds have provoked controversy in Iowa ever since operators such as the Hansens began to build them during the 1990s. Many rural communities, including people such as Julie Duhn, have campaigned fiercely against them, citing damage to health, livelihoods, property values, the environment, and the farm economy.[5] Although their efforts have yielded small victories, they have lost the war.

The state's hog industry, led by the Hansens, has cultivated close relationships with state politicians on both sides of the aisle to roll back regulations. Even as California has passed animal welfare laws and North Carolina has tightened its permitting program for confinement operations, the hog industry in Iowa goes almost unchecked. Today, Iowa raises about one-third of the nation's hogs, about as many as the second-, third-, and fourth-ranking states combined.[6]

Since Iowa Select was founded in 1992, the state's pig population has increased by more than 50 percent while the number of hog farms has declined by over 80 percent. Over the past thirty years, twenty-six thousand Iowa farms quit the long-standing tradition of raising pigs.[7] As confinements replaced farms, rural communities have continued to hollow out.

Pigs in Iowa now outnumber human residents by a ratio of more than seven to one, and they produce a volume of manure equivalent to the waste of nearly eighty-four million people, more than the populations of California, Texas, and Illinois combined.[8] One expert estimated that each confinement facility produces "the same amount of waste as a city of 90,000 to 150,000 people," spread over only 640 acres with no sewage system.[9]

The environment simply cannot handle so much pig shit. In theory, this manure, when spread on nearby crop fields, is a useful fertilizer. But residents and scientists alike point to evidence that this "Mt. Everest of waste," as one University of Iowa water researcher described it, is frequently mismanaged.[10] It filters through soil to underground pipes that discharge directly into rivers, and when manure is overapplied, rain and snowmelt can quickly channel it into waterways.

As a result, as confinement operations have come to dominate pork production, they've degraded Iowa's water quality. Watersheds that are dense with livestock have a higher nutrient overload. Most summers, the state closes two-thirds of its state park beaches to swimming for a week or more, citing the health risk of toxins or bacteria.[11]

Closer to the confinements, many rural residents say they've been plagued—and others pushed out—by the stench, the flies, and the health hazards that accompany the facilities. "We know what hog manure smells like, but this is like a sewer," one retired farmer who lived next to an industrial hog facility told the *Washington Post*.[12]

The Hansens likely can't see—or smell—any hog buildings from their seven-thousand-square-foot mansion, which is nestled inside a gated community in suburban Des Moines.[13] Their view is dominated by the golf course at the exclusive Glen Oaks Country Club, which abuts their backyard. In 2020, the Hansens' company jet recorded over two hundred flights, including several trips to Naples, Florida, where until recently they owned multiple homes on the coast.[14]

When Americans think about farmers, they probably don't have jet-setting millionaires such as Jeff and Deb Hansen in mind. But businesses like theirs are increasingly the norm in farm country: huge, regional-scale corporations owned by just one or a few families who use their political connections to overpower both local democracy and local businesses.[15]

Iowa Select became a behemoth as the result of decades of deregulation that allowed power to concentrate in our food system. And it's not just smelly. It's a sad story of the corporate capture of my home state.

Metal Shed Farmer

Jeff and Deb Hansen grew up in Iowa Falls as typical farm kids. They graduated from the local high school in 1976 and soon married. Both went straight to work: Jeff helped on his father's farm while Deb worked in a local farm insurance office.[16]

During the Hansens' childhoods, Iowa's rich soils supported a constellation of diversified single-family operations. Farmers grew corn and soybeans, but many also raised a flock of chickens, milked a small dairy herd, or grazed beef on pasture. As with many long-term investment portfolios, diversity was a farm family's lifeline.

Many family farmers considered pigs to be a cornerstone of their farms. Farmers raised a variety of breeds in barns and in pens. Although many farmers kept hogs in every stage of the life cycle, others specialized in "farrowing"—breeding sows and raising the litters—or buying "feeder" pigs, fattening them to maturity, and then auctioning them at the sale barns spread in a grid across the Iowa countryside. These competitive markets ensured a fair price for farmers.

It was likely at just such a sale barn that newlywed Jeff Hansen bought his first three sows, which he kept in a converted barn on his father's property.[17] As the herd grew, the couple found the work grueling, particularly Deb, who had quit her office job to manage the pigs. To lighten her load, the Hansens purchased labor-saving equipment such as "elevated farrowing crates with steel slats, a feed pan and automatic waterers," according to *National Hog Farmer*, a trade magazine.[18] Quickly grasping the potential of mechanized livestock equipment, Jeff Hansen founded his own business to build confinement systems.

Animal warehouses had already transformed the poultry industry in the South during the 1950s and 1960s, and the model soon spread to other sectors and regions.[19] They were first extensively used with hogs in the late 1980s in North Carolina, where a state legislator deregulated the industry for his personal benefit.[20] Dairy followed shortly thereafter, starting in California.[21]

A consistent theme in this warehouse animal model is that one state moves first, triggering others to follow suit. After confinements were deregulated in North Carolina, Iowa followed closely behind, desperate not to lose its status as the nation's top pork producer. As the race to the bottom sped up, the US Department of Agriculture failed to stop it.

Big meatpackers, which purchase and slaughter pigs and package pork, were enthusiastic about the shift to this model. The meatpackers prefer to buy from confinement operations through production contracts because they offer a steady stream of pigs in predictable sizes that are ready for slaughter on a precise schedule. The model is vastly more profitable than buying from a patchwork of independent growers, who sell pigs of various breeds and sizes at local auctions. Today, two-thirds of Iowa hogs are grown on contract with big meatpackers.[22] Consequently, the sale barns that dotted the Iowa countryside slowly closed, and so did the competitive market for selling hogs.

Meanwhile, trade agreements that cut tariffs and sidelined import restrictions in places such as Asia and Mexico swung open the doors of a world market for livestock products, particularly eggs and pork. Wall Street took notice; outside investors played a critical role in financing the expansion of confinement operations in Iowa.[23]

Hardin County, where the Hansens were raised, was the perfect place to take advantage of this hog boom. Although nearly 90 percent of Iowa's land area is devoted to agriculture, its north-central region, smoothed by glaciers, has the flattest, richest cropland, which means it can accommodate copious amounts of manure and produce huge quantities of cheap feed.[24] The region also has abundant groundwater (hogs are thirsty).[25]

"At that point, there were two things I knew for sure," Jeff Hansen told *National Hog Farmer*. "Iowa was best suited to build an integrated pork production system and, second, I knew I could figure out how to do it."[26] The Hansens carved out a niche by building the confinement sheds that would take over Iowa's hog industry. By the early 1990s, they were bringing in $90 million per year assembling these confinements, known as concentrated animal feeding operations, or CAFOs for short.[27]

But after steadily expanding their confinement-building business, the Hansens decided they could also make money by raising their own hogs. In 1992, Jeff Hansen incorporated a new company, Iowa Select Farms, signed a contract with a meatpacker, and launched operations with a herd of 10,000 sows. During its first four years, Iowa Select more than quintupled its herd to 62,000 sows, enough to rate among the top ten largest pork producers in the country.[28] By 1999, with 96,000 sows, it was selling 1.7 million pigs per year.[29] Today, Iowa Select Farms is the fourth-largest hog producer in the country.[30]

Dirty Water

As Iowa Select built its empire, the impacts of its warehouses on the environment and surrounding communities quickly became apparent.

On a very basic level, the stench produced by confinements can be overwhelming. Within the sheds, powerful exhaust fans are necessary to constantly suck out poisonous gases rising from the manure lagoons. If the fans are shut off, the hogs die within hours. This is exactly what happened during the spring of 2020, when the COVID-19 pandemic disrupted slaughterhouse operations and Iowa Select needed to quickly kill hundreds of thousands of animals.[31]

In Iowa, confinements are often as close as a quarter mile from homes, schools, and businesses. In interviews and in years of news coverage, Iowans living near confinements have complained about air quality too poor for their kids to play outside; about clouds of flies attracted to the giant manure pits and lagoons; about the exploding population of rats infesting homes, drawn by the vast stocks of animal feed; and about vultures that snatch carcasses from animal warehouse dumpsters and then drop pig parts in backyards.[32]

Scientists have also documented negative health effects among people who live near confinements. One study of North Carolina residents who lived within a few miles of clustered confinements found that they had a lower life expectancy and higher rates of infant deaths, asthma, kidney disease, tuberculosis, and blood poisoning than those who lived farther away.[33] Dangerous levels of ammonia, which causes burning in the eyes and respiratory tract as well as chronic lung disease, have been measured in the air near massive hog sites in Iowa since the early 2000s.[34] Communities near hog operations also report higher rates of headaches, sore throats, runny noses, coughs, and diarrhea than comparable areas without hog confinements. A 2012 study found higher rates of neurobehavioral and pulmonary impairment in people living within 1.9 miles of a massive hog facility and manure lagoon in Ohio than in a control group in Tennessee.[35]

As of 2023, the US Environmental Protection Agency still hadn't even estimated airborne emissions from confinements in order to regulate them under the Clean Air Act, despite numerous instances of workers falling into manure pits and dying from the fumes.[36] Confinement applications sometimes promise to plant tree barriers to reduce air pollution, but the trees take several years to mature enough to be effective, if they are ever planted at all.[37]

The confinements have also caused economic devastation in surrounding communities. It's no secret that rural American economies have struggled for decades with high poverty rates and anemic job growth.[38] Confinement operators argue that the jobs they bring are beneficial to rural areas. Iowa Select might point to a 2017 study that it commissioned from Dermot Hayes, an Iowa State University economist with a long record of supporting agribusiness (and of business transactions with Jeff and Deb Hansen).[39] In the study, Hayes credited the company with "reversing economic decline" in rural communities where it built giant sow barns.

Yet economists such as Hayes often fail to disclose their corporate funding and support. Kate Conlow, an attorney and former journalist, has documented how extensive this problem is among economists working in agriculture. Although many universities have disclosure policies, Conlow noted that they are hardly ever enforced.[40] This failure warps the public debate.

Meanwhile, a different economist at Iowa State found that the overall economy in these communities continues to degrade in spite of all the jobs that Iowa Select claims to provide. Rather than stemming the decline, "they're actually one of the key mechanisms for driving people out of rural areas, despite the claims to the contrary."[41]

Even putting aside their economic impact, jobs at confinements are tough. Employees at sow farms monitor food, water, and ventilation; castrate, euthanize, artificially inseminate, and perform pregnancy checks on the animals; remove dead hogs; power-wash facilities to remove manure; and wean litters. One former Iowa Select driver told the *Guardian* in 2019 that he earned $23,000 per year working twelve-hour days with no overtime pay.[42] As Julie Duhn put it, "Is a job with Iowa Select what you want for your kids?" Given how difficult and poorly paid these jobs are, it's no surprise that Iowa Select has employed undocumented workers.[43]

Moreover, this production model depends on liberal use of antibiotics.[44] Overuse of these drugs is contributing to antibiotic resistance, not just in pigs but also among humans.[45] According to the Centers for Disease Control and Prevention, the United States now has a death every fifteen minutes from an antibiotic-resistant infection.[46] In response, public health officials have been ringing the alarm bell and calling for less use of these drugs in hogs.

But in Iowa, the most obvious impact of the confinements has been on the state's water. In a confinement facility, hog manure drops through a slatted floor and collects in a deep pool below. In some instances, that pool runs through a pipe to a manure pond or lagoon that holds the overflow. This waste can find its way into the watershed, adding to the pollution caused by fertilizer runoff. Gordon Garrison, a farmer in northwestern Iowa, told the *Guardian* that nitrate levels in the water on his property nearly doubled after a corporation built a shed housing up to 8,800 pigs in a neighboring field.[47]

Bob Havens, now in his seventies, learned to swim in Pine Lake and built his house near the lake twenty years ago. Now, he said, in the summertime, "the lake turns into this slimy green sludge" and billows of foam course through local culverts. Both are signs of a dangerous nutrient imbalance. As a result, Havens lamented, "you [can't] even canoe through it, let alone fish." Havens sees the pollution as a matter of equity. "A lot of folks in Hardin County can't afford a three-week vacation in the Bahamas," but they used to have Pine Lake for excellent swimming, fishing, and boating. Now, he said ruefully, "they just can't do it."[48]

The problem is bad enough during normal times, particularly with older facilities, but it can become a crisis in the wake of the sorts of natural disasters that are becoming more common as the planet heats up. After recent catastrophic flooding in western Iowa, for example, some livestock lagoons spilled over into nearby creeks, a process that can cause environmental devastation and threaten human health and well-being.[49] North Carolina faced a similar issue when more than fifty livestock lagoons overflowed in the wake of Hurricane Florence, according to NPR reporting at the time.[50] A recent report noted a large expansion of industrial animal facilities in Iowa's hundred-year floodplains even in the face of these risks.[51]

These two intertwined factors—overapplication of synthetic fertilizers, mostly to grow industrial animal feed, and pig waste from corporate farms—have created a water crisis in Iowa. To make water safe for human consumption, the Des Moines Water Works pays as much as $10,000 per day to treat it.[52] This problem isn't limited to Iowa. The US Department of Agriculture estimates that Americans pay almost $1.7 billion per year, mainly through higher water bills, to deal with this pollution.[53] The cost can be overwhelming for communities, particularly smaller ones with lower budgets and poorer populations.

But even cities such as Des Moines can barely keep up. The Raccoon River runs past cropland and corporate hog operations in northern Iowa and meanders east to Des Moines, where it provides five hundred thousand people in and around Iowa's largest city with drinking water. Of course, it likely carries much of the pollution with it, including from the manure produced by the Hansens' hog operations. In 2015, Des Moines experienced 177 days of high nitrate levels.[54] In response, it sought to spend $80 million on a new nitrate removal facility to handle its growing needs.[55]

Neutering the Backlash

As confinement buildings and their manure ponds spread across the Iowa countryside during the 1990s, a passionate rural backlash emerged, sparking a prolonged battle over the future of farming in Iowa. Protesters packed gymnasiums and crowded hallways in the statehouse. Coalitions of family farmers threatened by this new model, environmentalists, and neighboring residents and communities held rallies—one demonstration drew 1,000 supporters in a small town with a population of only 2,700—and lobbied legislators to enact a state moratorium on new confinement construction.[56]

The pushback against confinements came from all directions. Rightwing commentator Pat Buchanan even made opposition to confinements a key part of his 1996 presidential campaign in Iowa. "Farmers talk about it everywhere I go," he told the *Los Angeles Times* after the Iowa caucuses. "Whenever I bring it up, the audience explodes."[57] Buchanan's surprising close-second finish in the Republican Iowa caucuses—to Kansas senator Bob Dole—elevated him from protest candidate to legitimate contender.[58]

Although most big corporate animal warehouse networks operate in multiple states, the Hansens staked their entire operation on Iowa. But you'd be hard-pressed to say they were welcomed.[59] The fierce debate over confinements made the front page of the *Des Moines Register* year after year in the mid-1990s.[60] National newspapers frequently covered the story.[61] Even the Hansens' home county proposed a moratorium on new confinements.[62]

The Hansens and other industry leaders likely knew that this opposition posed an existential threat to their booming businesses. Regulations and restrictions against expansion were already being put in place in North Carolina, the state that had first deregulated the industry and kicked off the hog boom. Although Iowa's cheap corn remained attractive, its lax regulatory standards were—and remain—the Hog Barons' essential requirement for success.

It's easy to see why communities across the state revolted—and many continue to revolt—against the confinements.[63] In fact, a recent poll found that nearly two-thirds of respondents favored a moratorium on new corporate hog facilities.[64] But despite the popular resistance to animal warehouses, legislators faced pressure from business leaders to invite in even more of them. Agricultural economists sympathetic to large operators such as the Hansens argued that if the state were friendlier to hog operations, the growth potential would be enormous.[65]

In the summer of 1993, a report called "Project 21" was presented to the Des Moines business leaders who had commissioned it. The 111-page paper, authored by a Virginia-based consulting firm, chided Iowa's politicians and business leaders for "complacency" with the state's relative economic health and its low rate of unemployment. The report concluded that Iowa needed to do more to boost growth, which meant that the family farm needed to die. "Although it is politically popular to defend and protect the concept of family farms," the report proclaimed, "legislation limiting corporate investment is economic folly."[66]

The sentiment touched a nerve. "We're really tired of this type of nonsense," a leading organizer for an anti-confinement group called Prairiefire told the *Des Moines Register* in response to the plan. "And if they want a fight in the Legislature, we'll show them a fight they'd never imagined." One Iowa farmer asked, "Why are they trying to promote something that will both hurt the environment and sell our young people into lives of indentured servitude?"[67]

Forced to address the heated controversy, confinement operations marshaled their political power to fend off regulation. In 1994, the newly formed Iowa Pork Alliance enlisted Robert Ray, a Republican former governor, to remind Iowans of hogs' economic importance in statewide television ads.[68] Iowa Select Farms, for its part, emphasized repeatedly in the press that any efforts to stifle the growth of hog confinements would send production and jobs out of state.[69] Iowa Select and its employees also donated $41,000 to the campaign of Terry Branstad, the state's Republican governor at the time, and hired his former chief of staff, Doug Gross, as a lobbyist.[70] Branstad even appeared in an Iowa Select television promotion that year.[71]

The cozy relationship seemed to pay off. In 1995, Branstad signed a law that would prove to be pivotal for the Hansens, neutering local democracy to clear the way for his industry's development. The law, known as H.F. 519, offered token protections to neighbors of confinements: new buildings had to be sited at least a quarter mile from residences, and owners had to write plans—which had to be approved by the state—for disposing of their manure.

But the law also handed animal warehouse operators a huge victory by stripping counties of their long-standing authority to deny construction permits to confinement operators. Jeff Hansen described the law as a "fair compromise" and judged it sufficient to keep the Hansens' business in the state. "We're going to keep growing in Iowa," he told the *Des Moines Register*.[72]

The issue later became a prominent topic in the 2002 governor's race between Doug Gross, the Iowa Select lobbyist, and Democrat Tom Vilsack. While campaigning, Vilsack—who would later serve as secretary of agriculture for Presidents Barack Obama and Joe Biden—derided Gross as a champion of corporate hog lots. But as state senator, Vilsack had voted for H.F. 519.

Vilsack ended up winning the race. His second term, from 2002 through 2006, coincided with the largest confinement-building boom in Iowa's history.[73]

The Sacrifice State

After her rash cleared up—it took a month of topical treatments—Julie Duhn started attending meetings of the county board of supervisors and organizing people to oppose permits for proposed hog buildings. It frustrated and hurt Duhn to know that she could never take her grandkids swimming at Pine Lake. In all her activism, though, Duhn thinks she managed to stop only one confinement from being built. After a zealous campaign in 2017 and 2018 over a particular confinement, Iowa Select Farms withdrew its application.[74]

When Julie Duhn joined the fight against animal warehouses in 2016, activists and politicians had been campaigning—unsuccessfully—against them for more than twenty years. In Iowa, because of H.F. 519, counties have virtually no policy avenue for blocking confinements as long as the facilities meet the state's requirements.

Meanwhile, the Iowa Department of Natural Resources rubber-stamps permits for medium and large animal warehouses and levies only paltry fines for manure spills. The department's leadership is appointed by the state's governor. A recent state audit report determined that the Iowa DNR was "mismanaging a multimillion-dollar fund set up to help oversee Iowa livestock farms and their manure," but nothing has come of it.[75]

The department is also so critically underfunded that rigorous enforcement of management plans is all but impossible.[76] Implementation of state-sanctioned "best management practices" to reduce manure runoff is voluntary, and such efforts have not stopped the problem from worsening. In fact, 61 percent of Iowa's rivers and streams and 67 percent of its lakes and reservoirs do not meet basic water quality standards, according to a 2020 assessment by the Iowa DNR.[77]

In January 2018, Thomas Burkhead learned that Iowa Select Farms had applied for a permit to build its largest-ever sow complex a mile from his family's farm near Rockwell City, in Calhoun County. The proposal was for a hog mother ship: a three-shed breeding complex covering an area larger than four football fields and housing 7,498 pigs—5,200 of them gestating sows. Combined, the manure pits underlying the sheds would hold enough waste to fill three Olympic-size swimming pools.

Once weaned, the offspring of the sows would need to be fattened, and that meant even more confinements would soon need to be built. Calhoun County already had more than 150 facilities housing north of three hundred thousand pigs, and residents say the smell of their manure was already making the area unlivable. "There are a lot of days where I don't go outside, because it stinks enough to make you vomit," Burkhead said. "I mean, it will knock you on your knees."[78]

Burkhead launched into action. He rallied neighbors and community groups to fend off the industrial hog building. Although Burkhead figured they had almost no chance, the opponents persisted, eventually finding a mistake in Iowa Select's application. The group rallied people to a special supervisor's meeting and convinced the board to decline to recommend the proposal to the Iowa DNR. But the agency kicked the proposal to the Environmental Protection Commission, an oversight board appointed by the state's governor, which waved the company's application through.

With regulatory action blocked, activists have resorted to leaning on public scandal to shame companies into withdrawal. They create Facebook pages, write op-eds and letters to local officials and newspapers, crowd hearings held by county supervisors, and testify for hours. Anything to chip away at animal warehouse operators' standing with political leadership.

Bill Stowe, chief executive officer and general manager of the Des Moines Water Works, understood the need for drastic action. He had been warning elected officials for years that nitrate levels in the Raccoon River were getting dangerously high.[79] In response to waterway pollution concerns, the State of Iowa created a toothless plan called the Iowa Nutrient Reduction Strategy, which did not address the core issue. The plan had no specific goals, no deadlines, and no consequences for failure to address the issue. And consequently, the problem only got worse. Between 2003 and 2019, average pollution levels doubled across the state.[80]

The state's inaction forced Bill Stowe and the Des Moines Water Works to take matters into their own hands. In March 2015, the Des Moines Water Works filed a lawsuit against government entities called drainage districts in northern Iowa for their failure to control nitrate pollution in the Raccoon River.[81] "Iowa has become a sacrifice state," Stowe told reporters. "We and our land are collateral damage for [Big Ag]."[82]

Stowe faced immense opposition for taking such a drastic step. Rather than agreeing to regulate the pollution, the defendant counties dug in, incurring legal costs estimated at more than $1 million. Republican governor Terry Branstad called the lawsuit the equivalent of "declar[ing] war on rural Iowa." Republicans in the state legislature even proposed dismantling the Des Moines Water Works.[83]

But the truth of the matter was a lot more complicated than a war between rural and urban Iowa. Folks in rural Iowa—people like Julie Dohn and Thomas Burkhead—are just as threatened by water pollution as their counterparts in Des Moines. In fact, a 2018 national water quality study published in the *Proceedings of the National Academy of Sciences* reported that "violation incidence in rural areas is substantially higher than in urbanized areas."[84]

Besides, Branstad's solution to the problem involved raiding a fund that was established to finance new school construction with a sales tax.[85] This money would have been particularly meaningful for rural Iowa, which was in desperate need of an update to its decaying education infrastructure.

Polling by the *Des Moines Register* showed that over 60 percent of Iowans agreed with the Des Moines Water Works, including significant majorities of residents of small towns.[86] Another poll found that 73 percent of voters in the state supported limits on manure pollution runoff.[87] As Art Cullen, a local newspaperman, put it, "Anyone with eyes and a nose knows in his gut that Iowa has the dirtiest surface water in America."[88]

The Des Moines Water Works' court fight quickly became bitter. The agency indicated that it would settle the case if the parties agreed to higher water quality standards, but the counties swore off any settlement talks.[89]

At first, it was not entirely clear where the counties got the money to pay their massive legal bills, estimated to be upward of $1.4 million.[90] But an investigation conducted by the *Storm Lake Times* eventually revealed that the case was being financed by a secret fund created by the Agribusiness Association of Iowa.[91] As it typically does, Big Ag filtered money to the counties through front groups. When a newspaper and a local advocate for transparency sought to make the funding public, the counties fought them tooth and nail.[92]

Perhaps fearing that the lawsuit would lead to water quality regulations that would cut into its profits, the industry quickly mobilized to fight it. In addition to contributing to the defense fund, industry and its allies created another dark money group called the Iowa Partnership for Clean Water, which ran attack ads against the Des Moines Water Works, according to reporting by the *Des Moines Register*.[93] It's unknown whether Jeff and Deb Hansen contributed to this effort because membership of both the Iowa Partnership for Clean Water and the Agribusiness Association of Iowa is kept secret.

The lawsuit brought by Bill Stowe and the Des Moines Water Works was ultimately dismissed. But even though it wasn't successful, Stowe's efforts brought the issue and the corruption surrounding it into the light of day.

Bill Stowe passed away from pancreatic cancer in April 2019.[94] Not long before Stowe died, Art Cullen wrote a column in the *Des Moines Register* honoring him for accelerating "a conversation that had been taking place in quiet corners. . . . It took courage for him to challenge the chemical cabal that controls Iowa agriculture and politics." Art continued, "Not everyone would have had the steel."[95]

Sadly, Iowa's water crisis has not improved since Stowe spoke truth to power. In fact, the state has only added more confinement buildings. Every year since 2018, Iowa politicians, cheered on by activists, have introduced a bill in the state's legislature to halt animal warehouse expansions, and they've worked with Democratic senator Cory Booker of New Jersey to introduce a bill in the US Senate that includes a long-term phaseout of large animal warehouses nationwide. But so far, neither has had enough votes to pass.[96]

Coming up on its thirtieth anniversary, Iowa Select Farms is still expanding, along with the rest of the hog industry in Iowa.[97] The state is now home to at least thirteen thousand confinements, and applications for new ones hit the Iowa Department of Natural Resources at a steady clip.[98]

In the face of opposition, the Hansens have employed a number of tactics to maintain control over the political levers in the state. The Deb and Jeff Hansen Foundation has a long and well-publicized history of charitable giving. It donates thousands of pork chops to food banks, gives vouchers for hams to dozens of schools, and organizes Operation Christmas Meal, a series of drive-through pork handouts. It then posts photos of smiling employees, occasionally joined by a governor or US senator, on social media.[99]

It's not unusual for a sitting governor to attend a charity gala thrown by the Hansens. The 2016 spring gala for the Deb and Jeff Hansen

Foundation was a glittering event, packed with smiling faces and powerful personalities. Iowa's governor at the time, Terry Branstad, was in attendance, as was the president of Iowa State University.[100] The university, following a $2 million Hansen family donation, had dedicated the Jeff and Deb Hansen Agriculture Student Learning Center less than two years earlier.[101]

In 2019, Iowa's Republican governor, Kim Reynolds, contributed a tour of the state capitol and the governor's mansion, led by Reynolds herself, to the gala's auction. Iowa Select Farms requested her presence at the gala the day after Reynolds won election, likely aided by the Hansens' six-figure campaign contribution.[102]

The Hansen family's charitable efforts have seemingly solidified its power. During the outbreak of the COVID-19 pandemic in 2020, Governor Reynolds fought to keep packing plants open, prioritizing the interests of confinement operators such as the Hansens, who stood to lose millions as these sheds became overloaded with market-ready animals.[103]

And in July 2020, when Iowa Select's administrative headquarters in suburban Des Moines had an outbreak scare, the company reached out directly to the governor's office, which sent a rapid-response team to test thirty-two office employees.[104] Although Reynolds argued that the state offered testing to dozens of other businesses, the governor's rapid allocation of testing resources to political donors such as the Hansens stirred controversy, prompting an investigation from the state auditor.

In December 2020, Governor Reynolds spent a frigid day handing out Iowa Select pork packages at an Operation Christmas Meal drive-through event in Osceola, Iowa. But the Hansens weren't there to help. Their jet had landed a few days earlier in sunny Naples, Florida.[105]

CHAPTER 2

The Grain Barons

THERE IS A TEMPLATE FOR THE ALL-AMERICAN business success story. An immigrant family comes to the United States with little more than two pennies to their name, opens a small business, and works hard year after year. As the family members slowly build the business, successive generations take on the responsibility of running and growing it. The business prospers, and its leaders become prominent citizens, giving back to the community that helped them succeed. Museums, schools, and hospital wings soon bear their names.

The Cargill-MacMillan family, which owns Cargill, Inc., has told this story about its centuries-old business for decades now. William Duncan MacMillan, who served on the company's board of directors for over thirty years, published three books chronicling its saga, and the family even hired an Ivy League professor to write a three-volume version that spans over 1,800 pages.[1]

One aspect of Cargill's all-American narrative rings true: the corporation remains a family-owned business. In fact, for its size and age, Cargill has kept its ownership remarkably close. Today, nearly one hundred members of the Cargill-MacMillan family control about 90 percent of the company's shares.[2]

But Cargill is no ordinary success story. The company has grown and grown and grown, well beyond the bounds of the humble-family-business-made-good narrative. It is now the largest private company in America, larger even than the infamous Koch Industries.[3] For perspective, Cargill's annual revenue is equivalent to the *combined* annual state tax revenues of South Dakota, New Hampshire, Montana, North Dakota, Vermont, Rhode Island, Delaware, Maine, West Virginia, Idaho, Nebraska, New Mexico, Hawaii, Mississippi, Nevada, Oklahoma, Kansas, Arkansas, and Iowa.[4]

It's hard to pin down exactly how big Cargill is because, as a private company, it is not required to disclose its finances. In fact, Cargill produced public figures for the first time in 1969 only because Harvard Business School required it for an award it gave the company.[5] Nor is it easy to grasp the scope of Cargill's empire. The company employs over 160,000 people worldwide and operates in a seemingly endless list of industries, from salt to cocoa.[6] There's a good chance that some, perhaps most, of the ingredients of an average American meal were processed and sold by Cargill. The company likely transported most of the ingredients, too, via its massive shipping network.

To get a sense of how Cargill touches most aspects of the American food system, take it from one of the company's own brochures:

> We are the flour in your bread, the wheat in your noodles, the salt on your fries. We are the corn in your tortillas, the chocolate in your dessert, the sweetener in your soft drink. We are the oil in your salad dressing and the beef, pork or chicken you eat for dinner. We are the cotton in your clothing, the backing on your carpet and the fertilizer in your field.[7]

But despite the breadth of products and services that Cargill provides, I like to refer to the Cargill-MacMillan family as the Grain Barons. After all, the company's core business lines—food ingredients, shipping, animal feed, butchering, and financial services—revolve around a handful of commodities, especially corn and soy. Even the company's ancillary products, such as soybean candle wax, are derived from these crops. Although soybeans are technically a legume, not a cereal grain, they are often lumped in with corn as a "coarse grain" because of their similar role in the modern food system.[8]

Taken together, Cargill handles more than one-quarter of the world's grain trade.[9] Yet despite this dominance, the company is largely unknown to most Americans. I certainly never grasped its true size, even though it has been a constant backdrop in my life. I grew up in Cedar Rapids, Iowa, an industrial city in the eastern part of the state that forms a key cog in corn and soybean processing. I was born near a Cargill soybean mill and went to church near a Cargill corn mill. I even played soccer next to a Cargill grain elevator.

But as much as my physical surroundings, Cargill shaped the food that I grew up eating. In the late twentieth century, the American food system began to revolve around the processing of the same grains— corn and soy—on which Cargill has built its empire. Cargill's power is illustrated by the fact that it's easier to get a healthy, locally sourced meal in Washington, DC, or New York City than it is in my home state of Iowa, surrounded by some of the world's most productive agricultural land.[10]

This profound shift in the American diet can be traced back to a dramatic reconceptualization of the Farm Bill and of food policy in the United States. These same changes helped fuel Cargill's transformation from a robust family-owned business into the behemoth it is today. As a result, the story of Cargill is inextricably linked to the history of the US

Department of Agriculture and, more specifically, to the development of what I call the "Wall Street Farm Bill."

The New Deal Farm Bill

Cargill and the USDA are, coincidentally, almost the same age. Cargill was founded in 1865, only three years after Abraham Lincoln established the US Department of Agriculture as part of a series of actions that reshaped America's Heartland and the broader food economy.[11] That year, in the midst of the Civil War, Lincoln also signed the Homestead Act of 1862, which distributed the land that had been (or eventually would be) stolen from its American Indian inhabitants through displacement and genocide.[12] The law granted 160 acres to anyone who paid a small filing fee and agreed to work on and improve the land over a five-year period.

In theory, any American who went west could become a farmer and property owner.[13] In practice, however, land was distributed almost entirely to White male applicants. In all, some 270 million acres were distributed, about equivalent to nearly 213 Delawares.[14] The Homestead Act resulted in the creation of millions of farms, many run by recent immigrants to the country. Immigration to the United States increased sharply during this era, in part because the Homestead Act was highly publicized overseas.[15]

The rush of small farmers to the Heartland created opportunities for others as well. Across the region, all sorts of businesses adjacent to agriculture popped up. A whole economy developed to help move the crops grown and the animals raised by farmers to market.

William Wallace Cargill was one of the entrepreneurs who stepped into the void. He established Cargill, Inc. in 1865 when he purchased a grain elevator in Iowa.[16] Grain elevators are the first stop on a crop's long journey from a farm to an eater's plate. They're used to store grain while it waits to be transported and processed. In Cargill's early years, most of that transport took place via train, which is why Cargill grain elevators dotted the landscape near railroads.

As it happened, William Wallace Cargill's first grain elevator was just seventeen miles down the road from my ancestors' farm in Bluffton, Iowa. My grandma's family immigrated from Ireland around this time to escape the Irish Potato Famine. My ancestors likely farmed a typical mix of animals and grains, including corn and oats. It's very possible that the grain they grew spent time at this Cargill facility before heading to market.

For decades, Cargill was just one among many successful grain-hauling companies. The family grew its business by building and buying grain elevators across the Midwest. It owned or controlled more than one hundred elevators just twenty years after William Wallace Cargill made his first purchase.[17] Although the company took some tentative steps outside this niche, including by purchasing a small seed company in 1907, it remained a regional grain hauler at its core.[18]

Meanwhile, the USDA's role in its early years was mostly as a distributor of farming information.[19] Its role expanded as a result of World War I. The fighting on French fields, coupled with interruptions in Russian trade routes, left Britain and France heavily dependent on American food imports. Adopting the slogan "Food Will Win the War," President Woodrow Wilson's USDA told farmers that increasing production was their patriotic duty.[20] In only five years, farmers plowed eleven million acres for the first time, an area twice the size of New Jersey.[21] Farmers' incomes more than doubled over the course of the war.[22]

But when the war ended and European farmers returned to their fields, prices plummeted. In the summer of 1920, the price of corn fell by 78 percent while the price of cotton and wheat dropped by 57 percent and 64 percent, respectively.[23] These low prices were the worst-case scenario for many farmers who had borrowed heavily to expand production during the war, and so the entire decade featured a steady wave of bankruptcies and consolidations.

The bleakness for farmers only worsened with the Great Depression and collapsing financial markets. One in every four family farms were sold between 1920 and 1933.[24] My grandma's family was part of this statistic; they sold their farm and moved into town during this time. It wasn't until the Dust Bowl crisis became known worldwide that pressure for intervention became impossible to ignore.

For Cargill, however, this period presented an opportunity. During the dozen years between the crash of the US stock market in 1929 and the country's entry into World War II in 1941, the company transformed "from a medium-sized regional grain company to a large national corporation with many links abroad," according to the historian who the family hired.[25]

The primary architect of this transformation was John MacMillan Jr., a grandson of William Wallace Cargill. Although John Jr. did not formally become president of the company until 1936, he assumed control long before then because of his father's poor health.[26] John Jr. espoused a vision of an "endless belt," which Cargill's official history described as "control of the movement of grain from the time it left the farmer until it reached the final buyer."[27] He pushed for the company to control not just the physical handling and storage of grain but also transportation, insurance, and a variety of other key cogs in the grain trade.

The crisis facing the industry gave John Jr. an opening to put this vision into action. With distress spreading throughout agricultural markets, he understood that assets could be purchased "on an astonishingly cheap basis."[28] Cargill seemingly took advantage of the situation to build, buy, and lease grain terminals in new regions.[29] Because of these efforts, the company more than quadrupled its grain storage capacity in just a decade.[30]

Cargill also expanded in new directions. The company entered the shipping business by buying its first boat in 1935.[31] Not long thereafter, Cargill started building its own boats.[32] As the company brags on its website, "Not only had Cargill moved with the flow of grain down the Mississippi, the company had invested in all aspects of transporting grain along the river."[33] Eventually, the company expanded from rivers to oceans. It even built boats for the United States Navy during World War II.[34]

Cargill's rapid growth allowed it to consolidate power within the industry, and it began to display a certain ruthlessness in extracting profits. In 1938, the company and three of its officials, including John MacMillan Jr., were expelled from the Chicago Board of Trade after being found guilty of manipulating corn prices.[35]

But the crisis that had fueled Cargill's growth in the first place also led to new challenges. As part of President Franklin D. Roosevelt's New Deal, the Agricultural Adjustment Act of 1933—the first version of what is now known as the Farm Bill—paid farmers to reduce production of the most overproduced commodities.[36] The law was intended to wean farmers off the high demand the war had artificially provided and create a balanced, stable farm economy.[37]

The Roosevelt administration also understood that without government intervention, farmers had an incentive to overplant their land. To prevent further dust bowls, the administration successfully lobbied Congress to pass the Soil Conservation and Domestic Allotment Act of 1936, which offered money to farmers to reduce acreage and to plant soil-friendly crops that replenished and preserved the soil instead of depleting it.[38]

Cargill and other grain processors hated the Roosevelt administration. To finance the Agricultural Adjustment Act of 1933, the federal government levied a tax on corporations such as Cargill that processed agricultural commodities.[39] The idea of paying taxes for a program that would limit their business was anathema. Cargill MacMillan Sr.—John MacMillan Jr.'s brother—proposed shifting 10 percent of Cargill's assets out of the country. John Jr. went even further, arguing that the company would "be well advised to liquidate entirely our business in the United States."[40]

Luckily for Cargill, the predominantly Republican-appointed United States Supreme Court struck down the Agricultural Adjustment Act of 1933 in *United States v. Butler* (1936) on the basis that the tax on processors was unconstitutional. In response, Congress passed the Agricultural Adjustment Act of 1938.[41] The law was almost identical to the Agricultural Adjustment Act of 1933, with one key change: the program was financed by the US Department of the Treasury rather than by a tax on processors. To this day, farm subsidies are paid by all taxpayers' dollars, not specifically by companies like Cargill.

This cluster of laws shaped farm policy for decades. The programs stabilized prices, saving countless family farms, and became the bedrock of an era of strong government intervention in agriculture. While imperfect, they brought prosperity for many White farmers. But the New Deal Farm Bill had devastating flaws. Black farmers, especially those in the South, did not enjoy the same support. Sharecropping, adopted in the South after the Civil War, replaced slavery as an institution for perpetuating White control. Wealthy landowners who had virtually no connection to the land and rarely farmed relied on the labor of tenant sharecroppers for most of the planting and harvesting.[42] These landowners accrued nearly all the profits while sharecroppers endured perpetual poverty.[43]

This system of exploitation was perpetuated by the New Deal Farm Bill. Rather than paying subsidies to sharecroppers directly, the USDA disbursed them to White landowners. Meanwhile, a disproportionate number of Black tenant farmers were forced to plant less as part of the initiative to reduce overproduction. In other words, Black tenant farmers absorbed the sticks of the New Deal Farm Bill while their White landlords enjoyed all its carrots. Moreover, the New Deal Farm Bill relied on local White officials to administer its programs, including its extension of low-interest loans. These offices cheated and excluded Black farmers from public benefits across the country for decades.[44]

Yet for all these flaws, the New Deal Farm Bill accomplished its goal of protecting White farmers, and for a while, it produced a relatively balanced farm economy. For Cargill, the New Deal Farm Bill did not threaten the company's power or force it to pay a penny to limit overproduction.

But as soon as these policies were put in place, Cargill and its corporate brethren still worked to destroy them. Even without a tax on processors, the New Deal Farm Bill placed a ceiling on the growth of companies such as Cargill that benefited from processing commodities on a large scale. After all, the incentives in the New Deal Farm Bill that limited the production of commodities in turn limited the grain crops that companies like Cargill could store, process, and transport. For decades, their allies slowly took it apart, and fifty years on, they found a way to pass what I call the Wall Street Farm Bill.

The Wall Street Farm Bill

During his 1948 reelection campaign, Harry Truman spoke to an audience of over eighty thousand people in a field outside the tiny town of Dexter, Iowa, just west of Des Moines. In a speech that was broadcast on national radio, Truman defended the New Deal Farm Bill and proclaimed that Republicans wanted a "return to the Wall Street economic dictatorship."[45] Truman went on to win reelection. During his presidency, he protected the New Deal Farm Bill and the balanced food system that it curated, but Cargill and its allies began to gain ground soon after Truman left office.

John MacMillan Jr. wrote privately to a fellow grain executive at General Mills that America would never have a "sound economy" until it eliminated laws like the New Deal Farm Bill system.[46] The businessmen found an ally in their effort when Dwight D. Eisenhower, Truman's successor, appointed Ezra Taft Benson as his secretary of agriculture.

Benson was a conservative firebrand who accused the civil rights movement of advancing Communist causes, called the income tax Marxist, and believed that a Mormon woman's place was in the home.[47] He opposed any government intervention to protect family farms on the grounds that it subsidized inefficiency.[48] Instead, he urged these farmers to "get big or get out."[49]

Accordingly, as soon as he entered office he sought to undercut the New Deal Farm Bill, which normally comes up for renegotiation every five years.[50] In 1958, he forged a compromise that resulted in Congress passing a bill that watered down some of the law's protections for family farmers.[51] He also reorganized the USDA to orient it away from the sorts of policies that underpinned the New Deal Farm Bill.[52]

But Benson faced intense opposition from family farmers across the country. An October 1958 article in the *New York Times* reported that Benson's name "was pronounced in sour tones, often in anger" in rural America.[53] He also warred with members of Congress, including midwestern Republicans from Benson's own party who decried the secretary's attempts to undermine family farmers.[54] In the face of this opposition, Benson failed to get traction in his attempts to dismantle the New Deal Farm Bill, though he did succeed in weakening it.[55]

His efforts were continued by Earl Butz, who served as assistant secretary of agriculture under Benson and who Richard Nixon appointed secretary of agriculture, a position he held through the administration of Gerald Ford.[56] Butz shared Benson's philosophy of promoting industrialization in agriculture at the expense of the family farm. He adopted Benson's driving philosophy to "get big or get out." He pared back the program that paid farmers not to overplant their land and instead urged them to plant commodities "from fencerow to fencerow."[57]

Butz then took steps to encourage the sale of these commodities abroad. He liquidated the country's grain reserves, which temporarily propped up prices for farmers, by selling the crops to a handful of large exporters, including Cargill, at favorable prices.[58] The exporters turned around and sold the commodities abroad for "unusually large profits."[59] As a result, export sales nearly doubled during his tenure under Nixon.[60]

Because of these policies, Butz was beloved by agribusinesses, particularly food processors and distributors like Cargill. Carol Tucker-Foreman, executive director of the Consumer Federation of America at the time, pointed out that Butz was "a spokesman for the big corporate farmers, for the food processors and for the grocery people. He's not on the side of farmers or consumers. He's on the side of people who buy from farmers and sell to consumers."[61]

Yet despite Benson's and Butz's success in gradually chipping away at the New Deal Farm Bill, its core components persisted, though in a severely weakened state. Whitney MacMillan, who became chairman and chief executive officer of Cargill in 1976, pushed the company to be more active in national politics. His main goal was to remove the production controls from the Farm Bill. He organized national conferences, pushed the issue in the media, and got politicians on board. He also enlisted fellow agricultural giants to help him fund a lobbying group.[62]

This more concerted approach began to find some success. The Ronald Reagan administration tried to administer the final blows to the New Deal Farm Bill but faced opposition in Congress, particularly from Iowa senator Tom Harkin, who pushed for reinstating old protections.[63] Although Reagan didn't have the votes to replace the New Deal Farm Bill entirely, he chipped away at the program.[64] In the name of reducing the cost of government, the president took advice from a task force that included Cargill officials to reorganize (i.e., deregulate) the USDA.[65]

Eventually, Cargill's efforts paid off, and the last vestiges of the New Deal Farm Bill were repealed entirely. When Newt Gingrich ascended to Speaker of the House of Representatives after the 1994 election, agribusiness finally had the votes to gut the New Deal Farm Bill. Over one hundred Big Ag corporations, including Cargill, joined forces to lobby for the Federal Agriculture Improvement and Reform Act of 1996, or the Wall Street Farm Bill, as I like to call it.[66]

The law passed both houses of Congress with bipartisan support. Tom Harkin was one of only twenty-five Democrats and one Republican—John McCain—to vote against it in the Senate.[67] Family farmers and consumer advocates held out faint hope that President Bill Clinton would hold the line and veto the bill, but he signed it into law on April 4, 1996, just months before he gutted public assistance for poor mothers and children.[68]

Commodities and Consolidation

The Wall Street Farm Bill was precisely the sort of law that President Truman warned about in 1948. The sort of balance encouraged by the New Deal Farm Bill preserved economic stability and insulated farmers from fluctuations in prices. But the new law neutralized or eliminated all provisions that were designed to maintain balance.[69] Instead, the Wall Street Farm Bill directed most of the subsidies to incentivize overproduction of a handful of key commodities, particularly corn and soy.

Under the New Deal Farm Bill, a farmer faced with low corn prices could switch to another crop or even idle a portion of farmland in exchange for financial support. The new law removed any motivation to conserve land. Instead, farmers were encouraged to grow corn and soy whether prices were high or low, even on the most marginal land.[70]

The incentive to grow corn under the Wall Street Farm Bill is so strong that processors like Cargill have sought out new uses for the crop.[71]

Production of ethanol—a fuel typically derived from corn—exploded in the years after the Wall Street Farm Bill was passed.[72] In fact, it's now the single largest use of American corn.[73] Yet the idea of burning corn in cars as an effective fuel source is largely known to be a farce.[74] The Museum of Failure even included a display on ethanol.

Instead of growing a variety of crops and raising animals, most farms now rely on a commodity crop or two. That's why less than 10 percent of farms still have animals.[75] Previously, it was cost-effective for farmers to graze their cattle or grow their own feed. But the grain surpluses incentivized by the Wall Street Farm Bill led to subsidized cheap feed, giving rise to the sorts of industrial factory farms that make up the Hog Baron's empire.[76]

One problem with this system is that growing only corn or soybeans year after year is like investing all your savings in one company, which any financial advisor would tell you is a bad idea. During an economic shock, family farmers relying on one or two crops often wind up bankrupt, while the big boys are more likely to have the resources to withstand the downturn. The exhortation by Benson and Butz for farmers to "get big or get out" finally came to fruition, with the average size of a farm nearly doubling from 650 acres in 1987 to 1,201 acres twenty-five years later.[77] Meanwhile, Black ownership of farmland has declined significantly, from 16–19 million acres in 1910 to fewer than 3 million today. Black farmers now represent just over 1 percent of all American farmers.[78]

As farms consolidate, more and more of the wealth leaves rural communities and flows to the Cargills of the world.[79] Most land in Iowa is not even farmed by owners anymore.[80] The loss has choked local economies and hollowed out towns. While he was fighting President Reagan's attempt to gut the New Deal Farm Bill, Senator Harkin pointed to a study that compared two agricultural communities: one composed mostly of family farms and another crowded with giant corporate producers. At the time, and even more so in a follow-up study conducted decades later, the community composed of family farms was healthier in every sense of the word, from higher income levels to more locally owned businesses and a more robust civic life.[81]

The Wall Street Farm Bill was justified as a "free market" approach that would reduce costs, but these massive subsidies made it the most expensive Farm Bill yet. In truth, the only farmers who truly operate in a free market are the local community-supported agriculture (CSA) farmers, who usually grow a variety of produce with almost no government financial support.[82] The phrase "free market" takes on a dark double meaning when you realize that these farmers earn so little that they are practically working for free.

Although the Wall Street Farm Bill has been repeatedly extended and tweaked since 1996, the core of the law has remained the same. The interlocking programs that used to be part of a larger scheme designed to diffuse power in the system, give a leg up to family farms, and protect the health of the soil and the environment now exist just to heavily subsidize a handful of coarse grains. And no company was better positioned to take advantage of this new system than Cargill.

The Cargill Playbook

"Agriculture policy does not protect the person you or I think of as a farmer," Tom Buis of the National Farmers Union told the *New York Times* in 1999. "It benefits the largest operations and the processors. And the processors want cheap grain."[83] With the incentives under the Wall Street Farm Bill putting downward pressure on corn and soy prices, production of these commodities exploded in subsequent years. This boom meant that companies like Cargill saw record profits in the years following passage of the law.[84]

The Wall Street Farm Bill's massive government subsidies for corn and soy at the expense of almost everything else seemingly gave Cargill the rocket fuel it needed to consolidate its power over agricultural markets. More than half a century after John MacMillan Jr. outlined his dream of an endless belt, the company could finally make it a reality.

The company's approach was similar to the one pursued by Standard Oil decades earlier. John D. Rockefeller's Gilded Age behemoth controlled most of the oil supply chain, from the producers who extracted oil from the ground to the trains and pipelines that transported it across the country, to the refineries that turned it into a usable product, to the stores that sold it to consumers.[85] This sort of vertically integrated business empire let Standard Oil use its control over one link of the supply chain to exert pressure on competitors in another.

Like Standard Oil, Cargill came to dominate by being a middleman. Its primary business is moving grain and transforming it into other products, just as Standard Oil did for oil. The last family member to run the company, Whitney MacMillan, even compared grain markets to petroleum markets.[86] With the burst provided by the record profits it accumulated in the years after passage of the Wall Street Farm Bill, Cargill entrenched itself as the dominant middleman in the grain trade and then used this position to amass economic and political power through an aggressive acquisition strategy.

In 1998, Cargill announced its purchase of Continental Grain Company grain-handling assets, one of its chief rivals in the grain elevator business, the same niche in which Cargill got its start. At the time, Cargill handled about 20 percent of America's grain exports and Continental Grain moved about 15 percent.[87] The Clinton administration waved the acquisition through when Cargill agreed to sell a few grain elevators to provide a pretense that competition was somehow being maintained.[88] Yet for American farmers, this sort of consolidation has meant lower and lower prices for their crops as the number of potential buyers has collapsed. The share of each dollar spent on food that winds up in the hands of farmers has fallen from 53 cents in 1946 to 15 cents today, the lowest level ever recorded.[89]

The company also expanded into new industries and regions. When it identifies an opportunity, Cargill typically buys a small company or a mere stake in a dominant company. This beachhead approach allows Cargill executives to get an inside view of the area or business and decide whether they want to double down. Once they commit, Cargill seeks full domination by aggressively buying up large firms.

One example of this strategy is the company's expansion into beef slaughtering. Building on its animal feed business, Cargill bought a small beef feedlot in 1974.[90] Once it seemingly understood the industry, Cargill acquired a massive slaughtering company called MBPXL and then made several more purchases in the beef business. The subsidiary company, now known as Cargill Protein, is the second-largest beef packer.[91] These sorts of takeovers are why Cargill is now one of the four largest companies in beef slaughtering, beef feedlots, pork slaughtering, turkey slaughtering, animal feed, flour milling, corn milling, and soybean processing.[92]

They are also why allegations of price-fixing and collusion have become a normal occurrence for the company.[93] In 2004, Cargill settled a class action lawsuit for $24 million after being accused of colluding with two other companies to fix the price of a food sweetener.[94] In 2022, the company, along with two others in the chicken business, agreed to pay $84.8 million to settle a lawsuit claiming that the companies violated antitrust law by sharing information about worker pay and benefits.[95]

The lawsuits haven't slowed Cargill down, but the company does seem to know when to fold its hand if a beachhead seems unviable. If it can't become one of the top three or four players in a concentrated industry, it throws in the towel and sells off those assets. It seems to understand that operating in concentrated markets isn't profitable if it isn't one of the big boys. For example, Cargill sold its chicken hatcheries, feed mills, and slaughterhouses to Tyson Foods Inc., perhaps because it became clear that it could not compete with its rival's dominance of the space. Although Cargill decided to concede the American chicken market, it didn't give up on birds entirely.[96] The company still maintains a massive American turkey operation as well as chicken operations abroad.

And when market conditions change, so does Cargill. In 2021, the company decided to return to the chicken market. In conjunction with one of its grain competitors, it spent $4.5 billion to create the third-largest chicken-slaughtering company in America.[97] Although Joe Biden talked about the dangers of consolidation on the campaign trail, his administration signed off on the deal.[98]

Cargill has also been forward-thinking about co-opting innovations in the food system, including ones that might be seen as threats. Many companies avoid investing in new products or industries that could cannibalize their business. But Cargill would rather be in the room in a nascent industry to see if it is economically viable.

Two of Cargill's more recent investments have been in lab-grown meat and insect farming.[99] If the cost of growing cells into muscle meat ever dips low enough, it could cut into or even eliminate Cargill's slaughtering businesses. Similarly, insect farming could undermine its massive soybean-milling operation used to produce animal feed. Cargill is pursuing both ventures as a sort of hedging strategy. The company may be competing with itself, but at least it will never be left behind.

Shaping Diets and Policy

Cargill's massive empire has shaped countless aspects of the American food system, but none more so than the nation's sweet tooth. Cheap grain made it possible for Cargill to turn vast amounts of corn into high-fructose corn syrup at a much lower price than traditional sugar produced from beet and sugarcane crops.[100] Cargill first produced corn syrup at its plant near my church.[101] This new product significantly decreased the price of sweeteners and likely explains why America now consumes more sugar per person than any other country.[102]

The explosion in cheap sugar is the reason corn syrup is used to make everything from ketchup to pop to bread to dog food.[103] Grocery store aisles are filled with the sorts of unhealthy processed foods that might be economically viable only because of the structure of subsidies under the Wall Street Farm Bill. The relative cost of grain-derived products fell sharply between 1982 and 2008: by 10 percent for fats and oils, by 15 percent for sugars and sweets, and by 34 percent for carbonated beverages. Over the same period, the price of fresh fruits and vegetables increased by 50 percent.[104]

As Farm Bill subsidies started propping up processed foods, the nation's obesity rate skyrocketed. These rates had stayed flat through the 1960s and the early 1970s. But as the New Deal Farm Bill framework collapsed, they began a steady trajectory upward.[105] People are eating more unhealthy foods because these foods are subsidized by the government while healthier foods largely are not.[106]

It's no wonder that the country is facing an obesity crisis. Struggling families make rational economic decisions in order to put food on the table. As one prominent nutritionist explained, "If you have only a limited amount of money to spend, you're going to spend it on the cheapest calories you can get."[107] Numerous studies have documented that nutrition quality goes down alongside incomes. "Across the country, bodies got bigger as pay envelopes shrunk," remarked historian Bryant Simon.[108]

A recent study published in the *New England Journal of Medicine* predicted that half of all Americans would be obese within the next ten years.[109] Widespread obesity leads to a whole host of problems across society. Four of the top ten killers in America today are chronic diseases linked to diet: heart disease, stroke, diabetes, and cancer. One recent study estimated that obesity-related issues cost the American health-care sector about $173 billion each year.[110] Even the military has expressed concern about the impact of obesity on troop readiness.[111]

Cargill certainly is not taking any responsibility for these profound changes in the American diet. Instead, the company has financed organizations that push back on the notion that the United States has an obesity epidemic.[112] It used the same practices in Brazil when the country considered enacting regulations to curb obesity.[113] Any government action to address nutrition could threaten Cargill's bottom line, given that it is one of the largest global producers of corn sweeteners.

Cargill has even been using a front man strategy to corrupt academic research. In 2012, a Stanford University study claimed that organically grown food was not more nutritious than conventionally grown food.[114] This outlandish claim was later largely disregarded, but not before it was revealed that one of the institutes that supported it was funded by Cargill.

In another instance, Cargill funded a front group that, in turn, financed studies disputing any special health consequences associated with corn syrup.[115] It also financially supported a researcher who highlighted the benefits of farmed fish, which are largely fed a soy-based animal feed produced by Cargill.[116] In this last instance, the researcher's financial relationship to Cargill was not initially disclosed in the story and the reporting on it.[117]

Cargill has spent millions of dollars on top of its lobbying budget to finance these middlemen.[118] Its goal is to muddy the waters regarding the health and environmental impacts of the company's products and, ultimately, to influence policy governing them. For instance, the company supported an organization that tried to underplay the contributions of beef production to climate change.[119] At the same time, a Cargill representative sits on the executive board of the North American

Meat Institute, a trade association that fights efforts to regulate the American meat industry.[120] These examples are likely only the tip of the iceberg in Cargill's lobbying efforts, given the lack of disclosure about who funds these groups.

And Cargill hasn't just shaped laws to its advantage. In certain instances, it has been accused of flat-out breaking them. For example, Oxfam International released a report in 2013 revealing how Cargill secretly evaded land reform efforts in Colombia. For context, Colombia pursued land reform because many observers viewed concentrated landholdings by the wealthy and corporations as an "underlying cause" of a civil war that had displaced millions and killed more than 220,000 people over half a century. Cargill circumvented the land reform laws by using three dozen shell companies to buy farmland intended for family farms. The company ended up exceeding the legal limit on landownership thirtyfold.[121]

Subsidized corn and soy helped turn John MacMillan Jr.'s vision of an endless belt into reality. As a result, Cargill is now arguably the most powerful private corporation in modern history. The company operates its global empire out of a newly renovated 488,000-square-foot office complex in the upper-class Minneapolis suburb of Wayzata.[122] The compound is hidden in a patch of woods near a creek that the US Environmental Protection Agency has labeled impaired.[123]

It's hard to square the company's portrayal of itself as an all-American success story with the behemoth that emerged in the wake of the Wall Street Farm Bill. Because of this dominance, I think of Cargill as the twenty-first century's version of Standard Oil. But given Cargill's size, power, and geographic scope, that comparison might undersell it. A better analogy might actually be the British Empire in the nineteenth century.

After all, the sun never sets on Cargill grain.

CHAPTER 3

The Coffee Barons

You may not have heard of JAB Holding Company, but there's a good chance you've been in one of its stores. The Luxembourg-based conglomerate, controlled by members of the reclusive Reimann family in Germany, owns coffee chains and bakeries from sea to shining sea—and beyond. The list is extensive: Peet's Coffee, Caribou Coffee, Einstein Bros. Bagels, Bruegger's Bagels, Manhattan Bagel, Noah's New York Bagels, Krispy Kreme, Pret A Manger, Insomnia Cookies, and Panera Bread. In fact, the company now sells more coffee than Starbucks.[1]

Even coffee drinkers who try to patronize small neighborhood cafés are probably giving their dollars to JAB because many independent stores buy their beans from roasters owned by the company, including seemingly local ones such as Stumptown Coffee Roasters, La Colombe Coffee Roasters, Intelligentsia Coffee, and Green Mountain Coffee. JAB also sells directly to customers who prefer their beverages at home through its ownership of Keurig Dr Pepper Inc., the largest maker of single-serve coffee pods in the United States, and Trade Coffee, an online retailer.[2]

Together, JAB companies employ 180,000 workers and the conglomerate trails only Nestlé in the global market.[3] Even more amazing is how quickly JAB acquired so much control over the industry. Although the company dates back to the early 1800s, it entered the coffee business only in 2012, with its purchase of Peet's Coffee.[4] JAB became the world's second-largest purveyor of coffee (excluding coffee sold in stores) within seven years of selling its first bean.[5]

The Reimann family—more than any other baron portrayed in this book—is good at keeping secrets. The family has studiously avoided the sort of media coverage and public appearances that have proved irresistible to the other barons. In fact, rumor has it that when family members turn eighteen, they sign a pledge not to show their face in public, which is why no photos accompany their names in the annual *Forbes* list of the world's wealthiest people.[6] As the *Economist* put it, the Reimanns are "faceless," letting the wild success of their coffee empire speak for itself.[7]

Yet just a few decades ago, this guarded German family likely could not have assembled its empire. Its acquisition spree was made possible by seismic shifts in the law, with profound consequences for JAB's competitors and customers and even those who never drink a sip of coffee.

A Faceless Family, a Ruthless Strategy

The Reimann family fortune dates to the nineteenth century. Ludwig Reimann, great-great-grandfather of the present-day Reimanns, married the daughter of an industrial chemicals magnate named Johann Adam Benckiser, or JAB if you go by his initials. Ludwig Reimann took over the company when Benckiser died, and it stayed under the family's control for generations.[8]

Ludwig's descendants, Albert Reimann Sr. and his son Albert Reimann Jr., controlled the company as Germany descended into fascism. Both were ardent anti-Semites and became members of the Nazi Party, as well as early and enthusiastic supporters of Adolf Hitler, as Katrin Bennhold reported extensively in the *New York Times*.[9] The younger Albert Jr. hitched his wagon to Hitler as early as 1923, when he heard the future dictator speak in Munich. He even wrote a letter to Heinrich Himmler, the main architect of the Holocaust, describing the family as "unconditional followers of the race theory" and their company as "a purely Aryan family business."[10]

Once the Nazis came to power, the company became enmeshed in the regime's racial project. One of its factories was held up as a "model [Nazi] plant," and Albert Sr. even took a leadership position in a committee that "helped orchestrate the Aryanization, expropriation and expulsion of Jewish businesses."[11] Both Albert Jr. and Albert Sr. used forced labor, not only in their factories but also in their homes. Female workers were "forced to stand at attention naked outside their barracks, and those who refused risked sexual abuse." At the time, forced labor was common among companies such as the Reimanns', but this level of abuse stood out.[12]

Despite his unbridled anti-Semitism, Albert Reimann Jr. had an affair with a half Jewish employee. Emilie Landecker was born to a Jewish father and a Catholic mother, who died when Emilie was just six. As her father witnessed the Nazis' rise to power and was stripped of his rights as a citizen, he decided to protect his children by baptizing them in the Catholic faith and putting the family property in their names.

Because her father was not allowed to work, Emilie supported the family by getting a job, at the age of nineteen, in the accounting department of the Reimann family's company. She was working there in 1942 when the gestapo sent her father to a death camp. At some point, she became romantically involved with Albert Reimann Jr. and ultimately had three children with him.[13] Two of those children now own a large portion of JAB Holding Company.

Wolfgang Reimann remarked of his mother, "She lived through the horror show happening in our own company."[14] In interviews with the *New York Times*, Wolfgang recounted being shushed by Emilie when he asked about his Jewish grandfather. He said the children knew little about the company's sordid past until media reports began to surface.[15]

In 2018, a British newspaper broke a story about the Reimanns' historical ties to the Nazi regime. Soon after, the family members who own JAB released an interim report they had commissioned to investigate those ties.[16] To atone, the owners of JAB announced a one-time donation of ten million euros to organizations that help former forced laborers and their families. They also pledged to give twenty-five million euros annually to their family foundation to fund projects that "honor the memory of the victims of the Holocaust and of Nazi terror."[17]

The family's contrition appears to be genuine, and their willingness to dredge up and publicly acknowledge such a dark history deserves to be commended. Yet they have not always backed up this sentiment with action. When Russia invaded Ukraine in 2022, many Western companies, including Starbucks, ceased operations in Russia, citing moral and ethical concerns. As of August 2023, JDE Peet's, one of JAB's core portfolio companies, still operated in Russia, based partially on the reasoning that coffee is essential to "sustain health or life."[18]

JAB is by no means the only company that built its wealth by supporting the Nazi regime. As a report by America's secretary of war noted, Hitler's Germany was characterized by "a great series of industrial monopolies in steel, rubber, coal, and other materials."[19] These companies include several firms still around in some form today, such as Bayer, Deutsche Bank, Siemens, and Bosch. Few firms were more closely associated with the regime than the chemical giant IG Farben. America's chief war crimes prosecutor called IG Farben "the men who made war possible . . . the magicians who made the fantasies of

Mein Kampf come true."[20] The company even built a factory next to Auschwitz to take advantage of slave labor provided by the concentration camp.[21]

These giants and their wealthy owners were instrumental in the Nazis' rise. In 1947, shortly after the end of World War II, the Library of Congress prepared a report that analyzed the reasons the Nazis came to power in Germany. It found that cartels provided critical financial support to the party at key moments.[22] IG Farben, for example, gave the Nazis their largest individual donation before an election when the party was short on funds.[23]

Monopolies supported Hitler even when he had few other backers because they knew he would preserve the economic order and help their bottom line.[24] They weren't just opportunists who cozied up to the regime once it took control. People like Albert Reimann Jr. recognized that if they did their part to bring the regime to power and supercharge its war machine, they would reap the benefits. Sure enough, the Reimanns' close ties to the party resulted in a financial windfall, with sales more than tripling during the decade after the Nazis took power.[25]

It would be simplistic to attribute the rise of fascism in Germany, or elsewhere, solely to corporate consolidation. But it would also be naïve to ignore its role. The Reimann family's history of cozy relations with a genocidal dictator shows what can happen when corporate and political power reinforce each other at the expense of the public. Monopoly and democracy, it turns out, don't easily coexist.

Busting the Gilded Trust

The idea that corporate consolidation threatens democracy is not a new one. As US Supreme Court Justice Louis Brandeis put it, "We may have democracy, or we may have wealth concentrated in the hands of a few, but we can't have both."[26]

While monopolies were supporting the rise of fascism in Germany, Brandeis and other reformers in the United States were working to limit industry's power. In the early years of the twentieth century, they created a regulatory framework to promote fair markets and prevent corporate behemoths like JAB from bullying workers and influencing politics.

Brandeis, the son of a Jewish immigrant, was a lawyer who cut his teeth during the Gilded Age, a time of massive inequality. During this era, companies entrenched their power by monopolizing a single industry or by holding a dominant position in related industries. An example is the way John D. Rockefeller's Standard Oil built a template for the Grain Barons' endless belt by controlling most of the oil supply chain.[27]

Brandeis rose to prominence because of his opposition to one of those companies: financier John Pierpont Morgan's transportation monopoly. Around the turn of the century, Morgan's New Haven Railroad began gobbling up its competitors to consolidate over three hundred ferry and rail transportation companies into one regional monopoly that stretched from New York City to Boston.[28] Brandeis became the leading public figure for the opposition to Morgan's plans.

In 1913, a federal commission unearthed evidence of significant accounting fraud and bribes in Morgan's consolidation spree. In response, the US Department of Justice threatened an antitrust lawsuit against the New Haven Railroad. The company ultimately conceded the battle and began selling off its holdings.[29] In the face of seemingly impossible odds, Brandeis had won.

The battle with J. P. Morgan cemented Brandeis's strong faith in decentralized systems and organic growth. He was far from a critic of business: his father was a businessman, and he was a prominent business attorney, after all. But he saw firsthand how a big corporation could use its economic power to steamroll its rivals and corrupt the political process. Because of his fights against these barons, Brandeis became known as the "people's attorney."[30]

Brandeis was not alone in this fight. He formed part of a reform-ist movement with people such as muckraking journalist Ida Tarbell, whose book about Standard Oil brought public attention to the dan-gers of unchecked corporate power.[31] A consensus developed for taking action to combat the "trusts," as monopolies and cartels were known, and political pressure began to build around the issue.

Years earlier, the US Congress had enacted the Sherman Antitrust Act of 1890 to provide tools to curb anticompetitive behaviors. Senator John Sherman, the bill's namesake, explained that "if we will not endure a king as a political power, we should not endure a king over the produc-tion, transportation, and sale of any of the necessaries of life."[32]

Yet these tools were hardly used for years.[33] Presidents Benjamin Har-rison, Grover Cleveland, and William McKinley brought only eighteen suits under the Sherman Act *combined*.[34] President Theodore Roosevelt understood the popular desire for action on the trusts better than his predecessors and brought more than forty cases.[35] He also broke up Standard Oil into thirty-four companies.[36]

Reformers such as Brandeis ultimately saw competition policy as an issue of power. Brandeis articulated this vision in a speech to the New England Dry Goods Association:

There is no way to safeguard the people from the evils of a pri-vate transportation monopoly except to prevent the monopoly. The objections to despotism and to monopoly are fundamental in human nature. They rest upon the innate and ineradicable selfish-ness of man. They rest upon the fact that absolute power inevitably leads to abuse.[37]

In Brandeis's telling, mere safeguards were not the answer because big corporations have the time and money to outlast and undo any regula-tions that hurt their bottom line. Whereas some thought that regulation could channel the power of big corporations into productive ends, Brandeis argued that power must be challenged head-on; otherwise, it would compound itself and ultimately corrupt democratic values.

In 1916, President Woodrow Wilson nominated Brandeis to the Supreme Court, but corporations and their allies waged an intense battle against the nomination by smearing Brandeis as a radical and dabbling in anti-Semitic tropes. His nomination was under consideration by the US Senate for 125 days, which held the record for the longest period for a Supreme Court nominee until it was broken by Merrick Garland a century later.[38] Ultimately, the Senate confirmed his nomination by a vote of 56–28.[39]

Brandeis's appointment to the Supreme Court gave him a powerful platform to push American law in a new direction. He worked to get like-minded individuals appointed to high-level government positions during Democratic administrations.[40] One senior official in the Franklin Roosevelt administration called Brandeis the "old man in the shadows."[41]

His economic vision was also built into the DNA of many legislative reforms of the New Deal era. One famous example was the Glass-Steagall Act, which was inspired by his writing.[42] President Franklin Roosevelt signed this legislation into law in response to the Wall Street crash of 1929. At its core, this legislation diffused power in the American banking system by prohibiting banks from operating as both commercial banks and investment banks. The law effectively broke up big banks and hindered consolidation in the sector for decades. Some have credited it with helping to keep the US financial system safe from a major crash until after its repeal in 1999.[43]

Brandeis's impact on the American legal system had so many economic ramifications that the *Economist* called him a "Robin Hood of the law."[44] His framework for diffusing power went on to dominate American politics for decades and helped locally owned businesses flourish across the country. By ensuring competition within and across industries, it sparked broad economic growth that benefited workers throughout the economic spectrum. And, maybe most important, Brandeis's framework helped check industry's influence over American politics.

Empire Building

After the war, Allied occupying powers arrested Albert Reimann Jr. Even though he still professed a belief that Hitler would prevail as late as a month before the end of the war, he brushed aside allegations of his ties with the regime and insisted that he was a victim of the Nazis. The French government attempted to bar Albert Reimann Jr. from continuing his business operations, but the Americans overruled them.[45]

For the next thirty years, Albert Jr. helped run the company. When he died, in 1984, he left equal stakes to his nine children, who took the company public and ultimately merged it with another firm. His children then founded JAB Holding Company as a vehicle to invest their wealth.

Instead of investing in the normal mix of stocks, bonds, and real estate, the managers of JAB pursued a different approach.[46] With its pile of money and outside investors—including the endowments of Stanford University and the University of Pennsylvania—JAB bought companies directly, focusing on rolling up as many firms as possible in the same industry and then combining them into one new megafirm.[47]

The next step was to restructure the firms they had purchased, which likely entailed realizing as many "efficiencies" as possible. This playbook, which is common for buyers like JAB that take over a company and want to make it pay better for them as an asset, often involves a combination of layoffs and leveraging of size and market power to squeeze suppliers and the workers that remain. The strategy is most famously—and controversially—employed by private equity firms.

JAB initially focused on perfume and luxury goods, but in recent years it has pivoted to coffee and cafés. With the flowering of independent stores, and Americans' taste for distinct brands, the coffee business was highly fragmented and innovative, a sign of a healthy, competitive industry. This abundance of profitable businesses presented an opportunity for JAB. The company went on a buying spree, spending $30 billion in just four years, capped off by its $13.9 billion purchase of Keurig Green Mountain in 2015.[48]

JAB isn't the only company to try to consolidate control of an industry through this sort of naked power grab. In fact, JAB mimicked the strategy of conglomerates in the beer industry, which is dominated by two global firms. As one financial analyst pointed out, it seemed as if JAB was on a mission to become "the Bud(weiser) of the coffee space."[49]

In fact, once you start looking, you can find concentrated industries everywhere in the American economy. In 2016, the *Economist* collected data on almost a thousand industries and found that market concentration increased in nearly two-thirds of them over a fifteen-year period.[50]

Many institutional economists suggest that when five firms control more than 60 percent of a market, it is no longer competitive.[51] Yet we've blown past these thresholds in many sectors, including some unexpected ones. Just two companies sell 74 percent of all milk.[52] One company—Whirlpool—manufactures 58 percent of all washers and dryers.[53] And just two companies control 82 percent of the market for coffins and caskets.[54]

Often, consolidation in a sector is obscured by one company using many different brand names, just as JAB conceals its power through ownership of many seemingly independent companies. Corporations use different brands to cater to different socioeconomic classes. These brands create the illusion of choice.[55] It may seem as if shoppers have options, but all they're really choosing is their preferred price point. That's why LensCrafters, Sunglass Hut, Pearle Vision, Target Optical,

Glasses.com, FramesDirect.com, EyeBuyDirect, Clearly, Ray-Ban, and Oakley are all owned by one foreign-based company, EssilorLuxottica.[56]

Although concentration is rampant across the economy, it's a particularly bad problem in the food sector. One company sells 73 percent of baby food; one company sells 47 percent of pet food. It just so happens that it's the same company: Nestlé.[57] And the nation's meatpacking industry is now more concentrated than when Upton Sinclair wrote *The Jungle*.[58] Four companies, two of which are foreign owned, now slaughter more than half of all meat consumed in the United States.[59]

You would never guess these markets are so consolidated from a casual trip to the grocery store. You can look at a shelf of peanut butter and think you're seeing a competitive market, with a range of options like Jif, Smucker's, Adams, Laura Scudder's, and Santa Cruz Organic. But all these brands are owned by the J.M. Smucker Company, which now sells nearly one in every two jars of peanut butter directly.[60]

That statistic doesn't even account for the fact that many store-brand versions of the product are likely manufactured by large producers like J.M. Smucker. Although the exact numbers of store-brand items that the company produces are not publicly known, a 2022 recall illustrated its success in penetrating this segment of the industry. In addition to recalling Jif, the company recalled store-brand items that it made for large grocery store chains, including Giant Eagle and Safeway.[61]

The illusion of choice means that even when consumers think they are opting for a brand that sounds like a local, independent option, like Stumptown, they are really just buying from JAB. Nearly eight in every ten coffee stores are now owned by just three companies. Not surprisingly, JAB is one of them.[62]

Even as it fends off allegations that it has monopolized the coffee space, JAB is plotting its next monopoly play: pets.[63] It recently spent $1.4 billion to buy a pet insurance business, and it has acquired over 1,400 local veterinary practices and care centers.[64]

Obtaining control of a market to create an illusion of choice has formed the heart of JAB's strategy in recent years. The Reimann family has seen its wealth explode during this period of expansion, with a yearly return rate higher than 15 percent.[65] *Forbes* estimated the four siblings' net worth in 2022 at $23.2 billion, making them one of Germany's richest families.[66]

But JAB's strategy likely would not have been possible before changes in the law profoundly altered the American and international economic landscapes. For much of the twentieth century, antitrust laws influenced by Brandeis's framework promoted competitive markets and prevented companies like JAB from concentrating their economic power. Today, those protections have been brushed aside by a new worldview.

The Bork Apocalypse

Since the late 1970s, judges, politicians, and bureaucrats have waged an all-out war on Brandeis's competition framework, and their efforts have transformed the structure of our economy. One man in particular personifies this movement: a controversial academic and judge named Robert Bork.[67]

Americans were first introduced to Bork in the aftermath of Richard Nixon's Saturday Night Massacre, when Bork served as the president's hatchet man in the cover-up of the Watergate scandal. Nixon ordered the firing of Archibald Cox, the special prosecutor appointed to investigate wrongdoing by the Nixon campaign, but both Deputy Attorney General William Ruckelshaus and Attorney General Elliot Richardson refused to carry out the order and resigned in protest. Bork, who was solicitor general at the time, was the only person willing to put principles aside to do Nixon's bidding. Nixon had promised to appoint him to the Supreme Court.[68]

After Nixon's resignation, Bork briefly retreated to academia before returning to public life when President Ronald Reagan nominated him to the Supreme Court in 1987. Bork's involvement in the Watergate scandal and his controversial views—including previous support for a poll tax, literacy tests for voting, and opposition to the Civil Rights Act of 1964—quickly became a political flashpoint. The Senate voted down his nomination, but Bork endured as one of the most influential legal activists of the past few decades.

As a law professor and later as an appellate judge, Bork focused his energies on dismantling the long-standing competition framework associated with Brandeis. Bork earned his undergraduate and law degrees from the University of Chicago, a school founded by oil baron John D. Rockefeller. The university is infamous for its association with a deeply conservative economic worldview known as the "Chicago school" that is attributed to the influential work of many of its faculty members. One of the foundational beliefs of the Chicago school is in the merit of paring back laws protecting competition. Milton Friedman, a leading Chicago school economist, even quipped that "we would be better off if we didn't have [antitrust laws] at all."[69]

In 1978, Bork published a book called *The Antitrust Paradox*, in which he criticized the Brandeis framework and argued that the only purpose of competition laws is to maximize economic efficiency.[70] In Bork's view, regulators and courts analyzing mergers should ignore harm to workers, locally owned businesses, and communities, as well as exclusionary practices that entrench a company's economic power.

Instead, Bork advocated for an exclusive focus on the impact on consumer prices, an approach known as the "consumer welfare standard." This framework considers a monopoly detrimental to society only if it leads to higher prices for consumer goods. As long as an economist can argue that prices may go down as a result of a merger, a company's accumulation of market power and the disappearance of its competitors doesn't matter.

This framework represented a radical reorientation of antitrust policy, and its core principles were wholly unrelated to the original criteria and intentions of antitrust and competition laws. The consumer welfare standard does not appear anywhere in the Sherman Act. According to Columbia Law School professor Tim Wu, "not a single statement in the [original] legislative history comes close to stating the conclusions that Bork drew."[71] Bork simply rewrote history to match his laissez-faire, pro-corporate ideology.

Unfortunately, *The Antitrust Paradox* was enormously influential in shaping the development of competition policy. Bork and others like him provided an intellectual cover for today's robber barons to weaken the rules protecting competitive markets. He was a key member of the Federalist Society, an organization that bills itself as a nonpartisan educational effort. A blockbuster *Washington Post* investigation found close ties between the Federalist Society, which is funded by wealthy donors, and other nonprofits that support conservative judges and policies. These reporters calculated that the network collected over $250 million between 2014 and 2017 alone.[72]

The judiciary has become filled with judges associated with the Federalist Society and Bork's ideology who have pared back the sorts of protections that Brandeis fought for. As Adam Cohen recounts in his book *Supreme Inequality: The Supreme Court's Fifty-Year Battle for a More Unjust America*, the result has been "a systemic rewriting of society's rules to favor those at the top and disadvantage those in the middle and at the bottom."[73]

Bork acolytes also gutted the Federal Trade Commission, America's anti-monopoly watchdog. The agency's staffing levels declined by 46 percent over the course of the Reagan administration. In fact, as of 2021, staffing levels were still only two-thirds of what they were the year Reagan took office.[74]

Actions by the Reagan administration and a series of cases decided by the Supreme Court adopted Bork's novel, unprecedented doctrine not long after he invented it out of thin air.[75] Bork's philosophy has become firmly entrenched in legal scholarship, political ideologies, and regulatory practice in the federal government.

The reign of Bork's doctrine has led to exactly the sort of consolidation through unchecked acquisitions that reformers like Brandeis feared. Prior to Bork's anti-antitrust revolution, for example, the Grain Barons' acquisition of their chief rival in the grain elevator business likely would not have been approved. And without this radical reinterpretation of America's competition framework, JAB might not have been able to aggressively consolidate the coffee and café industry.

The irony is that the standard has not even succeeded at achieving its limited aims. A whole cottage industry has sprung up for economists—hired and paid by the merging companies—to produce studies showing that a merger will lead to lower prices. One hired gun has raked in more than $100 million for these services, according to the estimates of a ProPublica investigation.[76] The Federal Trade Commission and the Department of Justice relies heavily on these so-called studies, which are rarely even made public, to make enormously important decisions about whether to permit companies to merge.

Because of deference to these studies, the government often operates on the assumption that larger firms can create "efficiencies"—usually a polite word for layoffs—that will lead to lower prices for consumers. But the reality is that instead of lower prices, they often lead only to higher pay for executives and bigger profits for shareholders.

Meanwhile, the promised savings for consumers have a way of failing to materialize. In 2015, a researcher reviewed past mergers and found that eight out of ten resulted in higher prices for Americans.[77] A recent *Consumer Reports* investigation, for example, found that a one-month supply of five commonly prescribed drugs averaged $107 at independent pharmacies, but the same prescriptions cost $752 on average at Walgreens and $928 at CVS.[78] Similarly, Affordable Care Act marketplace premiums were, on average, 50 percent higher in areas with monopolist insurers than in areas with more than two insurers.[79]

The rapid consolidation that has occurred under the consumer welfare standard also makes it easier for companies to fix prices. A Bloomberg Law story published right before Thanksgiving in 2019 noted that turkey producers represented the only corner of the meat industry not under investigation for price-fixing. At that point, cases were pending against producers of salmon, pork, beef, tuna, and chicken.[80] But not long after the article was published, turkey producers were added to the list.[81]

On a more fundamental level, the consumer welfare standard undermines the core purposes of competition policy by systematically stacking the deck against locally owned businesses in favor of large foreign-owned corporations such as JAB Holding Company. In the words of Jeffrey Young, chief executive officer of a global coffee research firm, "There's never been so much control over the coffee market and power has never been so concentrated, so we're in uncharted territory. Regardless of whether we think we're going to have cheaper or better coffee, usually in economics, it's not healthy to have so much control across so few."[82]

At its core, the standard uses pseudoscience to mask moral judgments, giving license to courts to favor corporations based on the false notion of efficiency. It's one main reason why economic power is more concentrated today than at any other point since Brandeis was fighting J. P. Morgan's transportation monopoly. In fact, in a comical display of power, JAB's American operation is located across the street from the White House (the company is unsurprisingly headquartered in Luxembourg, a known tax haven).[83]

As firms have gotten bigger and industries have become more consolidated, local ownership has been disappearing. Locally owned businesses increasingly can't compete on these tilted playing fields. Even as barons like the Reimann family have garnered huge profits, the consequences for society at large have been profound.

Monopoly versus Democracy

I know firsthand the value of local business. After years of working as a hairdresser and then managing an outpost of a national chain, my mom, Kathy Frerick, dreamed of being her own boss. Around the time I started grade school, she decided to open a bakery and coffee shop near our house.

I have distinct memories of how much work my mom put in to get her bakery off the ground. My parents took road trips to various conventions and competitors to learn the ropes of the business and piece together their plans, leaving me and my brother with our grandparents. When the store was under construction, my mom picked us up from school and brought us to the site, excitedly pointing out where everything would go. In my memory, the grand opening was like Iowa's version of the Met Gala, with so many people dressed to the nines. My mom worked the room in a stunning white pantsuit, and my dad looked the sharpest I've ever seen him.

My mother took incredible pride in her business and did everything she could to make it a success. She built relationships with her regulars and organized events with the owners and managers of the stores nearby. Our family spent Sunday mornings scrubbing the place top to bottom. My dad cleaned the floor tiles while my brother and I wiped all the marks off the white tables and chairs.

You see this pride of ownership in all sorts of local businesses. There's a level of care that just doesn't exist when the only goal is to generate better returns for distant executives and shareholders. It's why local businesses almost always seem to provide better products and services than their corporate competitors.

In my hometown, folks could get coffee anywhere, but they came to my mom's place because of the relationship she built with them. They knew all about our family, and my mom knew about the happenings in their lives. We attended their weddings, funerals, and everything in between.

It's an obvious but essential difference between corporate chains and mom-and-pop shops: local business owners live in the same community as their customers and their employees. Their children attend the same schools. They use the same public services and deal with the same problems. Unlike the reclusive Reimanns, they are literally the faces of their businesses, with their reputations and the health of their communities essential to their success. They have a stake in the places they serve in a way that a huge conglomerate does not.

My mom made a point of donating to any local nonprofit that asked. One year, she provided one of the winning prizes for the sweet potato pie contest fundraiser at the African American Museum of Iowa. She even served as a local celebrity judge.[84] The director of the museum was a regular; I used to ring up his orders.

Mergers, on the other hand, are often accompanied by a collapse in donations to local charities and nonprofits. After its purchase by InBev, based in Belgium, Anheuser-Busch reportedly reduced its local giving by 80 percent.[85] One longtime resident of a slaughterhouse town told me that the plant donated money to the community when it was locally owned, but the contributions stopped once the plant was swallowed up by a conglomerate. "If I wanted to run a big fundraising campaign, [the packing plant] would not be a big donor," one mayor noted. "They are not going to exert that kind of influence on the community."[86]

Local businesses cultivate a distinct identity and sense of place. My hometown, Cedar Rapids, is known for its kolaches, a product of the city's deep Czech heritage. Likewise, any Iowan can brag all day about our state's Maid-Rites (loose meat sandwiches) and tenderloins (breaded pork), even if folks outside the region have never heard of them. That's why you see signs urging people to "shop local" or expressing "love for local" in towns and cities across the country. A lot of these values can't be quantified in terms of efficiency or a benefit to a consumer. But they exist, and many people understand them intuitively.

The loss of local ownership has ripple effects that go far beyond where we shop. Researchers have documented that local businesses are closely associated with civic engagement and well-being.[87] They form part of a community's social and economic fabric in a way that multinational corporations often do not. I don't want to fetishize locally owned business, but there is a balance to strike here, and we've swung way too far on that pendulum. The sad truth is that our economy stacks the deck in favor of the big players over the local owners.

Our family bakery closed more than a decade ago. The business was always profitable, but sales started tumbling as multinational chains began popping up in the area. My mom remains close to her employees and many of her former customers. She continued to work in the food industry and eventually became the manager of one of her former competitors, an outpost of a large coffee chain located in a big-box store. My mother landed on her feet, but for many owners, shuttering their business takes a significant psychological (not to mention financial) toll.

As people lose power in their everyday lives, they become susceptible to the appeal of an authoritarian who offers a scapegoat for their troubles and a means to express the power they retain. Lee County, a community in Iowa that had seen almost all its major locally owned employers disappear since the 1970s, voted for Barack Obama in 2012 by a margin of 56 percent to 41 percent.[88] In 2016, Donald Trump won it by nearly 16 percentage points. In 2020, Trump's margin over Joe Biden jumped to 19 percent.[89]

Indeed, demographer William Frey has argued that Trump's campaign strategy was built on attracting voters in places losing population—in other words, rural communities that had been hollowed out by corporate consolidation.[90] Katherine Cramer, a political science professor at the University of Wisconsin, explained the rural attraction to Trump this way: "They feel like their communities are dying, and they perceive that all that stuff—the young people, the money, the livelihood—is going somewhere, and it's going to the cities."[91]

But even as his message appealed to disaffected voters in the Heartland, Trump won in 2016 because of the financial support he received from many of the billionaires and multinational corporations that benefited most from the shift to the Bork framework, which brought about the second Gilded Age. He mastered the art of speaking from both sides of his mouth. Even while promising to "drain the swamp" and to fix a "rigged system," Trump courted the financiers and monopolists who wallowed in the swamp and rigged the system.

Few people understand the connections between concentrated economic power and fascism better than the Reimann family. "In history, businesses have enabled populists," reflected Peter Harf, current chairman of JAB Holding Company. "We mustn't make the same mistake today."[92]

CHAPTER 4

The Dairy Barons

Sᴜᴇ McCʟᴏsᴋᴇʏ's ᴄᴏᴡs ɴᴇᴠᴇʀ ɢᴇᴛ ᴀ ᴄʜᴀɴᴄᴇ to roam on pasture. But, as she told *Food & Wine* magazine in 2018, she strives to keep the girls happy. Sue's husband, Mike McCloskey, is chairman of a dairy production facility and tourist attraction called Fair Oaks Farms, which has been referred to by some media outlets as the "Disneyland of agricultural tourism."[1] At the facility's vast complex of Amazon-like warehouses, the "happy girls" pump out more than four million school milk cartons' worth of milk per day, making Fair Oaks one of the largest dairy producers in America.[2]

But it is far from exceptional. For decades, huge operations like Fair Oaks have been replacing family dairy farms across America. Wisconsin, the longtime heart of dairy production in the United States, lost 38 percent of its dairy farmers during the past decade.[3] Today, more than half of America's milk is produced on less than 3 percent of its farms.[4] And those megafarms are like Fair Oaks: factories that are larger than any operations in agricultural history.

I visited Fair Oaks Farms in the summer of 2021. The complex is in Northwest Indiana, right off Interstate 65 between Chicago and

Indianapolis. Admission was $20 for children and adults when I visited and free for children under two. School group tours make up the backbone of the center's guests, providing nearly half of its six hundred thousand annual visitors, an attendance figure that equals that of the Indiana State Museum and Conner Prairie (a living historic farm) combined.[5]

Admission includes access to a big outdoor play area containing a bouncing pit, a ropes course, and a rock-climbing wall shaped like a milk carton. A farm-themed Marriott hotel and large restaurant are situated on the property to accommodate travelers, along with a gas station, gift shop, and ice-cream parlor. The complex is recognized as the number one agritourism destination in the Midwest. "We hope to be the agricultural hub for the United States," Jamie Miller, general manager of attractions at Fair Oaks, told *Pacific Standard*.[6]

The real attraction of Fair Oaks is the tour of nearby industrial pig and dairy factories, which visitors reach through a short tram ride from the main complex. I boarded my tram with a group of mostly schoolchildren and their chaperones, and after leaving the visitor complex, we turned in to one of the warehouses where thousands of the McCloskeys' girls spend their lives.

According to my tour guide, the warehouse is the most technologically advanced dairy in America. It is laid out almost like a parking lot. Each cow spends most of her day in her own parking stall, occasionally leaving to get milked and sporadically having her manure removed. In the newest cow warehouse, most of the operations are robotic, from milking to manure removal.

We drove down the center lane of one building and passed rows of lethargic cows in their pens. At the ends of the rows, lagoons collected manure, which we could smell from the tram. The guide reassured us that everything centers on "making sure the girls are happy" and touted the farm's sustainability measures involving the cows' manure.

These warehouses are essentially all the cows will know. Across the dairy industry, cows typically stay in such warehouses until the age of three, when their bodies begin to break down as a result of stresses caused by this environment and production model. For reference, this life span is nearly a year and half shorter than that of a normal pastured family farm cow.[7] As the cows approach the end of their lives, they are often sold to slaughterhouses, bound to be served as hamburgers topped with the cheese they might have once supplied.

At Fair Oaks, there is no mention of what these warehouses replaced: the family dairy farm. States such as Wisconsin and Vermont are dotted with abandoned idyllic red barns that formerly housed dairy herds of a few dozen. As the price of milk has dropped steadily over time—in large part thanks to increased production by industrial facilities—these family farms have thrown in the towel and closed by the thousands.[8] Pastures where cows used to graze are now planted with corn and soy, mostly to feed the cows now housed permanently inside these massive metal sheds.

The labor on these industrial operations is primarily performed by young undocumented men, whose bosses often also serve as their land-lords.[9] A 2017 report of immigrant dairy workers found that the average pay was $9 per hour, and 97 percent lived in housing provided by their employer.[10] One 2015 episode of the podcast *This American Life* documented a two-bedroom trailer shared by thirteen workers.[11]

These workers face difficult and often dangerous working conditions. While researching this chapter, I discovered an unreported incident in which a worker died on the McCloskeys' farm in January 2021, in the same barn I toured a few months later. Records from the Indiana office of the Occupational Safety and Health Administration described him as a forty-seven-year-old recent immigrant born in Honduras who spoke limited English. He had been working a twelve-hour shift near manure equipment when his clothing got caught in the machinery. He was pulled in and died from asphyxiation.[12] He left behind a wife and three children.[13] In response, OSHA fined Mike and Sue just $10,500.[14]

Even before I knew about this worker's terrible death, I found the Fair Oaks Farms tourist attraction to be an unsettling place. And so was its namesake town of Fair Oaks, a small, low-income community nearby. "I have lived in Newton County for twenty years and I feel that Natural Prairie Dairy [an organic industrial dairy operation with a neighboring facility] and Fair Oaks Farms has brought disgrace to the county I call home," Janice Lewandowski wrote recently in a local newspaper.[15] As I walked around this hollowed-out town, I could understand why she felt this way. I can barely smell, but on a summer day with no wind, the stench of manure was unrelenting.

While Fair Oaks Farms has become a regional destination, Mike and Sue McCloskey have emerged as leading spokespeople for the industry. *Good Housekeeping* named Sue McCloskey a 2017 Awesome Women Awards Honoree, and *Food & Wine* profiled her in 2018.[16] *Politico* referred to Mike McCloskey as "the closest thing to a rock star in the industry."[17] Mike and Sue have spoken across the country about their sustainability efforts, including at the South by Southwest Festival and Yale University.[18]

As tens of thousands of American dairy farms have folded, the McCloskeys have found huge financial success in the industry. They live in a nearly twelve-thousand-square-foot mansion about ten miles north of their cow warehouses, just far enough away to escape the waft of manure.[19] They also own a multimillion-dollar condo located blocks from Navy Pier in Chicago and list a condo at the Ritz-Carlton in Puerto Rico as a legal residence.[20]

The McCloskeys didn't become the vanguard of the industrial dairy industry by accident. For decades, they've shown foresight and boldness that kept them a full step ahead of their competitors. They've (improbably) created new dairy products, partnered with other giant corporations, hired the best public relations firms money can buy, and turned foul-smelling facilities into a tourist destination.

But a closer look at the McCloskeys' rise to power reveals that political savvy was as important as business acumen in building their empire. They perfected the art of using public resources—whether they were water, land, tax breaks, subsidies, or politicians themselves—for private gain. They are not self-made barons; the system made them, and continues to promote them, even as many family dairies have been lost.

West to Midwest

Sue and Mike McCloskey were not raised in the dairy business. Mike was born in Pennsylvania, but his mother moved the family back to her home in Puerto Rico after her husband died. In Puerto Rico, McCloskey met an uncle who was a veterinarian and decided to follow in his footsteps, earning a doctor of veterinary medicine degree from the National Autonomous University of Mexico and the University of California, Davis.[21] Sue McCloskey, on the other hand, grew up in the suburbs of New York City west of the Hudson River.[22] The two met when she was an art student in San Diego, where he was her landlord.[23]

The couple began their ascent by building a successful veterinary business in California. But Mike McCloskey had developed his own ideas about the dairy industry and wanted to put them into practice. So the couple started their own dairy in California with only 250 cows. Soon, they moved the operation to New Mexico.[24]

Dairy farming in arid New Mexico might sound strange, but the state produces nearly three times as much milk as Vermont. For the past few decades, dairy production has been shifting from family farms in New England and the Midwest to industrial factories in the West and Southwest. Western dairies now produce nearly half of America's milk.[25]

Many of these businesses are massive factories with thousands of cows in the middle of the desert. Cheap, heavily subsidized feed is trucked in from miles away, and low-wage workers, usually undocumented, perform most of the work. At a traditional family dairy farm, it's practical to put cows on pasture and let their waste fertilize the grass that serves as their feed. But industrial dairy operations in the desert benefit from a key advantage: they can rely on the sun to quickly dry out the manure, which is then applied to fields as fertilizer. There are also hardly any neighbors to complain about the smell.

The ongoing water crisis in the West raises serious concerns about these facilities. Cows consume thirty to fifty gallons of water per day.[26] In California, industrial dairies require more water every day than what the state suggests that all residents of San Jose and San Diego use, according to Food & Water Watch.[27] Water for these factories is pumped from aquifers below, which are quickly being depleted.[28] In Arizona, the dairies are causing residential wells to run dry.[29] And in a twist on history, the town of Dalhart in the Texas panhandle, which was featured in Ken Burns's documentary on the Dust Bowl, is now home to several massive, water-intensive dairy operations.[30]

In the growing dairy hub of the Southwest, the McCloskeys expanded their operation to thousands of cows. Their business seemed to be thriving, but in 1999, the McCloskeys zigged where others zagged and moved again, this time to Northwest Indiana.[31] A move to the Midwest was unheard of in the industry at the time; most dairy production was migrating in the opposite direction. But it was in Indiana that the McCloskeys went from wealthy owners of a megadairy to titans of the industry.

Their new dairy operation was located at the former site of the Grand Kankakee Marsh, often called the Everglades of the North. This massive wetland covered nearly a million acres across Northern Indiana and a portion of Illinois.[32] In 1838, the Indiana government forcibly removed the Potawatomi people who lived in the marsh, in a massacre that became known as the Trail of Death.[33]

White settlers then drained 95 percent of those wetlands to convert them to farmland.[34] That's why drainage canals outline most of the McCloskeys' farmland. Those canals have been labeled impaired by the US Environmental Protection Agency for having excessive levels of *E. coli* bacteria in the water, which indicates contamination with animal waste.[35] The government recommends that people, especially children and the elderly, avoid drinking the water because of the risk of severe illness.[36]

For the McCloskeys, the former marshland provided several key advantages. The area has lots of sand, which their operation needs for the cows' bedding, and the water supply is much better than in New Mexico.[37] Moreover, corn and soy, which constitutes a part of their cows' diet, grows for hundreds of miles east and west, lowering feed and transportation costs.[38]

The location also presented an opportunity to take advantage of regional price differences to game the infamously complex federal milk subsidy system. Subsidy payment is based on where dairy is processed, with lower prices in heavily industrialized regions. The move to Indiana likely meant that the McCloskeys would receive higher subsidies than in New Mexico, where the surrounding region was dotted with industrial dairies.[39]

But the McCloskeys' new location in Indiana might have also provided an opportunity to sell milk in different geographic regions, depending on which ones paid more. One expert told me that a common strategy for large dairies like the ones owned by the McCloskeys is to sell into regions with fewer industrial operations, which tend to have higher rates. With lower production costs than family farms because of exploitive labor and environmental practices, the move to Indiana may have meant that the McCloskeys had the best of both worlds.

But even though they'd grown their herd by thousands, built a huge complex of dairy warehouses, and set up their permanent home in the former Grand Kankakee Marsh, the McCloskeys acted as if they were on the run from oblivion.

Milk production has increasingly become a race to the bottom. As farms have grown bigger and bigger and federal subsidies have increasingly encouraged more production, the dollar value of milk has declined. Oversupply has been catching up with the industry big-time, and thousands of operations have been calling it quits as prices have pushed out family farms that couldn't—or wouldn't—get bigger by stuffing their animals into metal sheds so their operations could stay in the black. It's the same phenomenon that decimated the pork industry.

If the McCloskeys' income depended on their participation in a market where prices were stuck in a doomed downward spiral, they'd never get off the treadmill. The McCloskeys' solution was to create a unique brand identity, a new product that American consumers would want more than the traditional milk.[40] That brand eventually became Fairlife.

Game Changer

The road to Fairlife was long and winding. The effort went through different names, formulas, and branding strategies. The first variation appeared in 2004 under the name Mootopia, which was sold at H-E-B, a grocery chain based in San Antonio with locations across Texas.[41] The McCloskeys also tried a sports drink called Athletes HoneyMilk in Chicago-area Wal-Marts.[42]

Eventually, they launched the Fairlife brand, a new milk product resembling Mootopia, and rebranded Athletes HoneyMilk as Fairlife Core Power.[43] The company started Fairlife production in a former General Motors plant in Michigan and opened corporate offices in the chic West Loop neighborhood of Chicago.[44]

Milk has been going through hard times for a while in American shopping baskets. Since 1975, milk consumption per capita has declined by roughly 40 percent, with plummeting sales of whole milk driving this decline.[45] Grocery shoppers increasingly avoid buying foods perceived as high in fat and look for items dense with protein.

Fairlife addressed these problems with an ultra-filtered milk—essentially, milk put through a special filtration process—to make its nutritional profile more attractive to health-obsessed shoppers. According to Fairlife, the product has 63 percent more protein, 38 percent more calcium, and half the sugars of normal 2 percent milk.[46] It's also lactose free and can sit in the fridge unopened for up to 110 days, compared with just a few weeks for normal milk.[47] The "added value" over normal milk allowed the McCloskeys to charge higher retail prices and slowly foster brand loyalty with higher-income, mostly urban consumers.[48]

Fairlife hit shelves in 2014, with an initially rocky public response.[49] Stephen Colbert described it as "like they got Frankenstein to lactate."[50] In a taste test conducted by BuzzFeed, most people preferred normal milk, and the writer observed that "Fairlife is a little bit creepy to drink."[51] The biggest difference I notice is the color. Whereas a glass of pastured milk has a rich off-white color, Fairlife has an unnatural pure whiteness to it. Unlike the traditional glass bottle or clear plastic jug, Fairlife comes in a plastic container obscured by a full-bottle label, so shoppers can't see this unappealing coloring before they buy the product.

To turn Fairlife from a niche product into a famous brand sold in grocery stores across the country, the McCloskeys enlisted the support of the beverage world's most powerful partner: the Coca-Cola Company. Before launching Fairlife, the McCloskeys struck a deal for the multinational beverage giant to distribute the drink and buy a minority stake in the company.[52] For Coca-Cola, Fairlife represented an opportunity to add another non-soda beverage to its growing roster of grab-and-go options.

Coca Cola's strategy for Fairlife mirrored the one it had implemented for its highly successful premium juice brand, Simply.[53] Unbeknownst to most American consumers, Coca-Cola owns both the Minute Maid juice brand and the Simply premium juice brand. Both brands sell orange juice but at two different price points, aimed at different types of consumers.

That was the plan for Fairlife, which the company hoped would serve as its fancier, more expensive line of milk products. That's why the president of Coca-Cola North America referred to it at a conference as "a milk that's premiumized."[54] As one Coca-Cola executive said bluntly, "We'll charge twice as much for it as the milk we're used to buying in a jug."[55]

The strategy was wildly successful. Sales went from $143 million in 2015 to $702 million in 2021.[56] Fairlife has since expanded to other bottling locations across America and even one in Canada.[57] In January 2020, Coca-Cola purchased the rest of Fairlife.[58] The terms of the deal were not disclosed.

With the launch of Fairlife, the McCloskeys earned their status as Dairy Barons. They reinvented milk, developing a patented process that ultimately brought in hundreds of millions of dollars every year. But the environmental cost of their supersized dairy farms started to draw public attention, and once again, the McCloskeys had to defend their empire.

Wasteland

Dairy cows are eating machines, each consuming 110–120 pounds of wet feed per day.[59] And with this intake comes a lot of waste. The cows at Fair Oaks Farms produce about 430,000 gallons of manure every day.[60] For reference, that's more manure than is produced by the entire human population of Austin, Texas.[61]

The methane gas emitted by industrial dairies like Fair Oaks is an extreme driver of climate change. In fact, methane traps more than eighty times more heat than carbon dioxide over a twenty-year period.[62] As industrial dairies began to pop up, climate scientists started to draw attention to the issue. In 2006, the Food and Agriculture Organization of the United Nations highlighted dairies' climate footprint, and three years later, the Worldwatch Institute issued a report that found that the problem of livestock emissions was even worse than the United Nations recognized.[63]

With this increased scrutiny, the McCloskeys faced a public backlash from the high-income consumers of Fairlife. So the McCloskeys took their weakness and turned it into a selling point, using the old strategy that the best defense is a good offense. Perhaps to preempt the critique that their industrial production model results in higher greenhouse gas emissions, they began promoting a new technology, manure digesters, as a solution to their methane problem.

The theory behind these digesters is simple. They are essentially giant, airtight manure tanks. Manure from the company's cows is pumped into a digester, where it remains for a few weeks. Inside, the manure is heated so that bacteria can thrive and consume solids, replicating what takes place in a cow's stomach.[64] Biogas produced by the manure is captured and converted to methane, which can be used as a source of energy.[65] The leftover matter from the digester is applied to the fields as fertilizer.[66]

The McCloskeys spoke to anyone who would listen about the sustainability of their operation and the digesters. As Mike once warned in a speech, "If we don't already have a script and are preaching it daily, . . . things can get out of hand."[67] One *Fortune* article headline celebrated "how a huge dairy is solving a major pollution problem."[68] The *Chicago Tribune* ran stories on the McCloskeys' desire to power their trucks with energy from cow manure.[69] The McCloskeys even appeared on the popular television show *Dirty Jobs*, where host Mike Rowe sold their environmental narrative like the items he used to sell on QVC. "At the end of the day when the dust settles, or in this case the poo," Rowe proclaimed, "Fair Oaks Farms turns out to be one of the greenest factories in the country."[70]

If it sounds way too good to be true, that's because it is. There are three catches with digesters. On a very basic level, some have argued that digesters do not make sense financially without massive government subsidies, for which industry leaders such as the McCloskeys have been lobbying for years.[71] In congressional testimony in 2020, Mike McCloskey stated, "The primary impediment to on-farm digester adoption is the lack of financial incentives available to farmers. I strongly believe that once the proper incentives are in place, digesters will be adopted throughout the industry."[72]

Even more important than cost are questions about digesters' effectiveness. A recent study published in *Nature* found significant methane emissions from digesters, which the researchers assumed was from leaks.[73] The McCloskeys themselves have experienced this problem. The Indiana Department of Environmental Management fined their dairy operation for releasing too much gas from its digester equipment.[74] There have also been incidences of digesters exploding, which is not surprising, given the flammable nature of the gases involved.[75]

But above all, the digesters "solve" a problem that doesn't even exist outside industrial dairy operations. On a traditional pasture-based dairy farm, cows defecate on grass and the manure serves as a natural fertilizer. The manure slowly breaks down through a process of aerobic decomposition, which releases carbon dioxide but little methane.[76]

In an industrial dairy operation, manure is commonly stored in a pit or lagoon and undergoes a very different decomposition process. Manure releases methane only when it decomposes in anaerobic—

oxygen-free—conditions, as found in these pits and lagoons.[77] As a result, a pasture-based dairy farm doesn't produce anywhere near the amount of methane per cow as an industrial dairy does.

And yet, "green" payments to industrial factories for their manure digesters have begun. The US Department of Agriculture spent more than $200 million on digesters in 2021 alone to help offset the cost.[78] A recent news story noted that in California, some industrial dairy farms could make more money from manure than from milk because of the state's cap-and-trade system.[79]

These incentives mean that operators may be being paid to pollute more. It also gives another unfair advantage to industrial operations over family-owned pastured farms, entrenching the industry's worst practices. We're looking at a future in which pollution becomes an extra revenue stream that helps industrial dairies drive even more family farms out of business.

The story of digesters goes a long way toward explaining how barons like Sue and Mike use public coffers—and funding meant to help *all* dairy farmers—to go from wealthy to ultra-wealthy while polluting more and endangering workers and animals. A lot of the money that enriches large operations comes from obscure programs known as checkoffs. Few Americans know about these programs, but they affect our entire food system in stunning ways.

Checkoffs: Agriculture's Dark Secret

Checkoffs are entities financed by a mandatory tax levied on farmers. A dairy farm, for example, must pay the dairy checkoff a set dollar amount for every gallon of milk it produces. The money is then used—in theory—to collectively improve sales of a particular commodity. For example, the checkoff might conduct an advertising campaign to encourage Americans to buy more of the product.

Although commodity checkoffs are almost unknown outside the industry, most Americans are familiar with their work. For example, the famous "Got Milk?" advertising campaign was financed by the dairy checkoff. Fair Oaks Farms displays a gallery of "Got Milk?" celebrity photos in its hotel lobby. "Beef. It's What's for Dinner" and "Pork. The Other White Meat" are also famous campaigns developed and implemented by checkoff programs.

Commodity checkoff programs originated at the state level. During the Great Depression, the Florida legislature tried to boost consumption of citrus fruits produced by struggling farmers through a program funded by taxes on growers of oranges, grapefruits, and tangerines. Revenues were administered by a board appointed by the governor called the Florida Citrus Commission. The commission used some of these revenues to employ a national advertising firm to convince Americans to drink more Florida orange juice.[80]

Other states soon followed suit and passed similar legislation approved by farmer referendums. The programs included one in Idaho for vegetables, one in Iowa for milk, and another in North Carolina for tobacco.[81] The first federal checkoff was created for wool with the enactment of the National Wool Act of 1954, followed by a checkoff for cotton in 1966.[82]

Although growth of the programs was slow at first, they expanded rapidly just as the food system was deregulated toward the end of the twentieth century. The growth of checkoffs overlapped perfectly with the replacement of the New Deal Farm Bill framework with one that incentivized overproduction. After all, one of the key missions of the checkoffs is to get Americans to buy more. As the government began encouraging overproduction at the behest of corporate interests, the checkoffs played an important role in stimulating demand that would consume the increased output. In the 1980s and early 1990s, Congress passed laws creating new checkoffs, including one for dairy in 1983 and one for pork in 1985.

The 1996 Farm Bill streamlined the process to establish new check-offs and empowered the USDA to oversee these programs.[83] In the wake of these changes, new checkoffs proliferated like dandelions. By the 1990s, nine out of ten farmers were required to contribute to a check-off.[84] As of 2022, twenty-one categories of food products, from dairy to watermelons to popcorn, had an associated federal checkoff program.[85]

Most of the individual federal checkoffs are small entities. In 2016, about half of the federal checkoffs operated with less than $10 million in revenue.[86] But dairy dwarfs its counterparts. Dairy-related programs alone accounted for nearly half of the $885 million collected by check-offs in 2016.[87] Because of a lack of transparency in these institutions, their size is rarely reported.

This model leads to clear ethical issues. The most extreme case involves cigarettes. In *The Cigarette: A Political History*, historian Sarah Milov described in vivid detail the critical role that tobacco checkoffs played in seeding doubt about the dangers of smoking.[88] Food policy experts worry that food checkoffs send similarly problematic messages, as with the dairy checkoff encouraging Americans to eat more ice cream amid an obesity crisis.[89]

The money collected by checkoffs may even be used to fund junk science to support bogus health or climate claims. One former checkoff director noted that his checkoff shifted its resources from promotional campaigns to these sorts of "scientific" studies because it found them to be a better use of funds.[90] "The old way of telling [our] story through advertising is dead," Tom Gallagher, chief executive officer of the dairy checkoff, told an audience at the World Dairy Expo in 2016. "If we showed up with an ad . . . , people [would] go, 'That's big agriculture. I don't trust big agriculture. Those guys are lying to me.'"[91]

Gallagher laid out an alternative approach to checkoff spending during the same talk. He pointed to efforts by the dairy checkoff to push back against attempts to regulate the greenhouse gas emissions of industrial dairies: "There were those groups out there like WHO that were saying we were contributing eighteen percent to the carbon emissions, and we were able to correct that record." He even bragged about how the Obama administration relied on the research financed by the checkoff in its decision not to regulate industrial dairies. In 2023, an investigation by the *Guardian* detailed how checkoff funds were used to spread climate misinformation.[92]

Although the programs are supposed to benefit all food producers, that's true for only a small segment of the industry. Deregulation in the past few decades has led to massive vertical integration in agriculture. For example, WH Group of Hong Kong, through acquisitions of companies such as Smithfield Foods, both owns the most hogs in America and is the largest slaughterer of hogs.[93]

The largest agricultural corporations pay the most money into the checkoffs and consequently have gained disproportionate control over how the checkoffs operate. Recently, a vice president of Smithfield served as vice president of the pork checkoff.[94] Accordingly, the money spent by these checkoffs often bolsters corporate interests rather than the interests of all farmers who pay in.

In effect, the checkoffs force family farmers to pay a tax to their more powerful competitors. Often, these programs use this money to fight against the same family farmers who fund it. It's as if union dues paid by workers went toward their employers' efforts to bargain down wages, strip benefits, and fire employees.

It's not a coincidence that nearly a quarter million hog-raising family farms left the business during the first twelve years of the pork checkoff's existence. As agricultural expert John Ikerd noted, farmers "didn't realize the money was going to be spent to promote a kind of agriculture that was going to end up driving the independent producers out of business."[95]

But pork farmers grew wise to what was happening and momentum grew to end the pork checkoff program in the late 1990s. In theory, farmers can vote to end a checkoff, but even that process seems rigged. Hog farmers in the Midwest organized and collected over nineteen thousand signatures asking for a referendum.[96] In response, the pork checkoff hired a Washington, DC, corporate communications firm— whose previous clients included large tobacco companies—to defeat the referendum. The pork group ultimately spent around $4 million on the election.

Despite this lobbying effort, the farmers voted to terminate the pork checkoff in September 2000.[97] But Ann Veneman, secretary of agriculture under President George W. Bush, threw out the vote. The courts stepped in and forced the USDA to ask farmers whether they wanted to hold another referendum.[98] The USDA claimed that the renewed effort fell short of the required threshold, but it never released the final vote totals.[99]

Anger against checkoffs continues to this day. A 2019 investigation by the *Milwaukee Journal Sentinel* found that the dairy checkoff was paying its ten top executives an average of $800,000 each in 2017, even as a large number of Wisconsin dairy farmers were going out of business. "These high-priced marketing people sitting in fancy offices in suburban Chicago were driving up to the meetings in luxury foreign SUVs," said Sarah Lloyd, a struggling Wisconsin dairy farmer. "They were using my money and (other) farmers' money when farmers' kids are on free and reduced lunch."[100]

The USDA is supposed to rein in these sorts of abuses, but it has largely disregarded its oversight role, as recent reports by the US Government Accountability Office and the USDA Office of Inspector General have found.[101] The result has been several highly publicized scandals of funds being used in questionable—if not illegal—ways.[102] One checkoff paid for the spouse of a "'senior staff member' to accompany him to New Zealand for a 'meeting.'" Another used payments to a subcontractor as a mechanism for paying its employees over $300,000 in unauthorized bonuses.[103] Given the high degree of secrecy in these organizations, this misuse of funds is likely the tip of the iceberg.

It's not entirely clear why the USDA works so hard to protect check-offs, but one theory is that it results from the cozy relationship between the checkoffs and USDA officials. It's a common career path for USDA officials to work at a checkoff after leaving government service. Tom Vilsack, between stints as secretary of agriculture in the Obama and Biden administrations, made nearly a million dollars per year as an executive at the dairy checkoff. He waited only four days after resigning as secretary to announce his new job.[104]

The McCloskeys have not always had a cozy relationship with the dairy checkoff. In fact, the couple may have been involved in a lawsuit challenging the constitutionality of the program. The suit was filed in 2002 by their longtime lawyer Benjamin Yale on behalf of Pennsylvania family dairy farmers Joe and Brenda Cochran.[105] According to Brenda Cochran, Yale made it very clear that Mike McCloskey and his organization had an interest in the case.[106]

The lawsuit may have represented an effort by the McCloskeys to get out of their obligations to pay into the dairy checkoff. It was around the time of the lawsuit that the McCloskeys launched Mootopia, the early prototype of Fairlife. Perhaps they worried about paying into a program that would essentially help their competition by advertising generic milk.

But in 2005, the US Supreme Court threw out the Cochrans' lawsuit, which meant the McCloskeys had to keep paying into the checkoff.[107] For unclear reasons, the dairy checkoff started provided special funding to the McCloskeys to help them build their empire. Millions of dollars were routed to privately owned Fairlife.[108] Checkoff money also went into the Fair Oaks tourism complex that advertises an industrial dairy model driving family farms into bankruptcy.[109] And a portion of the science behind digesters was financed by the checkoff.[110] A détente seemingly had been reached.

Shock Wave in the Dairy World

During most of the 2010s, the McCloskeys' sustainability publicity train kept on chugging down the track. It took an undercover team led by a Florida man to finally put a dent in their professionally crafted reputation.

In early June 2019, an organization called Animal Recovery Mission posted numerous photos and videos taken at warehouses owned by the McCloskeys.[111] According to one media summary of the investigation, "violence towards the animals appeared to be commonplace, typically stemming from frustration over the calves' unwillingness to feed from artificial nipples."[112] Another article described "a four-minute video [that] depicts young and newborn calves being stabbed, kicked and stomped, some left with obvious injuries. The animals were beaten with steel rods and burned with branding irons."[113]

The videos received substantial press coverage, including in the *Chicago Tribune*, undermining the eco-friendly image the McCloskeys had carefully cultivated. As one headline put it, the story "destroys Fair Oaks Farms' charming facade."[114] With national outlets covering the leak and the videos going viral on social media, Mike and Sue had a public relations crisis on their hands.[115] Several Chicago-area grocery stores soon announced that they planned to pull Fairlife products from their shelves.[116]

Mike McCloskey responded quickly. In a video and written statement posted to the company's Facebook page, he took full responsibility for the actions in the footage and promised a series of reforms, including contracting with an animal welfare organization to conduct routine and regular audits.[117]

The fervor eventually subsided. The Chicago area grocery stores that pulled the product ended up putting it back on their shelves.[118] No new laws or regulations were enacted. The McCloskeys were taken at their word when they promised to do better.

But on closer inspection, the promised reforms seem like a farce. Mike McCloskey is listed as a staff member of the dairy welfare certification firm that Fairlife uses.[119] The audit was also performed by a rubber-stamping organization, according to Andrew deCoriolis of Farm Forward, an anti-industrial animal organization:

> As far as I can tell, one of [the audit company's] primary roles is to help companies like Fairlife recover from bad publicity. My recollection is that Fairlife was not working with [it] until the investigation of Fair Oaks broke in the media. Basically, Fairlife's response to documented incidents of animal abuse was to hire an auditing company to audit their supplier farms to industry standard practices that Mike helped craft.[120]

Following this scandal, Fairlife sales did dip, according to data from nationwide retail checkout scanners. But sales recovered in less than a year, and by August 2021 they were up more than 50 percent since the scandal broke.[121] The company also settled claims for $21 million that it falsely advertised its milk as coming from humanely treated cows.[122]

On a TEDx stage in 2018, Sue McCloskey said, "If you can't pull back the curtain and explain with confidence to your consumer, and describe what you're doing, then you may need to rethink what it is that you're doing."[123] The curtain was pulled back on the McCloskeys, but there's little evidence that they did any serious rethinking of their business model.

Dorado Beach, a Ritz-Carlton Reserve

The McCloskeys' dairy empire is certainly the product of ingenuity. Who but a visionary could imagine a theme park entirely devoted to industrial agriculture? And yet the record shows that the couple had a lot of help along the way, particularly from politicians.

According to one dairy expert, the McCloskeys "are the most powerful and politically influential dairymen in the US."[124] One dairy publication even said, "Mike's fingerprints are on virtually every program and policy in the industry today."[125] They are also very active in Republican politics. Over the past few decades, they've made more than two hundred political donations totaling nearly half a million dollars to almost exclusively Republican candidates. Their financial support included a $25,400 donation to Donald Trump weeks before his surprising upset victory in 2016.[126]

The McCloskeys seem to have been rewarded for their contributions. Mike McCloskey served on Trump's agriculture advisory committee and was even under consideration to be his secretary of agriculture, according to *Politico*.[127] Although he didn't get the job, he did meet privately with Secretary of Agriculture Sonny Perdue and with President Trump at the White House.[128] The McCloskeys have also sat on well-connected boards, including the secretary of defense's Defense Business Board and the Indiana Economic Development Corporation.[129]

Administrations on both sides of the aisle have tried to benefit from the McCloskeys' talent at public relations. As governor of Indiana, Mike Pence held a town hall at the Fair Oaks facility.[130] Tom Vilsack, secretary of agriculture under both Barack Obama and Joe Biden, visited around the same time to preview a new exhibit financed by an agribusiness corporation. He told the *Indianapolis Star* that "what we see here at Fair Oaks is the broad scope of opportunity."[131]

The McCloskeys are friendly to government when it is subsidizing Band-Aid remedies for industrial agriculture's environmental issues and helping them launch their most famous product. Checkoff money—essentially a tax on milk—produced big windfalls for the McCloskeys.

They've constantly dipped into taxpayer-funded programs and lobbied Congress for money.

But boy, does Mike McCloskey hate taxes. McCloskey is chairman of Consulting & Ancillary Services of Puerto Rico (CASPR), a company that advises rich Americans on how to lower their tax bills, guiding them through a new tax avoidance program on the island. Here's how the company sells itself on its website: "As high-income earners, we cringe every time we sign over a significant chunk of our salaries to the government. . . . Rather than accepting this raw deal, we searched for an effective method to reduce our tax burden."[132]

According to Jesse Barron in *GQ*, this new tax program "makes Puerto Rico the only place on U.S. soil where personal income from capital gains, interest, and dividends are untaxed. . . . To qualify for Act 22, individuals must prove to the IRS that they have become bona fide residents of Puerto Rico" by being on the island for a specified number of days. Most local residents are not eligible for the exemption.[133] The program might explain why the McCloskeys list a condo at the Ritz-Carlton in Puerto Rico as a legal residence.

The McCloskeys seem convinced that their work benefits the common good and the wealth their family accrues from the deal isn't too relevant. But when the organization that runs Fair Oaks Farms applied for nonprofit status, the Indiana Board of Tax Review rejected it. The board pointed out that that the attraction ultimately promotes something for private gain.[134] It makes one wonder why the USDA ignored what the Indiana Board of Tax Review viewed as a red flag.

If you were being generous, you could argue that Mike McCloskey's tax schemes are in a moral gray area, but he's also been accused of crossing legal lines. In 2004, McCloskey settled with the US Securities and Exchange Commission for insider trading. He agreed to pay a penalty of $185,000 without admitting or denying the allegations.[135]

As for what the future holds, the McCloskeys' empire has never looked stronger. In recent interviews, Mike McCloskey mentioned that he wants to enter the Chinese market and expand dairy production to Puerto Rico.[136] The COVID-19 pandemic hit industrial dairy hard at first, but the USDA stepped in with massive bailouts.[137] The McCloskeys also received $2.9 million in Paycheck Protection Program (PPP) money.[138]

According to the dairy publication *Milkweed*, Mike McCloskey seems to be back in business with the Coca-Cola Company too, despite the soft drink giant's attempts to distance itself from the McCloskeys in the wake of their scandals. In 2022, he visited industrial dairies in the Northeast as Coca-Cola scouted for a new Fairlife plant in the region.[139] In May 2023, the company announced plans to build a 745,000-square-foot production facility in upstate New York, funded by the state to the tune of $21 million in tax credits and up to $20 million in additional capital grants.[140] The justification for this taxpayer-funded generosity: 250 new jobs.

Meanwhile, the future of America's dairyland is similar to what has played out in Iowa: industrial, corporate food production that will further hollow out communities and encourage reactionary right-wing politics. More wealth will leave the places that produced it, and anger will fill the void.

You can go see it all for yourself at the "Disneyland of agricultural tourism."

CHAPTER 5

The Berry Barons

On March 27, 1977, a bomb planted by a separatist group known as the Canary Islands Independence Movement detonated at the Gran Canaria Airport. In response, air traffic controllers diverted flights to a small airport on a nearby island called Tenerife. As planes crowded the airport's single runway, the area was beset with waves of fog.[1]

Among the disrupted passenger jets was Pan Am flight 1736, en route to the Canary Islands from Los Angeles. The plane was eventually given clearance to taxi down the foggy runway to fly to its original destination, but because of a pilot error, another Boeing 747 plane took off without clearance at the other end of the runway. A few seconds later, the two planes collided, resulting in 583 fatalities.[2] It is the deadliest recorded aviation accident to this day.[3]

Among the deceased were Joseph "Joe" and Glovie Reiter, owners of the Driscoll's, Inc. berry company.[4] The couple had two adult sons, J. Miles and Garland.[5] Both had grown up helping in the family business, but the tragedy forced them to take the helm.

The Reiter brothers took control of Driscoll's at a pivotal point in the company's history. As the US Congress and a string of presidents deregulated the Farm Bill and gutted competition protections, the brothers faced a choice: get big or get out. They decided to get big as fast as possible.

J. Miles and Garland Reiter now control about one-third of the $6 billion US berry market. If you buy raspberries or blackberries in a grocery store anywhere in America, you're probably buying from them.[6] They sell organic and conventional berries of all kinds, but they built their empire on strawberries, or, as strawberry workers refer to them, *la fruta del diablo*—the fruit of the devil.[7]

The brothers built this empire and fought off takeover attempts by the other fruit giants—Chiquita, Del Monte, and Dole—by figuring out a way to sell strawberries, blackberries, blueberries, and raspberries year-round.[8] As the *New York Times* noted, Driscoll's year-round strawberry crop, thanks to its global production system, "gave the company a crucial advantage with supermarket chains, which prefer to deal with only one supplier."[9] To solve the seasonality problem, the company leaned on a model of production that shifted responsibility for growing berries to third-party suppliers.

Given the company's prominence, you might be surprised to learn that Driscoll's doesn't grow any berries. Although it sells berries under the familiar Driscoll's brand in grocery stores around the world, the company itself does not actually cultivate the crop. Instead, it buys them from 750 growers in nearly two dozen countries, operations that together employ more than one hundred thousand people.[10]

This model helped J. Miles and Garland turn the regional company they inherited into a global powerhouse. Even more amazing, they did so while evading responsibility for water and labor issues that, as one berry expert told me, underlie everything in berry production.

The Nike Model

To understand Driscoll's, it's helpful to think of it less as a farm business than as a genetics and marketing company. Driscoll's owns the patents to the berry's genetics, which it licenses to approved growers on an exclusive basis. The company then markets these berries under the Driscoll's brand.

This involvement with genetics is deeply embedded in the company's DNA. The Reiter family has farmed berries in California for generations.[11] In the early 1900s, J. Miles and Garland's grandfather, Joseph "Ed" Reiter, teamed up with his brother-in-law, Richard Driscoll, to develop and market a variety called the Banner. The berry stood out from the crowd. But at that time, there was no way to patent a plant's genetics, which meant that anyone could cultivate the variety, so Reiter and Driscoll had competition.[12]

This hurdle was removed when President Herbert Hoover signed the Plant Patent Act of 1930, which enabled Reiter and Driscoll to claim ownership of breeds they engineered. The Banner variety was ultimately hit hard by disease—a common issue with monocultures—but the business model had been proven.[13]

Driscoll's isn't alone in exploring advances in strawberry genetics. The University of California system has long run a strawberry-breeding program to boost the industry.[14] As Dana Goodyear described in the *New Yorker*, the operation "is Driscoll's antithesis—public, open, nonexclusive—supplying, for a nominal royalty fee, any grower wishing to use its plants."[15]

Yet despite the UC lab's commitment to open-access science, the Reiter family found a way to privatize its efforts. The program ran into problems in the middle of the twentieth century. Most of the strawberry growers in California at the time were Japanese, and when over 120,000

Japanese Americans were imprisoned during World War II, there was suddenly a severe shortage of growers. The disruption likely hurt the lab's finances. In the Reiters' telling, the problems were so serious that the strawberry lab at UC Berkeley was making plans to abandon its work, though ultimately it never did.[16]

It was in this void that the Reiters sowed the seeds of their fortune. Two key researchers quit the university program and went to work for the family.[17] With these hires, the Reiters grabbed the knowledge and skills that had previously been directed toward building intellectual property available to the public and instead put them to work producing privately owned varieties of strawberries.

Driscoll's was established in 1950 when Ed's son, Joe Reiter, joined forces with a few other berry growers.[18] Not long after, some wily genetic maneuvering produced a patentable strawberry that could be shipped to the East Coast, which was the holy grail of strawberry breeding.[19] The variety also fruited later than its competitors, giving it a seasonal advantage that creates a temporary and lucrative monopoly. That's one reason why California currently grows 90 percent of domestically produced strawberries.[20] Before the variety was patented, the state ranked only eighth nationally in terms of acreage used in strawberry production. In fact, Arkansas once had three times the acreage of California.[21]

Driscoll's focus on genetics resembles the business model described by Naomi Klein in her book *No Logo: Taking Aim at the Brand Bullies*. Klein deconstructed the rise of the brand and the logo, with a particular focus on the example of Nike, a multibillion-dollar company that doesn't actually manufacture anything. Instead, it pays to put its logo— the infamous swoosh—on clothing that other companies make.[22]

Nike's competitive advantage is not in its products but in its brand. Nike spends most of its time and energy putting together ad campaigns featuring the swoosh. A generic gray shirt might sell for $10, but the same shirt made in the same factory with a swoosh printed on it sells for three times more. The price difference reflects customers' willingness to pay a premium for a piece of clothing to associate themselves with the image created by Nike's ad campaign.

The Driscoll's business model is in many ways akin to those of Nike and some of its neighbors in Silicon Valley. Its niche isn't to grow the strawberries but to breed, brand, and transport them and rake in profits from everyone else's sweat. A senior vice president at Driscoll's summed up this philosophy, pointing out that "[berry] growers are sort of like our manufacturing plants. We make the inventions, they assemble it, and then we market it, so it's not that dissimilar from Apple using someone else to do the manufacturing but they've made the invention and marketed the end product."[23]

Although Driscoll's does not farm the berries it sells, it maintains control over the fruit throughout the process. Driscoll's likely dictates how the fruit is grown and, of course, sets the price it will pay to the farmers. This model of production has deep roots in American agriculture. Professor Douglas H. Constance refers to it as the "Southern Model" and argues that it emerged in chicken production in the South in the 1940s before becoming the norm in that industry by the late 1950s.

Under this model, a corporation controls almost every aspect of the production chain. In the case of chicken, the corporation owns the breeding, hatching, feed mills, transportation, and processing plants, meaning that it does everything but raise the bird, which it usually contracts out because it is the riskiest part of the production process. The farmer, meanwhile, is required to use the corporation's hatchling and feed and then sell the bird back to it. According to Constance, "contract [chicken] production is but a formalized form of sharecropping." As a result, Constance considers the Southern Model to be "a remnant of slavery in the U.S. South."[24]

The Southern Model quickly spread across the food industry and around the world, with nuances specific to crop and locale. The relationship between Driscoll's and its approved suppliers is not necessarily as exploitive as the one between chicken farmers and companies like Tyson's. After all, Garland Reiter is the chief executive officer of an entirely separate company that grows berries for Driscoll's as an approved supplier.[25] Yet ultimately, by owning its brand and the genetics of the berries, Driscoll's maintains control over the entire production chain even as it disclaims responsibility for growing the berries.

These days, Driscoll's employs about thirty people at nine locations across the globe to do this breeding.[26] The company refers to these scientists as "Joy Makers," referring to the ecstasy of biting into a delicious, perfectly engineered berry.[27] J. Miles bragged in a company promotional video that "it is unusual in our industry to commit as much as we do to R&D, but it was really the basis for founding Driscoll's."[28]

The Essential Ingredient

Driscoll's headquarters sits at the end of a cul-de-sac in a generic building in an office park in Watsonville, California, right next to Highway 1, the iconic coastal highway. There are no tours or company store or even a berry statue. You would never guess that a berry empire is run out of this nondescript slab of concrete but for the Driscoll's sign out front. But once you start poking around, you begin to see the tendrils of the empire snaking out.

The California Strawberry Commission is located just up the road, in the same office park as Driscoll's. California strawberry growers founded the organization in 1955 to try to get more people to eat strawberries.[29] Eventually, the group evolved into a powerful state-level checkoff program, similar to the checkoff the Dairy Barons used in building their empire. It's hard to imagine that when the California Strawberry Commission is deciding how to spend its dollars, executives from Driscoll's don't take a stroll down the parking lot.

Surrounded by berry fields about fifteen miles east of Santa Cruz, Watsonville is nestled in the heart of the Pajaro Valley, a key center for agricultural production in the state.[30] Even aside from Driscoll's suppliers, many of the valley's large employers have some connection to farming. Watsonville's population of about fifty thousand is mostly working-class Latino.

In honor of its berry heritage, Watsonville hosts an annual Strawberry Festival each August. There's a strawberry pie–eating contest and a strawberry-themed amusement park ride. Driscoll's has been a sponsor of the festival for the past several years. When I attended the 2022 festival, it reminded me of the St. Jude Sweet Corn Festival thrown by my church each August in Cedar Rapids, Iowa. The Watsonville Strawberry Festival is a celebration of the crop that surrounds the city but also an excuse to ride a Ferris wheel, eat a funnel cake, and play some carnival games. You can even get your picture taken with someone dressed up as a strawberry.

Watsonville is in one of the two big strawberry-producing regions in America. The other is farther south, near the cities of Oxnard and Santa Maria, just north of Los Angeles.[31] In both areas, "the natural air conditioning of the Pacific Ocean keeps the [coastal farmland] cool and foggy."[32] Berries love this climate. It means they live in a perpetual spring, so they end up producing strawberries for much longer than the berries in my grandpa's Iowa backyard, which fruit for only a short time.

But while the temperature may be perfect for strawberry production, the rainfall isn't. In fact, Watsonville gets only about an inch of rain between May and September.[33] That's a problem for water-intensive crops such as strawberries. After all, 91 percent of a strawberry is water.[34]

Because Driscoll's suppliers aren't getting their water from the sky, they're largely pumping it from underground. Roughly 90 percent of the water supply in the Pajaro Valley comes from groundwater. Driscoll's acknowledges that most of the fields in which the company's fruit is grown are irrigated with groundwater.[35]

Those wells have contributed to the aquifers becoming severely overdrafted—more water flows out than in—and to salt water being drawn in from the ocean.[36] That's a problem for the farmworkers and other residents who rely on wells for drinking water, particularly when drilling new, deeper wells in California can run to $55,000, according to the *Washington Post*.[37] It's also bad for the farms themselves; some farmers in the Pajaro Valley have found that the groundwater is too salty to use for irrigation.[38]

The groundwater problem has reached crisis proportions not just in Watsonville, which at least enjoys a coastal climate with wet winters, but throughout the state. Unlike states like Iowa that typically get enough annual rainfall to support crop production, many parts of California do not. In fact, large swaths of California's farmland receive less than ten inches of rain annually, meeting the technical definition of a desert.[39]

And the farther south you go, the drier it gets. Seventy percent of Californians live in the southern part of the state, where only 30 percent of the water originates, but they use only a fraction of the limited water reserves. Farmers in the state, on the other hand, suck up approximately 80 percent of all water used in California.[40] Berry production isn't even the most harmful. In fact, almond production in California uses more water than all the people in Los Angeles and San Francisco combined, according to calculations by *Mother Jones*.[41]

Driscoll's certainly didn't create California's water shortage, but the company's rise parallels the development of a byzantine system that uses more water than nature can provide. In the 1930s, as Ed Reiter and his son Joe were branching out into raspberries, California began building the dams, aqueducts, and canals that would move water from the northern tip of the state to the south. Most of the water in this system comes from snowmelt from the Sierra Nevada range. But there's only so much snowmelt, and when it's not enough, farmers and others start drilling and pumping. Because the snowmelt replenishes those underground water reserves, a dry year means shortages all around.

From the earliest days of California's water projects, lack of regulation created a vicious cycle. More infrastructure and wells allowed California farmers to move onto ever drier, poorer ground that required even more irrigation.[42] As investigative reporter Mark Arax noted, "the more water [they] got, the more crops [they] planted, and the more crops [they] planted, the more water [they] needed to plant more crops, and on and on."[43]

Two generations later, the Reiter brothers recognize the bind. J. Miles has called a severe lack of water "the single greatest risk to the future of farms in California" and acknowledged that "California has to deal with groundwater, or we're going to ruin this state."[44] When California passed a law in 2014 requiring local agencies to regulate groundwater, Reiter griped that "this is going to be the most miserable of all regulations I've ever dealt with. But the consequences of doing nothing are beyond our imagination."[45]

To their credit, the Reiters aren't doing nothing. The company has worked with its growers to adopt conservation techniques, including using microsprinklers and soil moisture sensors to use water only when necessary. In 2010, Driscoll's helped establish a community-led forum to address the overdraft issue in the Pajaro Valley.[46] The signature project was a wireless irrigation network that, according to Driscoll's, led participating farmers to reduce their water consumption by 30–40 percent.[47]

Yet these efforts, while admirable, can't change the fundamental fact that Driscoll's suppliers and their berries are part of an agriculture system currently demanding more water than the local environment can support. California enacted legislation in 2014 to curtail water use to a sustainable level starting in 2040, but experts think that does not go nearly far enough.[48] The state will likely need to fallow hundreds of thousands of acres of farmland to achieve a sustainable aquifer, but few want to face that reality.[49] After all, California supplies 90 percent of the country's strawberries, not to mention three-quarters of its fruits and nuts.[50]

For Driscoll's, the specter of drought will continue to hang over the strawberry fields that supply its core product. J. Miles Reiter has called water the company's biggest priority, rivaled only by labor: California agriculture's other, even more shameful legacy.

A Modern-Day System of Indentured Servitude

In May 2020, in the early days of the COVID-19 pandemic, berry pickers at Rancho Laguna Farms, a Driscoll's supplier in Santa Maria, went on strike. They pushed for a raise of ten cents per box of berries collected, up from $1.90 per box, which rarely added up to minimum wage. Because strawberry pickers are paid piecework rate, they must work fast to make a decent living, typically between $70 and $150 per day. But the managers at Rancho Laguna were requiring their pickers to select only the best berries, which slowed them down and cut their wages to roughly $50 per day.

Workers at Rancho Laguna were concerned not only about low wages but also about a lack of COVID-19 protocols. One woman, called Rosa in the press because she feared giving her real name, heard that some of her coworkers had tested positive but that the foremen were ordered to "keep it quiet." According to Rosa, the farm had originally spread out workers, but by May 2020, that caution was out the window.[51] The situation had gotten so bad that the nonunionized workers joined together to demand better pay and conditions. Rosa acknowledged that "it just made sense to unite as workers because it gave us more power to influence the company."[52]

That influence has never been welcomed by the Berry Barons or their compatriots. You can trace corporate resistance to worker power in the industry all the way back to the passage of the National Labor Relations Act of 1935, which forbade employers from firing workers for joining or organizing a union but made an exception for farmworkers and domestic workers.

Three years later, farmworkers were again denied the protections guaranteed for their counterparts in other industries when they were shut out of the minimum wage and overtime pay requirements of the Fair Labor Standards Act.[53] Given that these jobs were dominant forms of employment for Black Americans at the time, it's important to acknowledge the role of structural racism in these decisions.[54]

Today, 95 percent of agricultural workers in California are immigrants.[55] Beginning in the 1940s, the United States and Mexico signed a series of agreements that arranged for Mexican laborers to temporarily work in American agriculture. The Bracero Program, as it was known, was supposed to ensure that workers had decent meals and housing, wages equivalent to those received by US-born employees, and transportation back to Mexico. But in reality, the program enabled growers to take advantage of vulnerable people to break strikes and undercut workers' bargaining power.[56]

There was a moment of hope in subsequent years as leaders such as Cesar Chavez and Dolores Huerta fought for the rights and well-being of agricultural workers. Chavez and Huerta cofounded the United Farm Workers union, which attempted to organize California farmworkers, including berry pickers.[57] They made significant gains in the 1970s, including stronger legal protections, increased wages, and greatly improved working conditions.[58]

But as large corporations gained power and consolidated, they began to claw back the gains that these workers had fought for.[59] The Immigration Reform and Control Act of 1986 created a formal vehicle for businesses to import low-wage, temporary farm labor under the H-2 visa program. The creation of the H-2A visa fundamentally altered the American food system.[60] During the past twenty-five years, the number of workers who migrate to the United States under this program has grown exponentially, with the total doubling between 2011 and 2016 alone.[61]

Many of these workers are former farmers who were forced off their land in their home countries. Upon signing the North American Free Trade Agreement in 1994, with the encouragement of Big Ag, Mexico fully opened its borders to American grain exports.[62] NAFTA represented a windfall for the Grain Barons and their ilk, but the influx of heavily subsidized American grain undermined local farming economies, particularly family farms.[63] As a report by Oxfam International put it, "there is a direct link between government agricultural policies in the US and rural misery in Mexico."[64]

Mexico lost over 1.9 million farming jobs in the first decade after NAFTA.[65] These farmers were forced to "migrate or starve," so they streamed across the border either under the H-2A guest worker program or as undocumented immigrants.[66] The pain was particularly felt by Indigenous communities, which is likely why a large number of migrant workers and undocumented immigrants from Mexico and Central American countries such as Guatemala do not speak Spanish.[67]

"Rosa," who joined the strike at Rancho Laguna Farms, is a Mixteco mother of three from Oaxaca, in southern Mexico. Like most pickers in California, she is undocumented, making her particularly vulnerable to the whims of her employer.[68] When she returned to work after the strike, she and her coworkers were sent to one of worst fields, ordered to pick only the best berries, and given larger boxes to fill, which sliced their pay even further. If she didn't like it, supervisors told her, she could be easily replaced.[69]

Undocumented workers are the most vulnerable, but even being "legal" doesn't provide much protection. The H-2A guest worker program essentially encodes second-class citizenship by creating a mechanism for these folks to live in the country with limited rights.[70] The Southern Poverty Law Center has called the guest worker program a "modern-day system of indentured servitude," except that guest workers have no pathway to American citizenship and instead are forced to leave the United States when their temporary work visas expire.[71]

The workers at Rancho Laguna were at least supported by a local advocacy group called Central Coast Alliance United for a Sustainable Economy (CAUSE). Most crop workers do not have access to lawyers.[72] Instead, they are essentially held captive by their employers or by labor brokers, who control their documents. Former US representative and House Ways and Means Committee chairman Charles Rangel called the guest worker program "the closest thing I've ever seen to slavery."[73]

Corporations can take advantage of undocumented and guest workers because they fear deportation, which may be why farmworker union membership has fallen from around eighty thousand to ninety thousand members in the 1980s to essentially zero today.[74] It's not a coincidence that the average farmworker in California made only $31,770 in 2021.[75]

Guest workers are also less likely to report workplace abuse or injuries. Federal reports list agricultural work as a profession with high mortality rates from workplace injuries.[76] Berry picking is not an easy job. Picking strawberries requires workers to be stooped over for hours at a time, often under a hot sun. Hence the phrase *la fruta del diablo*. In 2019, Human Rights Watch issued a report that documented what working in the industry entails:

> [The farmworkers] showed the scars, scratches, missing fingers, or distended, swollen joints that reflected these stories. Some broke into tears describing the stress, physical pain, and emotional strain they regularly suffer. Almost all explained that their lives, both in the plant and at home, had grown to revolve around managing chronic pain or sickness.[77]

The H-2A system hurts all working Americans, not just migrant workers. In its report on the subject, the Southern Poverty Law Center pointed out that "as long as employers in low-wage industries can rely on an endless stream of vulnerable guestworkers who lack basic labor protections, they will have little incentive to hire U.S. workers or make jobs more appealing to domestic workers by improving wages and working conditions."[78] By putting downward pressure on wages, the H-2A program provides a huge windfall to the largest producers at the expense of pretty much everyone else.

The Reiters have been very vocal supporters of the H-2A program, advocating for its expansion and for loosening of restrictions.[79] Not unrelatedly, the labor organizer I spoke with told me that he's heard plenty of horror stories about the farms that produce berries for Driscoll's, with wage theft being the most common issue.

When the laborers at Rancho Laguna Farms tried to go up the chain of command and protest outside the Santa Maria office of Driscoll's, a spokesperson sidestepped the issue. The company shared a statement with the *Santa Maria Sun* that tried to minimize its role, arguing that "Driscoll's does not have a role or legal standing in this process."[80]

Later, when the petition at Rancho Laguna ballooned to fifty-seven thousand signatures, and after the workers and the farm reached a settlement, Driscoll's was compelled to issue a new statement. On its website, the company posted: "Driscoll's is always fully committed to protecting the health and safety of those who work across our broader enterprise, including the harvesters employed by our independent growers. . . . Driscoll's swiftly followed-up on these concerns and will continue to monitor Rancho Laguna Farms' progress in this area and ensure all commitments are fully implemented."[81]

At times, public pressure forces the company to engage with the issue of labor. But Driscoll's can always disclaim responsibility for the acts of its suppliers, even though its model incentivizes farmers to squeeze workers as hard as they can. By focusing on breeding and contracting out the actual farming, the company can claim plausible deniability for how growers treat the workers. The handy part about being brand managers and owners of intellectual property is that you can rake in the profits from indentured servitude without employing a single farmworker.[82]

The Quest for Physical Perfection

In early September 2022, farmworkers and other residents of the Pajaro Valley held a press conference on a thirty-foot-wide dirt road that separated berry fields from an elementary school.[83] Parents and children held a printed banner pleading "Stop Poisoning Our Kids: Go Organic!"

The group called on berry growers to stop spraying traditional, non-organic pesticides near schools and residential areas, which they believed were responsible for neurological and other diseases affecting local children. They didn't seem to buy the industry-funded studies that claimed the chemicals were perfectly safe.[84]

A few months later, J. Miles Reiter and other Driscoll's employees met with the activists. Reiter acknowledged that over time, going organic was a worthwhile goal. But the company made no commitment to require its growers located near schools, parks, and hospitals to do so.[85] Reiter had earlier argued that it was up to the growers, not Driscoll's, to decide whether or not to go organic.

Once again, being the seller of berries, rather than the grower, proved useful. Yet Driscoll's has set up a system that makes these chemicals if not necessary, certainly expedient. It all comes back to producing as many identical berries as cheaply as possible.

To understand why fumigants are particularly attractive to Driscoll's suppliers, and strawberry growers in general, it helps to know a little about the plant itself. If you've ever grown strawberries in your backyard, you might have noticed that the plants sprout horizontal stems that run above the ground and generate new plants at varying intervals. The main plant is known as the "mother," and the horizontal stems bolting above the ground are known as "runners." The runners are effectively clones of the mother plant.

I used to help my grandpa with his strawberry patch behind his house in Iowa. He would till every other row so that the runners could fill in that space. It's a common practice with strawberries because younger plants tend to produce more berries, which of course is the goal for a global supplier such as Driscoll's.

Many breeders like Driscoll's truck the mother plants up to the mountains along the Oregon and California border to expose them to cold air, priming the runners for maximum production. When it's time for growing season, they plow under the mothers and ship the runners to growers on the coast. These offspring will produce the berry crop you see in the grocery store. Growers also constantly cut their runners so that the plant can focus its energy on growing the biggest berries possible. At the end of the season, the runners are also plowed under, and each year the land is planted with a new batch.[86]

The Reiter brothers use this system to accommodate the particularities of strawberries, which are fickle and research intensive to breed. Like hybrid corn seeds, strawberry seeds don't yield the same plant they came from but instead produce a slightly different variety. To get exactly the same berry they patented, the Reiters need clones.

The downside of planting clones is that they create the potential for disease to spread rapidly because of their genetic similarities. To prevent crop loss, berry farmers fumigate their land before planting the runners. If you've ever driven near strawberry fields, you might notice rows of black plastic mounds. The mounds make it easier for pickers to collect the berries, and the dirt is enclosed in plastic to capture the fumigation gases injected into the soil. This process kills essentially everything in the soil, including insects, weeds, and fungi.[87]

Organic strawberry fields are typically not subjected to these chemicals. Instead, an organic farmer might grow berries in a different field each year, returning to the original plot only after several years to make sure remnants of diseases don't remain in the soil. Driscoll's does control about 60 percent of the US market for organic strawberries, but this is likely a small portion of its total business.[88] After all, the fumigation approach requires less land, which is key when you're supplying a global market. For most of Driscoll's suppliers, fumigants are just part and parcel of farming.

The most powerful and important fumigant—methyl bromide—was widely used dating back to the 1960s. Sociologist Julie Guthman, who wrote a book on the subject, believes that this highly effective odorless, colorless gas fueled the strawberry industry's growth. But then scientists discovered that it eats away at Earth's ozone layer. Despite years of industry resistance, this finding led to restrictions on the use of methyl bromide for strawberries grown outside nurseries.[89]

Methyl bromide has largely been banned, but other fumigants have taken its place.[90] The use of these gases has stirred protest not just in the Pajaro Valley but across California, where berry fields often abut schools, parks, and hospitals.[91] For context, one district in the state has eighteen schools located directly adjacent to farmland.[92] That's significant because some studies have linked fumigants to lower IQs in kids, along with other health problems.[93]

Eventually, the chemicals can make their way into nearby waterways. As with the area around the Dairy Barons' Fair Oaks Farms complex, the US Environmental Protection Agency has classified most of the canals that surround Driscoll's and the California Strawberry Commission as impaired, largely because of the presence of bacteria and toxic chemicals.[94]

For the most part, farmworkers and their families have dealt with the brunt of this pollution. J. Miles and Garland Reiter certainly don't live near the berry fields; they own coastal estates in Santa Barbara and Santa Cruz.[95] In fact, a lot of "farmers" in California don't live on farms. The largest farmer in California lives in Beverly Hills and controls almost enough farmland to cover the five boroughs of New York City.[96]

Increasingly, farm owners aren't even individuals or families but are corporations and other institutions. Harvard University bought thousands of acres of California farmland as part of its investment of its massive endowment.[97] The arrival of Wall Street money has only intensified inequality in an already unequal area.

Offshoring

Not long after J. Miles and Garland Reiter took control of Driscoll's after their parents' untimely death, a series of critical changes to the legal framework and the food retail market presented an opportunity for them to put the company's model into hyperdrive. The Reiters took advantage, outsourcing the farming of their berries not just to independent contractors but out of the country entirely.

Outsourcing production to overseas subcontractors is commonplace in corporate America, and Driscoll's is no different.[98] Today, the Reiters' network employs people on every continent except Antarctica.[99] As much as their ownership of intellectual property and their ability to create a brand, the Driscoll's model is based on shifting farming out of the country to companies that don't need to worry about US minimum wage laws or environmental regulations.

The model mirrors the way companies such as Nike benefit from unethical practices of overseas subcontractors. It is increasingly common across the food industry. Recent investigations have uncovered the use of child workers and other shocking labor practices in the production of tomatoes in Mexico bound for America, along with the involvement of drug cartels in farming the avocados we eat.[100] Mexico is, incidentally, one the Reiters' favorite places for berry production.

Driscoll's began importing berries from Mexico around the time President Bill Clinton signed NAFTA and the Wall Street Farm Bill into law.[101] Meanwhile, the loosening of America's competition rules led to a roll-up of retail grocery stores. Consolidation in one part of the food sector added pressure for other sectors to consolidate. As one agricultural expert told me, big boys want to run with big boys. Walmart, after all, does not want to find a local berry farmer for each store.

A large portion of Mexico's berries come from the San Quintín Valley, an arid area 180 miles south of Tijuana.[102] In 1987, prior to passage of NAFTA and the Wall Street Farm Bill, this valley produced only 9,000 tons of berries. By 2020, that number had increased to 120,600 tons in Baja.[103] Anthropologist Christian Zlolniski refers to this area as an agroexport enclave because few of the berries produced there are eaten domestically. Instead, nearly all berries are exported.[104] As a result of this boom, Mexico surpassed Spain in 2019 as the world's leading strawberry exporter.[105]

What makes this feat more incredible is that the San Quintín Valley is one of the driest places in North America. Its annual average rainfall is less than three inches, about as much as that of Death Valley.[106] This climate means that farmers were forced to turn to groundwater to fuel the berry boom. In fact, agriculture uses more than 95 percent of the water in the area.[107]

But pumping groundwater is likely even less sustainable in the San Quintín Valley than in the Pajaro Valley, where the Driscoll's headquarters is located. According to Zlolniski, the industrial berry growers' political power has resulted in the local government looking the other way on their water use. It's unlikely that the same leniency is shown for local farmers.[108]

Accordingly, more water is being used than can be replenished. That's why the Reiter brothers built their own desalination plant to use ocean water; according to a Driscoll's representative, this represents the first time seawater has been used for agriculture in Mexico. The Reiters' investment suggests that berry production in the region will soon be dependent on it.[109]

Yet even taking these issues into account, the shift in production has likely led to a windfall for the Reiters. The biggest expense in berry production is labor, and the move of Driscoll's to Mexico and elsewhere helped defray that cost.

In 2015, the poor labor conditions in the San Quintín valley came to the attention of American media. The workers, mostly Indigenous people from some of Mexico's poorest states, such as Oaxaca and Guerrero, staged a massive strike.[110] They demanded wages of $13 per day and an end to crew bosses' sexual harassment of female pickers.[111] The strike eventually ended when the government sent in the military. With this show of force, workers were offered only a fraction of what they demanded.

One of the targets of the protest was BerryMex, a supplier to Driscoll's. At the time, workers received just over two cents for each dollar a shopper spent on organic strawberries.[112] But BerryMex isn't just any supplier; it is owned by the Reiters.[113] "I'm really proud of what BerryMex does and I would love to see it publicized accurately," responded J. Miles when asked about the protest in 2015. "It's really a lot to be proud of there."[114]

And this sort of abuse is not localized to Mexico. A 2022 investigation by the *Guardian* documented similar worker abuse by Driscoll's suppliers in Europe. They discovered workers who earned less than the legal minimum wage and far exceeded legal limits for working hours. A spokesperson for the Reiter brothers promised a "thorough audit" of these growers.[115]

The ability to send production offshore undermines labor reforms for American farmworkers and essentially reverses decades of hard-fought gains. As one produce farmer told me, any effort to improve the conditions of American farmworkers essentially means that more produce will be grown outside America. The recent Republican rhetoric against immigration heightens this trend. American fruit and vegetable imports almost doubled from when Donald Trump took office to when he was finally forced to vacate it.[116]

As American agriculture focuses on growing more and more commodities for processing and export, fruits and vegetables are increasingly imported from other countries. Following this trend, an ever-growing volume of strawberries consumed by Americans is imported, and the Reiters have a lot to do with that.[117]

But the problem is not specific to strawberries. Since the 1990s, the United States has been a net importer of fresh and processed fruits and vegetables, and the gap gets bigger every year.[118] More than half of all tomatoes sold in America are now brought in from Mexico, and nearly 60 percent of the apple juice sold in the United States comes from China, even though most of the United States has a climate conducive to apple production.[119]

The problem is so bad that salmon caught in the United States is shipped to China for processing and then shipped back to the United States for consumption.[120] And in California, fruit and vegetable fields are being replaced with nut trees intended for export; 70 percent of almonds and nearly half of pistachios grown in California are exported.[121]

The offshoring of the American food system has made our food more like the rest of the American economy: uniform, lackluster in quality, and highly consolidated. This restructuring is visible in every aisle of the grocery store. Eaters get a lower-quality, blander product; there's a night-and-day difference between a backyard strawberry and a bloated, tasteless Baja berry.

This system also exacerbates climate change. The farther food travels to get to your plate, the more carbon is put into the atmosphere via a fossil-fuel-intensive transportation system.[122] Meanwhile, farmworkers—including many berry pickers—are increasingly exposed to smoke from wildfires, which are becoming more common because of climate change. As Inside Climate News reported, these workers often "are forced to toil through fires that are not just more frequent and severe but more toxic than ever."[123]

The food system is dynamic and always shifting. But when corporations such as Driscoll's run the show, it shifts in whatever direction allows them to accrue maximum profits. That's the current trajectory of American agriculture. One place after another is destroyed just to keep profits up, no matter the cost to workers, to the environment, or to natural resources. Wall Street and large corporations such as Driscoll's have taken control of the agricultural sector, while the communities they operate in and the workers who pick their berries are left holding the bag.

As for their next move, the Berry Barons plan to grow their global empire even further. They recently purchased berry companies in the United Kingdom and one that operates in sub-Saharan Africa.[124] They also plan to triple their investments in China over the next five years.[125] And they even announced their intention to build an indoor farm meant to produce over four million pounds of strawberries per year in Virginia, near the large East Coast berry market.[126]

The Reiter brothers built their fortune on water-intensive farming that can't be sustained. But what elevated them to baron status was shifting production onto others and dodging responsibility for the havoc it causes. They are a pair of barons that only the twenty-first century could have created.

CHAPTER 6

The Slaughter Barons

On the night of March 7, 2017, Michel Temer, the president of Brazil, welcomed Joesley Batista, chairman of meatpacking giant JBS, into his home for a meeting. The pair made awkward small talk before turning to the urgent matter that brought them together: Temer's presidency was under threat.

A sweeping anti-corruption probe was roiling Brazilian politics, and investigators had already linked one of Temer's political allies, House Speaker Eduardo Cunha, to a graft scheme involving an oil company in which the Brazilian government owned a majority of shares. President Temer was likely worried that Cunha would implicate him in the scandal.[1]

Joesley Batista tried to soothe the president by telling him that he was "taking care" of the problem. His company had been sending bribes to Cunha "every month" and had even given one of Batista's personal helicopters to Cunha's fixer.[2] Temer replied, "You need to keep that up, got it?"[3] Batista agreed that he would.[4]

Temer felt reassured, but he was really being betrayed. Unbeknownst to the president, Batista had been wearing a wire as part of a plea bargain related to his company's role in the scandal. Two months later, leading Brazilian newspaper *O Globo* broke the story, based on audio of the conversation.[5]

In response, thousands of angry protestors demonstrated in the capital calling for Temer's resignation, and his approval rating cratered to 5 percent.[6] Temer finished his term in disgrace, and police later arrested him on corruption charges.[7] He was succeeded by Jair Bolsonaro, a controversial figure with ties to Brazil's far right.[8]

For Joesley Batista, the decision to cooperate with investigators was a saving grace. Batista, his brother Wesley, and a handful of other family members control not only JBS, the world's largest butchering company, but also a vast holding company called J&F Investimentos.[9] The deal may have preserved the Batistas' empire and kept the brothers out of jail.[10]

In addition to providing valuable assistance in ensnaring the president, they agreed to fess up to all their crimes. They admitted to paying over $150 million in bribes to 1,829 politicians between 2005 and 2017. One bribe included a $1.5 million Manhattan apartment.[11] The company pleaded guilty to US foreign bribery charges and agreed to pay a $256.5 million fine.[12] The Batistas also promised to do better. A new chief compliance officer was named, and a committee was created to ensure adherence to global regulations.[13] But the brothers could not resist their criminal tendencies. Before Brazilian officials even had a chance to publicly announce the plea deal, the brothers allegedly engaged in insider trading by dumping shares in the company ahead of the news.[14]

The lawlessness that brought Joesley to his meeting with President Temer that night in 2017, and that helped the brothers not only evade responsibility for their actions but also potentially profit from them, was nothing new. In fact, it was part of a pattern of behavior that helped them build their empire in the first place. After all, Joesley and Wesley became barons through a spree of criminality and a callous disregard for their workers that eerily parallels the slaughtering barons portrayed by Upton Sinclair in *The Jungle* more than a century ago.

Baron Status via Bribery

The Batista brothers control the largest slaughtering empire the world has ever seen. According to their own website, Joesley and Wesley are the largest global butchers of beef and chicken and are number two in pork.[15] In addition to their meat monopolies, JBS is the world's largest leather processor.

Bloomberg News estimates the Batistas' personal fortune at $5.8 billion.[16] They produce almost enough protein daily to give a four-ounce portion to every citizen of Australia, Canada, Poland, Spain, and Italy combined.[17] To keep all these kill lines running, the brothers employ a quarter million people globally.[18]

But JBS was a small player in the industry until relatively recently. The brothers' father, José Batista Sobrinho (whose initials inspired the name JBS in a branding strategy that mirrors that of the Coffee Barons), started the family's butchering company in 1953. He began modestly by killing five cattle per day at a small plant in central Brazil.[19]

José sensed an opportunity in the late 1950s when Brazil decided to build a new capital in the center of the country called Brasília, not far from his small plant. He moved quickly to feed the workers building this new city. Business boomed so much that he was able to acquire a larger second location.[20] Both brothers skipped college to help their father at his packing plants.[21]

For the next few decades, the company remained successful but nothing like the global behemoth it would eventually become. By the early 1990s, the family still operated only three slaughterhouses, with a total capacity of one thousand animals per day. Although this number was impressive for a four-decade-old family business, JBS was still a regional enterprise and a fraction of its size today.[22] By way of comparison, a single JBS cattle slaughterhouse in Greeley, Colorado, can kill up to 5,600 cattle per day.[23]

But this family business went through a sudden transformation at the cusp of the new millennium to become the largest slaughtering company in the world. Its growth was fueled by an aggressive $20 billion international acquisition spree funded, in part, by low-cost loans from state-owned and state-controlled banks.[24]

The Batista brothers did not obtain this incredible pool of government funding by chance. Instead, they spent roughly $148 million to bribe more than 1,800 politicians and Brazilian government officials. Their bribery enabled them to obtain cheap financing and make aggressive moves that others could not match.[25]

Using this illicit money, the brothers rapidly gobbled up rival meat-packing companies. In Brazil alone, they purchased Grupo Bertin, Seara, Independencia, pork assets from Brasil Foods, and the poultry units of Tyson Foods and Céu Azul. Their shopping spree extended abroad as well: Swift Armour in Argentina; Australia Meat Holdings, Rockdale Beef, Tasman Group, Primo, Andrews Meat, and Tatiara Meat in Australia; Rigamonti in Italy; Tyson's poultry unit in Mexico; and Moy Park in Northern Ireland.[26]

These purchases fueled the Batista brothers' meteoric rise from little-known regional players to global slaughtering barons. In 2005, the company butchered only 5,800 head of cattle per day.[27] Less than two decades later, it had the capacity to kill 76,550 cattle, 127,100 hogs, and 13.8 million birds per day.[28] To give some context to their sheer size, the brothers sold more food in 2021 than well-known global brands such as Nestlé, PepsiCo, Kraft Heinz, and Unilever.[29] JBS became one of the largest companies in the world seemingly overnight.

The brothers would later confess that bribery was critical to their expansion. When investigators with the Brazilian attorney general asked Joesley Batista whether their US acquisitions would have ever happened without the bribes, he responded, "Oh, no way. It wouldn't have happened. We wouldn't have made the deal."[30] According to the *Economist*, "as JBS was buying up rivals, the Batistas were buying politicians."[31]

The US Securities and Exchange Commission later charged them with violations of the Foreign Corrupt Practices Act on the basis of the company's conduct in its acquisition of Pilgrim's Pride Corporation, the second-largest chicken processor in the United States. The brothers' misconduct continued after they took control of the company; the SEC also alleged that it used Pilgrim's Pride's bank accounts to continue to pay bribes. The Batistas and their companies ended up settling the claims by paying just $28 million in fines.[32]

The American Way

The Batistas first entered the American market in 2007 with their purchase of the historic Swift & Company. JBS's purchase of Swift made it the third-largest seller of beef and pork in the United States overnight.[33] Shortly before this acquisition, Wesley Batista moved his wife and three young children to Greeley, Colorado, to be near one of the company's new slaughterhouses.[34] JBS also opened a headquarters for its American operations on the western outskirts of town, upwind from the slaughterhouse and massive feedlots.[35]

The plant had originally opened in 1960 under the ownership of a local family, the Monforts.[36] In 1987, the Monfort family sold their company to the food conglomerate ConAgra for stock valued at $365.5 million. ConAgra later sold its pork and beef business to Swift & Company, which in turn was acquired by JBS.[37] The Batista brothers soon followed this purchase by buying Smithfield Foods' beef slaughterhouse business, along with a controlling interest in Pilgrim's Pride.[38]

JBS faced little government opposition to any of these purchases. It ran into problems only with its proposed acquisition of National Beef Packing Company, which was then the nation's fourth-largest beef packer. The merger would have given the brothers control over nearly one-third of the American beef market in less than a year.[39] The George W. Bush administration joined attorneys general from thirteen states in an antitrust lawsuit to oppose the merger, a truly rare and unexpected move by such a pro-consolidation administration.[40] Likely in response to this lawsuit, the brothers dropped their plans to buy the company.[41]

Otherwise, the brothers continued their buying spree unfettered. The Barack Obama administration was as complicit as the Bush administration. In 2013, JBS bought two more beef plants from Canadian company XL Foods.[42] Two years later, it bought the pork assets of Cargill, Inc., including the slaughterhouse next to the water park in Ottumwa, Iowa, which I used to go to as a kid.[43] The US Department of Agriculture, then led by Tom Vilsack, did not object to any of these purchases.

It's a pattern that can be seen across the meat industry, which has been consolidating ever since about 1980. In fifteen years, the market share of the four leading firms in the cattle sector rose from 25 percent to 71 percent, blowing well past what academics consider to be a competitive market.[44] Four beef-slaughtering firms, including JBS, now control 85 percent of the industry.[45]

But even that shocking statistic doesn't capture the full extent of the problem. In most instances, ranchers have only one or two regional buyers to which they can bring their finished cattle. A Wyoming rancher is not going to sell cattle to a Pennsylvania slaughterhouse; it would cost more to truck the animals across the country than the rancher would make in profits. For many ranchers, JBS is the only choice they have.

Because the Batista brothers made it a point to maintain the brands they bought, most Americans do not know that they are actually buying meat from this Brazilian company. In fact, the brothers don't sell any meat under the JBS name in America. This hidden ownership obfuscates their control over the American meat market and mirrors the tactics of the Coffee Barons and the Grain Barons.

As of 2023, JBS listed forty-three different meat brands that it sold in America alone. This list included several high-end brands that give the illusion of sustainable family farms. One such brand is Grass Run Farms, which describes itself as working with a "small network of family farmers in America's Heartland to ensure high quality, grass fed beef through careful production and sustainable management."[46] The brothers also own Just Bare chicken, whose website proclaims, "We could tell you everything that goes into our products, but truth is there's nothing to see here. No antibiotics. No added hormones or steroids. No added preservatives. Just simple protein."[47] Both websites feature images of idyllic family farms.

The one that stands out most to me is Cedar River Farms, which I saw highlighted a few years back at a famous restaurant near the White House as one of its "family farm" providers. The name caught my eye because my hometown is named after the Cedar River, which runs through it. At the time, I figured that the operation must be based somewhere along the river. I only later discovered that it was actually based hundreds of miles away in Greeley, Colorado, Wesley Batista's adopted hometown and the location of JBS's American headquarters.

This false image comes at the expense of actual beef cattle ranchers, the only sizable group of family farmers who still play a substantial role in the American food system. Since 1982, America has lost 80 percent of its dairies and 90 percent of its hog farms, mostly small, independent family operations.[48] There are dairy and hog family farms selling into organic and fine dining markets, but they are the outliers, not the norm.

Beef cattle ranches were able to survive this wave of consolidation, albeit deeply wounded. During this same period, America lost 50 percent of its beef cattle operations, a substantial number but not quite as bad as their counterparts in dairy and hogs.[49] Their continued existence remains under threat.

Taking a cue from the Hog Barons, the Batistas are trying to eliminate the open market, in which ranchers sell their own cattle, and instead move to a contracting model that stacks the deck in favor of big meatpackers. It used to be the norm in the meat industry to bid on animals destined for the kill line, sort of like how one might try to buy an item on eBay. These markets were capitalism at its finest, and they often empowered farmers to secure the highest possible price for their cattle.

But meatpackers like the Batista brothers hate transparency. They prefer to negotiate behind closed doors with more opaque terms.[50] With their newfound market power, JBS and their peers have increasingly pushed to have prices for feedlot cattle set ahead of time via purchase contracts.[51]

In 2009, half of all cattle destined for slaughter were still bought on the open market.[52] A decade later, only 21 percent were purchased that way.[53] Members of Congress have introduced numerous bills over the years to preserve this collapsing open market, but none can muster enough support to overcome JBS and the other meat giants.[54] Unless Congress acts soon, one can assume that the open market for buying cattle will be effectively dead, just as it is for hogs.

Ranchers are not the only ones being exploited by these Slaughter Barons. You are too if you buy meat. As Bill Bullard, chief executive officer of an organization representing cattle ranchers, told the *New York Times*, "You're having consumers exploited on one end of the supply chain, cattle producers exploited on the other."[55]

In 2021, Pilgrim's Pride, the chicken company largely owned by JBS, pleaded guilty to price-fixing. Prosecutors accused it of coordinating with other chicken giants between 2012 and 2017 to suppress competition and raise prices for products typically found in grocery stores and fast-food outlets.[56] As a punishment, President Donald Trump's

Department of Justice fined the company $107.9 million.[57] Although that number might seem high, this division of JBS earned $456 million in profit in 2019 alone.[58] Yet again, JBS received a slap on the wrist and then continued happily on its way. Nothing was done about the underlying dynamics that created the conditions for price-fixing.

Unsurprisingly, the brothers kept doing what was working for them. In 2021 and 2022, they settled three pork price-fixing cases for more than $57 million over accusations that they were overcharging wholesalers, restaurants, and grocery store customers. Then, in 2022, JBS agreed to pay another $52.5 million for accusations of overcharging in beef markets.[59] Sadly, as in the chicken case, no structural fix was implemented. The Batista brothers simply absorb these fines as another cost of doing business. They commit the crime, pay up, and seem to know that they can do it again.

But as Louis Brandeis and other reformers have warned, underpaying suppliers and overcharging buyers isn't the only way that monopolies cause harm. Their newfound power can have disastrous consequences far beyond the predictions of economists tinkering with computer models. In the case of JBS, no one bears the brunt of concentrated power more than slaughterhouse workers.

Slaughterhouse Rules

My first experience of researching the American food system led me to slaughterhouses. At an internship in college, my boss tasked me with verifying numbers for a report on school districts across America. Naturally, I spent a lot of time playing with the Iowa figures.

Out of curiosity, I decided to sort the data on the percentage of students in the district receiving free or reduced-price lunch, a signifier for the proportion of low-income students. I noticed that many of the districts with the highest percentage of low-income students happened to be the most ethnically diverse, as well as the ones with the highest per-centage of non-native English speakers. The only geographic pattern to their distribution was that they were all located in rural areas. I looked up the communities on Wikipedia and quickly noticed what they had in common: each was home to a slaughterhouse.[60]

At first, I couldn't understand the connection. Working the kill lines has always been a tough job, often performed by immigrants. It consis-tently ranks as one of the most physically demanding jobs with some of the highest injury rates.[61] But during a large part of the twentieth century, it was a path to the middle class for families like mine. People on both sides of my family, including my grandfather, worked at the old slaugh-terhouse in Cedar Rapids, a plant that closed the year I was born. Why were these jobs now located in some of the poorest parts of the state?

With that question in mind, I decided to dig deeper and write my college thesis on what this phenomenon meant for rural communities. I spent the following summer crisscrossing Iowa and speaking with work-ers, teachers, mayors, and clergy members. I ultimately wrote two the-ses because I enjoyed the experience so much. What I found stunned me: these Iowa towns resembled company towns from the turn of the twentieth century.[62]

More than a century ago, Upton Sinclair published *The Jungle*, a novel about an immigrant slaughterhouse worker in the Chicago stockyards.[63] While writing the novel, Sinclair interviewed slaughterhouse workers and observed the horrific conditions of meat production. He saw how the most ruthless and corrupt companies—including ones like Swift & Company—succeeded at the expense of folks just trying to get by.

Despite fierce opposition from the meatpackers, who tried to bribe the publisher not to release the book and planted negative stories about Sinclair in newspapers, *The Jungle* was an instant success, selling millions of copies.[64] President Theodore Roosevelt even invited Sinclair to the White House to discuss the novel.[65]

Readers, however, reacted more strongly to the unsanitary conditions described in the book than to its depiction of worker abuses. Oddly enough, the book became more closely associated with food safety and meat quality than with the plight of slaughterhouse workers. But Sinclair wanted to capture the raw abuse of corporate power and leave the reader demanding change.[66]

The sort of structural change that Sinclair advocated for eventually did come. Swift & Company was an original member of the Beef Trust of the early twentieth century. In fact, Swift's participation in the sort of price-fixing schemes that are JBS's specialty gave rise to an infamous US Supreme Court case—*Swift & Co. v. United States*—that confirmed the federal government's power to regulate monopolies.[67] Antitrust action against Swift and its associates in the Beef Trust sharply curtailed the power of monopolies in the industry.

Moreover, New Deal pro-labor policies meant that most of the industry was unionized by the end of the 1930s.[68] At the peak, 90 percent of slaughterhouse workers were employed under union contracts.[69] They used this bargaining power to improve their pay and working conditions. By the 1950s, slaughterhouse work was one of the highest-paid manufacturing jobs in the country, according to journalist Eric Schlosser.[70] Standard benefits included vacation, holidays, sick leave, and a company-provided meal during shifts.[71]

But the tide started to turn as the industry reconsolidated beginning in the 1980s. As large monopolies such as JBS started to regain control of the industry, they pushed a new model that allowed them to leverage their power over workers.

Rural slaughterhouses are a recent phenomenon. The plants described in *The Jungle* and the ones where my family members worked were located in urban centers like Chicago and Cedar Rapids. As historian Wilson Warren documented in his book *Tied to the Great Packing Machine*, the move from city to country happened in recent decades.[72]

The shift began when Iowa Beef Processors (later known as IBP) built its first plant just outside Denison, a rural Iowa town, in 1961. Originally financed with a federal small business loan, IBP grew to become one of the biggest meat-processing corporations by rewriting the playbook for the industry.[73]

The company differed from its competitors in several key ways. Its model brought slaughterhouses closer to where animals were raised, which reduced transportation costs. It reconfigured the physical layout of the factory to combine several floors into one. It also eliminated the need for butchers in grocery stores by producing vacuum-sealed cuts of meat (a very wasteful practice, given the space and plastic involved).

But above all, IBP made its money by slashing labor at any cost. By moving slaughterhouses from urban to rural areas, IBP ensured that its slaughterhouses held a monopsony in the labor market.[74] Less well known than a monopoly but equally dangerous, a monopsony occurs when one party has near-total control of a market for an item or service. Just as monopolies take advantage of the limited choice available to their customers, monopsony employers exploit their employees' lack of options in order to drive down wages.[75]

Company towns are one of the clearest examples of monopsony. They emerged in the United States during the industrial revolution of the late 1800s and early 1900s, often involving extractive industries or manufacturing. At their peak, more than 2,500 company towns existed.[76] Most infamously, communities sprang up in West Virginia where coal companies offered the only source of employment. Because of their monopsony power, these companies came to dominate nearly every aspect of their employees' lives, from food to housing.[77]

To create a company town, IBP first had to destroy the unions that protected worker safety and fair pay. IBP and the other growing giants gobbled up unionized plants and reopened them without a union—and with considerably lower wages. In 1989, it bought an old Oscar Mayer plant in a small Iowa town and used this tactic to cut wages nearly in half overnight.[78]

A different company violated a variety of labor laws to the point of making a mockery of them. As journalist Eric Schlosser documented, this company

> threatened to close the plant if workers voted to join the [union]. It harassed workers who supported the union and paid other workers to spy on them. It forced union supporters to distribute anti-union literature. It fired workers for backing the union. It asked workers to lie during their testimony to the [National Labor Relations Board] and refused to hand over company videotapes that the government had subpoenaed. During a union election . . . two [United Food and Commercial Workers] supporters were beaten and arrested by security officers and deputy sheriffs.[79]

The advantage gained from these tactics, coupled with policymaking that favored consolidation, meant that meat companies could revert to the practices that made them infamous at the turn of the century. Although corporations were fined for overt violations, absorbing these light penalties was seemingly part and parcel of the new model.

As the packers expanded through unchecked acquisitions, their power over workers grew in tandem. When companies get bigger and more powerful, they tend do so at the expense of workers and the communities they operate in. Because they face less competition for labor, the bargaining power of their workers is undercut. That's why studies have shown that advertised wages decline by up to 25 percent as an industry consolidates.[80] You don't need to live in a company town to feel the impacts of corporate power.

By the late 1980s, the meat giants had "virtually broken the back of organized labor," and other protections that made meatpacking a solid middle-class occupation were "unraveling at breakneck speed," according to journalist Lynn Waltz in her book *Hog Wild: The Battle for Workers' Rights at the World's Largest Slaughterhouse.*[81]

As a result, what were once solid middle-class jobs became some of the lowest paying in the country.[82] Workers at a slaughterhouse in Austin, Minnesota, for example, made $10.69 per hour in 1985, equal to about $30.00 in 2023 when adjusted for inflation.[83] Since then, wages for slaughterhouse workers have barely budged.[84]

Meanwhile, as lower pay and deteriorating working conditions made slaughterhouse work less desirable to some native-born Americans, companies increasingly looked to immigrants to pick up the slack.[85] The racial composition of the slaughterhouses began to change in the 1980s, reflecting an intentional strategy by some in the industry.[86] Researchers Lourdes Gouveia and Donald Stull characterized this workforce strategy as "a *Field of Dreams* approach to labor recruitment—'build it and they will come.'"[87]

Although Hispanic workers have been the most frequently recruited group of laborers for these plants, slaughterhouses have also brought in other racial and ethnic groups, including workers from Somalia and Myanmar.[88] The "*Field of Dreams* approach" to staffing means that each packing community has more nuances than even the US Census can capture. These jobs are often a point-of-entry position for new immigrants to the United States, whether legal or illegal. Although rural America is often viewed in the popular imagination as lily-white, these company towns show that the reality is a lot more complicated.

The immigrant labor model means even more power in the hands of the Slaughter Barons. As the late sociologist Lionel Cantú pointed out, "many immigrants are willing to work for lower wages; they provide a flexible labor supply (e.g., willing to work overtime or at night, easy to hire/fire); and they have higher organizational flexibility (e.g., willingness to work in substandard environments)."[89] The monopsony of slaughterhouses combined with their workers' tenuous social position guarantees employers almost unlimited power to exploit their employees.

At the same time the industry was reversing gains made by unions in the years after the New Deal, it was working to unwind the safety protections put in place after Upton Sinclair wrote *The Jungle*. In particular, the industry has focused on removing restrictions on the speed of the kill lines.[90] A faster line means higher profits for companies such as JBS.

Unsurprisingly, the prioritization of billionaire greed over worker safety can have very dark consequences, as journalist Ted Genoways detailed in his book *The Chain: Farm, Factory, and the Fate of Our Food*. In the mid-2000s, researchers at the Mayo Clinic noticed a highly unusual set of symptoms in workers at a nearby slaughterhouse.[91] They were experiencing weakness, pain, and numbness in their legs and feet.[92]

The researchers found that all of the sick workers were stationed in or near the part of the plant where meat was cut from severed heads. They had been inhaling aerosolized pig brains, which caused their immune systems to produce antibodies that attacked their own nerve cells. The push to increase line speeds meant that pig brain mist was diffusing at higher quantities and causing the workers' symptoms.[93]

This effort has only intensified in recent years. The Trump administration attempted to turn pork kill lines into the slaughterhouse version of the autobahn by eliminating speed caps entirely. Pat Basu, chief public health veterinarian for the Food Safety and Inspection Service from 2016 to 2018, told the *New York Times* that this proposal reminded him of the decision by the Federal Aviation Administration to shift some of its airplane certification duties to manufacturers like Boeing, a move that came under scrutiny after two crashes of Boeing's 737 Max aircraft resulted in 346 deaths.[94]

A court later ruled that this speed increase was unlawful because the Trump administration did not consider worker safety.[95] Even so,

Tom Vilsack, President Joe Biden's secretary of agriculture, later revived the policy to allow six pork plants to increase their speed as part of a trial program.[96]

The treatment of meatpacking workers during the early months of the COVID-19 pandemic also illustrates how powerless they are in the face of companies such as JBS. When the virus began spreading like wildfire in the United States in 2020, nearly two dozen plants temporarily closed to reduce its spread.[97] The closures resulted in a 25 percent decline in the nation's pork-slaughtering capacity.[98] Tyson even published a full-page ad in the *New York Times* and the *Washington Post* declaring that "the food supply chain is breaking."[99]

Perhaps in response to this pressure, President Trump declared that slaughterhouses were "critical infrastructure," which required the plants to stay open. ProPublica later reported that the North American Meat Institute—a lobbying organization controlled by the meatpackers—had drafted a similarly worded executive order and delivered it to the US Department of Agriculture only a week earlier.[100]

In the following weeks, workers spoke to the press and even staged a wildcat strike protesting the disregard for their safety.[101] But those pleas fell on deaf ears. Between March 2020 and January 2021, 269 meatpacking workers died from COVID-19.[102] One can safely assume that some of these lives could have been saved had better safety measures been put in place. A congressional report later concluded that the companies could have taken more precautions to reduce infections and deaths in their plants, noting the following:

> Instead of addressing the clear indications that workers were contracting the coronavirus at alarming rates due to conditions in meatpacking facilities, meatpacking companies prioritized profits and production over worker safety, continuing to employ practices that led to crowded facilities in which the virus spread easily.[103]

Reporters also discovered that the slaughterhouses kept exporting record amounts of meat even as the food supply chain was supposedly "breaking." For example, JBS's American operation exported nearly 770,000 tons of meat, an increase of 19 percent from before the outbreak of the pandemic.[104] The big four meatpackers—including JBS—collectively paid out more than $3 billion in dividends to shareholders during this time.[105]

Even when laws aren't rolled back, corporations make a mockery of the ones still on the books and face few repercussions for doing so. "The consequences for a company that crosses the line are not that severe," said Wilma Liebman, chairman of the National Labor Relations Board from 2009 to 2011. "Fines and paying back pay is just the cost of doing business."[106]

Often, these companies have the sympathetic ear of politicians. President Ronald Reagan's administration, for example, began reducing safety inspections shortly after he took office.[107] The person Reagan appointed to oversee worker safety was a construction executive whose firm had been cited 138 times for violations.[108] The situation has only gotten worse; there are now about 240 fewer inspectors than there were in 1980.[109]

The consequences for workers can be horrific. On September 3, 1991, twenty-five workers died in a fire in a chicken slaughterhouse in the small town of Hamlet, North Carolina. It was an industrial tragedy with eerie parallels to the infamous Triangle Shirtwaist Factory Fire of 1911. Half of the victims were Black women.

Although politicians dismissed the Hamlet incident as a freak accident, historian Bryant Simon documented the extent to which the company that owned the slaughterhouse disregarded the well-being of its employees in his book *The Hamlet Fire: A Tragic Story of Cheap Food, Cheap Government, and Cheap Lives*.[110] The company had never applied for a building permit, never received approval for the water wells it dug, and never filed the necessary labor forms with the state's safety agency. The saddest part is that many of the workers died only because the doors to the plant were locked from the outside, preventing them from escaping once the fire broke out.[111]

Meatpacking is once again one of the most dangerous manufacturing jobs in the country, with wages generally regarded as no longer reflecting a middle-class standard of living.[112] IBP no longer exists; it was acquired by Tyson Foods.[113] But even though IBP might have started this race to the bottom, the Batistas aggressively copied it and perhaps benefited the most from it. As one rancher said to me, "JBS makes IBP look like an altar boy."

In August 2022, American investigators discovered that a contractor hired by JBS to clean slaughterhouses employed over a hundred children in "hazardous occupations."[114] These children cleaned kill floors, bone-cutting saws, grinding machines, and electric knives.[115] The facts seem as if they came straight out of *The Jungle*. One child was only thirteen years old. A fourteen-year-old, who worked from 11:00 p.m. to 5:00 a.m., five to six days per week, cleaned machines used to cut meat and suffered from chemical burns. School records showed that the student missed class or fell asleep in class because of the job at the plant.[116]

The tendency of concentrated industries is to squeeze workers. Without real structural limits on their power or actual enforcement paired with meaningful penalties, their outsize profits come at the workers' expense. In JBS's case, that sometimes means children. After all, few companies are as committed to pushing the limits of the law—and merely absorbing any fines as a cost of doing business—as JBS.

A Criminal Enterprise

JBS's sheer disregard for the law sets it apart from the other barons in this book. The Batistas' criminal tendencies are now seemingly infused into the DNA of their monopoly. It's no surprise, then, that the family continues to engage in the same sort of behavior that helped them build their empire in the first place.

In 2017, Brazil accused employees of several companies, including JBS, of bribing dozens of meat inspectors with cash and expensive cuts of meat. They did so to export salmonella-contaminated meat and allow rotten meat to be served in public schools. The inspectors also falsified sanitary permits. One federal investigator referred to this plot as a "powerful criminal organization" in his description of the case, according to the *New York Times*.[117]

This sort of conduct is so flagrant, and so recurrent, that Congresswoman Rosa DeLauro asked the USDA to ban the company from doing business with the US government.[118] "They entered illegally into our markets," DeLauro told *Four Corners*, the Australian equivalent of *60 Minutes*. "It is all through bribery and illegal activity that they have managed to put themselves in the place of being one of the largest meat-packing corporations in the country and in the world."[119]

That position means that the company has a tremendous environmental footprint. Beef production is the single largest contributor to climate change among agricultural products.[120] In fact, JBS's annual climate footprint is higher than Italy's and almost the size of France's.[121] There are several reasons for these stratospheric emission levels. Much of the grain fed to cattle, especially during the feedlot stage, when the animals cannot forage, is grown using an immense amount of chemicals that were created as by-products of fossil fuels.[122] Cattle also produce methane gas when they digest food.[123]

Most relevant to JBS, ranchers are clearing a vast amount of land in the Amazon rainforest to create more farmland. Studies suggest that up to 80 percent of land clearance in the Amazon is driven by the cattle industry.[124] JBS does not itself chop down the trees, but it does incentivize the cutting through its demand for more Brazilian cattle to feed its empire.

The Batistas know that climate change presents a major public image issue. That's probably why they signed an agreement with Greenpeace in 2009 pledging not to buy cattle from ranchers in newly deforested areas. Moreover, in a sponsored content article published in *Politico* in 2022, Tim Schellpeper, chief executive officer of JBS USA, bragged that the company was "first in the agriculture industry to commit to achieving net-zero greenhouse gas emissions by 2040."[125]

Yet it quickly became clear that none of these promises meant any real commitment on JBS's part. Not long after JBS pledged that it would reduce emissions to net zero by 2040, a study by several environmental groups revealed that the company's emissions had actually increased by over 50 percent in the five preceding years.[126]

Similarly, just like money, cattle can be laundered. For example, several *New York Times* reporters recently profiled a small rancher who laundered illegally ranched cattle by selling them to an intermediary, who then sold the same cattle to a packer with a clean record.[127] JBS claims that it has a system in place to prevent it from buying cattle produced on illegally deforested land, but it's clear that is only a fig leaf. In 2017, the US government fined the company for buying forty-nine thousand cattle from illegally deforested areas.[128] Researchers found that a landmass the size of Vermont and New Hampshire combined was deforested during the ten years after the Greenpeace agreement was signed. JBS's failure forced Greenpeace to pull out of the agreement.[129] In 2021, the *Guardian* published an investigation that found that big American grocery stores like Walmart, Costco, and Kroger have sold beef imported by JBS that was linked to deforestation.[130]

But despite JBS's repeated misconduct, the federal government has declined to pursue structural remedies that would dilute the company's power or impose real consequences for its illicit actions. In fact, the US government has actively rewarded the company. Since entering American markets, JBS has received more than $900 million from federal contracts, according to the *Washington Post.*[131] The USDA also gave the company an additional $67 million in bailout funds meant for struggling farmers.[132]

These payments are so excessive that Congresswoman Carolyn Maloney of New York sent a formal request demanding that Secretary Vilsack review the department's contracts with JBS, noting that "it is troubling to see taxpayer dollars going to a major agribusiness that has such an egregious record of legal violations." But Secretary Vilsack dismissed these concerns, arguing that removing JBS from its list of procurement partners would "potentially impair competitive choice for the taxpayer."[133]

The administration's stance on JBS runs counter to President Biden's promises on the 2020 campaign trail to strengthen antitrust enforcement and to his priorities once elected.[134] Brian Deese, at the time Biden's director of the National Economic Council, co-wrote a blog post on the White House website in September 2021 blaming the meat giants for price increases and noting that they have the "power to squeeze both consumers and farmers and ranchers."[135] Biden himself even jumped into the fray, arguing that "capitalism without competition" is "exploitation."[136]

But under the direction of Tom Vilsack, the USDA has failed to take any action that would even remotely improve the situation. Vilsack's signature initiative was to give out a billion dollars of taxpayer money to new or expanding slaughterhouses as a roundabout way of deconcentrating these markets.[137]

This plan is like dumping a billion dollars on Ask Jeeves and wishing the company good luck against Google. Even in the best-case scenario, this initiative doesn't meaningfully change the structure of the industry.[138] It does virtually nothing for the millions of Americans who are being overcharged by JBS and their ilk, or the ranchers who are forced to depend on a handful of companies to buy their cattle, or the workers on the kill line.

As I chatted with friends in the cattle industry, it became clear that this money is mostly being wasted on entities that have no hope of being financially viable. If that comes to pass, and these operations go broke in a few years, big companies such as JBS will be able to come in and buy their assets for pennies on the dollar.[139] Time will tell whether some of these plants will become the newest tentacles of the Batistas' empire.

The sad thing is that there is a template for making real structural changes to meat markets that disperse power in the industry. The actions that worked so well more than a century ago—antitrust enforcement, building of union and worker power, and clear bright-line rules that protect market participants—cost American taxpayers nothing in direct investments or subsidies.

But instead of following this proven approach, Vilsack squandered taxpayer money and missed a rare bipartisan moment to do something meaningful.[140] He refused to grapple with corporate power in an industry that's run amok. For JBS and the Batista brothers, it might as well be yet another slap on the wrist.

CHAPTER 7

The Grocery Barons

IN EARLY 2014, DOUG McMILLON, chief executive officer of Walmart Stores, Inc., gave his top executives a homework assignment. At the time, Walmart was in a rut. Sales were sluggish, and the company would soon report its first annual sales decline since 1980.[1]

McMillon's predecessor had left after only a short tenure, seemingly pushed out by the Walton family, who then handpicked McMillon to revive growth and chart a new course for Walmart.[2] The descendants of Sam Walton, the company's founder, still collectively own over 50 percent of the company and hold several seats on the board. For context, Jeff Bezos owns only 12 percent of Amazon.[3] Given this control, Walmart is still essentially a family operation, so what the Walton clan wants, they get, including their choice of the company's CEO.

McMillon directed his lieutenants to read *The Everything Store* by Brad Stone, a tell-all book about Amazon and its founder, Jeff Bezos. As detailed in *The Everything Store*, Bezos meticulously studied Walmart as he built Amazon. Now McMillon wanted his team to do the reverse: study the rise of Amazon.[4]

Although Walmart was still the world's biggest retailer, Amazon was gaining ground based on its dominance in online shopping, a terrain Walmart had previously neglected. At the time, only 2.5 percent of the company's sales came from Walmart.com, and for the first time ever, Amazon's stock market value surpassed Walmart's.[5] The *Financial Times* quipped that "Walmart is committed to the past, and is heading there fast."[6] In response, some analysts called on Walmart to sell some of its overseas locations or parts of its American business.[7] Warren Buffett even sold 90 percent of his Walmart stock because he thought Amazon was about to eat the company's lunch.[8]

But McMillon had a battle plan for fending off this new rival. At the company's annual meeting of shareholders in the summer of 2015, Doug delivered a message that boiled down to one word: "omnichannel." McMillon argued that Walmart needed "to stop talking about digital and physical retail as if they're two separate things. The customer doesn't think of it that way, and we can't either."[9]

With this announcement, McMillon signaled that Walmart would no longer be content to dominate physical store sales; instead, it would aggressively invest billions to increase its digital presence and capture sales wherever they occur. As McMillon put it, "one customer can shop with us in so many different ways—in stores, on their phones, at homes, a pick-up point. But they just think they're shopping at Walmart." McMillon hoped that growing the company's online business would in turn grow its in-store sales because customers who come to pick up their orders would likely stay to buy something else.[10] To show its seriousness, the company even dropped the word "stores" from its name, becoming, effective February 2018, "Walmart Inc."[11]

McMillon's plan for growing Walmart's omnichannel business centered on one product category: food. Although Walmart Supercenters sell everything from clothes to tires, they are, at their core, food retailers, with nearly 60 percent of Walmart's sales now coming from groceries.[12] Walmart dominates the American grocery market so thoroughly that it has about the same market share as the number two, three, four, five, six, seven, and eight grocery store companies *combined*.[13]

Maintaining the company's grip on grocery was key because Walmart already had a head start on Amazon in this area.[14] McMillon wanted the company's physical stores to be the heart of a flywheel in which sales from one part of the business drive the growth of another part, which in turn spurs an increase in sales in the original part of the business.[15] This flywheel logic may have also spurred Walmart's entry into other new sectors, from health care to banking. "When we get better in food, the whole box grows," said Charles Redfield, who oversaw food retail at Walmart US.[16] Walmart's strength in grocery would be crucial in its battle with Amazon.

At the same time, Amazon was moving in the opposite direction. The company knew that it was at a disadvantage because of the massive physical presence of its competitor, with a Walmart store located within ten minutes of 90 percent of Americans.[17] Amazon realized that it needed to expand its physical store presence to maintain its online advantage.

In a memo circulated within the company, Amazon sketched out an ambitious new physical grocery store chain with more than two thousand locations.[18] Only a few months later, it burst into the grocery business by buying food retailer Whole Foods, a purchase that catapulted it into the top ten players in the industry. As reporters for the *New York Times* noted, "Amazon has effectively started a supermarket war" with its purchase of Whole Foods.[19] Walmart's market capitalization declined by $11 billion on the news.[20]

For two decades prior to this moment, the two retailers had stuck to their lanes, one physical and one online. But now, each company was trying to move onto the other's home turf. Like Godzilla and Mothra, these two giants were ready to fight for control of the American retail market. And the battlefield would be centered on the grocery aisle.

From Five-and-Dimes to Supercenters

Walmart was founded in 1962 in Rogers, Arkansas, by a businessman named Sam Walton. Walton had entered retail years earlier, in 1945, when he bought a franchise of a chain called Ben Franklin and then gradually opened more locations across Arkansas.[21] Ben Franklin stores, like other five-and-dime stores, tended to be located downtown. But after visiting a competitor, Walton realized that the future of retail lay in one-stop shopping. Walton understood that instead of buying goods from a variety of downtown retailers, shoppers would increasingly prefer the convenience of finding everything they need in a single store.[22]

Sensing an opportunity, in 1962 Walton opened his own store: Wal-Mart Discount City. It sold a similar mix of merchandise as Ben Franklin but in a much larger building and with a broader selection. Instead of renting space downtown, Walton built his new store on the outskirts, where there was ample parking.

Walton challenged an orthodoxy of the era: that shoppers wanted a balance between low prices and an enjoyable shopping environment. Instead, Walton sought to charge the lowest possible price no matter what. This philosophy became the cornerstone of his new store, best captured in its tagline: "Every Day Low Prices." In his memoir, Walton wrote about learning this valuable lesson with his first store. He had, in his own words, a "truly ugly" sales area. But that meant that he could sell goods for 20 percent less than his competitors. Walton wanted to "find out if customers in a town of 6,000 people would come to our kind of a barn and buy the same merchandise strictly because of price. The answer was yes."[23]

Driven by these principles, Walton opened locations first across Arkansas and then slowly across the South. He expanded both through acquisitions of competing retailers and through organic growth. He initially opened stores in rural areas before slowly moving into the suburbs.

Walton also developed another innovation. From its founding, Walton wanted his company to have the most efficient distribution system possible, which he viewed as a key competitive advantage. His model followed a hub-and-spoke pattern of expansion, in which Walton would first establish a distribution center and then open stores around it. The goal was to keep everything close by so that transportation costs and restocking time remained low.[24] As one Walmart executive said at a Wall Street–oriented conference, "The misconception is that we're in the retail business. We're in the distribution business."[25]

This focus on the distribution system meant that Walton cared deeply about technology. Before most of his competitors in the retail industry, he invested in a digital database with a store-level point-of-sale system and a satellite network. He also discovered before others that using barcodes increased checkout productivity by more than 50 percent. He then combined these two ideas to instantaneously collect and analyze sales data, which enabled the company to give its buyers access to real-time sales data on their products down to the store level, eliminating the guesswork that had previously characterized the industry.[26]

Although Walton was often ahead of the curve, he also understood the importance of copying a good idea when he saw it. For example, after seeing the success of a precursor to Costco, he created his version of the model in 1983 by opening Sam's Club as a membership-only retail warehouse.[27] These stores sold a limited selection of groceries but in vast quantities.

His game-changing idea, expanding into the grocery business, came in part from the French.[28] On one trip, he stumbled upon the French retailer Carrefour and its pioneering European "hypermarket": a combination of a department store and a grocery store that created a truly massive one-stop retail experience. Sam Walton created his own version of the hypermarket, "malls without walls," by adding a grocery store onto a traditional Walmart store.[29]

In December 1987, he formally entered the grocery business with the aptly named Hypermart USA. The first store, near Dallas, was so big that one reporter pointed out that it could house a basketball court, a baseball field, a football field, three tennis courts, and a swimming pool.[30] The store was so enormous that employees used to roller-skate around to answer customers' questions.[31] Although these stores were profitable, they did not meet expectations; ultimately, Walton opened only a few and eventually pulled the plug on the idea.[32]

But the company did learn some valuable lessons from this experiment. Soon after opening the first Hypermart USA, Walton opened the first Walmart Supercenter near Washington, Missouri, an exurb of St. Louis. This store was like the Hypermart but pared down to a more manageable size. An executive at the time described it as "a small-town version of a Hypermart," and it proved to be the perfect scale.[33]

The shift into Supercenters and the entry into grocery marked a new era for Walmart. The grocery business is notoriously tough, with exceedingly thin profit margins. According to a Columbia Business School study, 3 percent to 4 percent margins are considered typical for grocery stores, compared with 20 percent for other types of retailers.[34]

But though margins are tight, people shop for food much more often than they shop for other goods, and grocery is a steady business. For Walmart, the addition of groceries proved to be a powerful traffic draw because by adding groceries, stores boosted non-food sales by 30 percent.[35] And even with its "Every Day Low Prices" mantra, profits generally still came from higher-margin non-food merchandise.

As a result, the company began replacing most of its traditional stores with Walmart Supercenters at a blistering pace. By 1999, it had opened 683 Supercenters, and by the mid-2000s, this figure had ballooned to 1,980. In 2002, Wal-Mart became the largest grocery chain in the United States.[36] There is now a Supercenter in every US state except Hawaii: 3,572 in total, with only 364 traditional stores remaining.[37]

The company has since introduced another grocery concept called Walmart Neighborhood Markets, which are about one-fourth the size of a typical Supercenter and are essentially just grocery stores.[38] The company found that they offer convenience to shoppers who want to avoid the sprawling Supercenters and that they are easier to build in congested urban areas. As one industry consultant put it, "the Neighborhood Markets are the traditional food retailer's worst nightmare."[39] The company now operates 781 Neighborhood Markets, compared with 600 Sam's Club stores.[40]

In less than a few decades, Walmart went from selling no groceries to becoming the largest grocery retailer the United States has ever seen. The company gained this dominance incredibly fast. As recently as 1997, American consumers bought only 21 percent of their food from the four largest grocers at that time.[41] Walmart alone now sells 30 percent of American groceries.[42]

And like a Great Plains tornado, Walmart's sudden dominance of the grocery industry left a path of destruction in its wake.

Path of Destruction

"Wal-Mart is responsible for changing downtown America more than any business in the 20th century," one small-town Texas chamber of commerce president told *USA Today* in 1990. "Sam Walton built his empire on going into small communities. As he went into a small community, overnight, buying patterns went from downtown to . . . Wal-Mart."[43]

The rise of Sam Walton's empire unleashed two waves of destruction. The first wave, long documented and well publicized, was the collapse of local retailers and small-town main streets as the company's empire of traditional discount stores expanded across the country. The company has a long history of using the classic monopoly trick of selling goods at a loss when it opens a new store or moves into a new product category in order to undercut existing (typically smaller, local) businesses.[44] With its massive balance sheet, Walmart can sustain a period of losses in way that its smaller competitors simply cannot.

In his memoir, Sam Walton brushed aside the backlash against his company, remarking that "of all the notions I've heard about Wal-Mart, none has ever baffled me more than this idea that we are somehow the enemy of small-town America."[45]

But reality tells a different story. Kenneth Stone, a professor at Iowa State University, drew national attention when he found that in the first ten years after Wal-Mart opened almost a hundred stores in Iowa, the state lost 298 hardware stores, 293 building supply stores, 161 variety stores, 158 women's apparel stores, 153 shoe stores, 116 drugstores, and 111 men's and boy's apparel stores. He noted that smaller towns bore the biggest losses.[46] One can reasonably assume that this pattern of destruction repeated itself across small-town America as Walmart blitzed the country.

I actually remember when the first Supercenter opened by the mall near my family's home.[47] My mom took me and my brother there on opening day because it was such a big local event. Today, more than two decades later, the location seems just as busy as when we first entered its doors. Meanwhile, the mall across the street, where my mom's bakery was located, died and closed.

Although the story of Walmart's march across America's retail landscape is well known, the second wave of destruction—the impact on grocery stores—is less familiar to most people. Stone and his colleagues found that new Superstores weren't causing people to buy more groceries. It wasn't as if people suddenly bought more milk or bread when Walmart came to town. They just stopped going to their old stores. "I see it pretty much as a zero-sum game," Stone told Bloomberg at the time.[48] Other scholars have found similar results.[49]

If the grocery business is a zero-sum game, the Walton family was capturing more and more of the pie. One writer noted that "in the 1980s, you could still visit almost any community in the U.S. and find a thriving supermarket. Typically, it would be a dynasty family grocery store, one that had been in business for a few generations. Larger markets usually had two or three players, small chains that sorted themselves out along socioeconomic lines: fancy, middlebrow, thrifty."[50]

But alas, Walmart's blitz into grocery destroyed many of these local pillars. The company was a catalyst for the bankruptcy of at least twenty-five grocery chains and the closure of thirteen thousand grocery stores in just a decade.[51] Walmart has captured 50 percent or more of all grocery sales in forty-three metropolitan areas and in 160 smaller markets. In thirty-eight of these regions, its share of the grocery market is 70 percent or more.[52] A recent US Department of Agriculture study echoed these findings, emphasizing that rural areas tend to be the most concentrated grocery markets in the nation.[53] In some communities, especially in rural areas, Walmart is the only grocery store left. For shoppers, this consolidation often resulted in higher food prices, according to studies by academics and the Federal Trade Commission.[54]

For the stores that survived, Walmart's entry triggered a consolidation spree as competitors strove to keep up.[55] Kroger, the third-largest American grocery seller, with a nearly 6 percent share of the market, was the most aggressive.[56] After several high-profile acquisitions, it now operates 2,720 grocery stores under its own name and under other brands that it has acquired, including Ralphs, Dillons, Smith's, King Soopers, Fry's, QFC, City Market, Owen's, Jay C, Pay Less, Baker's, Gerbes, Harris Teeter, Pick 'n Save, Metro Market, Mariano's, Fred Meyer, Food 4 Less, and Foods Co.[57]

But all these brands and stores were apparently not enough for Kroger to compete with Walmart. In 2022, Kroger announced its intention to buy Albertsons, which, like Kroger, operates under its own name and a number of other brands, including Safeway, Vons, Jewel-Osco, Shaw's, ACME Markets, Tom Thumb, Randalls, United Supermarkets, Pavilions, Star Market, Haggen, Carrs, Kings Food Markets, and Balducci's Food Lovers Market.[58]

Albertson's had aggressively tried to roll up the industry. Its purchase of Safeway is particularly infamous. According to journalist David Dayen, President Barack Obama's Federal Trade Commission approved the purchase only after the companies agreed in part to sell 146 stores to a small grocery store chain with only 18 stores to prevent concentration in a few cities. But the small chain formed mostly by the divested stores proved to be a disaster, and it declared bankruptcy soon after. Albertsons ultimately bought back nearly one-quarter of the stores it had divested within less than a year.[59]

This rapid consolidation was, in part, a response to the size and power of Walmart.[60] Albertsons' chief executive officer, Vivek Sankaran, even defended its consolidation efforts at a US Senate hearing by arguing that it was the company's best path to compete against Walmart.[61] He noted in his written testimony that "the marketplace for groceries over the past decade has completely transformed."[62] The dominance of one grocery baron is seemingly triggering the creation of others.

The empire that Sam Walton was able to build is admirable. But Walmart's early stores were not unique at the time. Thousands of Americans opened successful five-and-dime stores, and dozens of others even built regional chains because the regulatory structure at the time fostered the flourishing of local, innovative enterprises like Walmart. That system began to break down in the 1980s, and it's questionable whether a similar business could now be built from the ground up. Sam Walton is an American success story, but he probably wouldn't be able to succeed today because of the empire built by Sam Walton.

Vendorville

Walmart is based in Bentonville, Arkansas, just a few miles from Sam Walton's first Walmart store in Rogers. Although Walmart currently operates out of a nondescript building that doesn't seem to match its power and scale, the company is in the midst of building a massive new corporate headquarters on the east side of town. The new offices are designed in the style of a college campus, with twelve buildings spread over 350 acres, and with a price tag estimated to be $1 billion.[63]

Bentonville is sometimes called Vendorville because its economy is built around Walmart and all its vendors.[64] I've visited Bentonville several times over the years. I first popped in on a whim in 2018 after attending an agriculture show in Little Rock. It's a charming town of over fifty thousand people that struck me as something out of *The Truman Show*. During most of the twentieth century, the town's population hovered around two thousand to three thousand people, but it exploded in tandem with the growth of Walmart.[65]

In an ironic twist, Bentonville captures the Main Street, USA imagery that Sam Walton's Supercenters helped destroy in other towns across the country. Whereas most small-town squares in America are in a state of decay, Bentonville's is the only one I've ever seen with James Beard finalist restaurants next to offices for national brands.[66]

The family's name and money are everywhere in Bentonville. That's not surprising, given that the Waltons are not just the richest family in town, or in Arkansas, or even in the United States; they are the richest family on the planet, with a collective estimated net worth of $225 billion.[67] They are so wealthy that members of the family own two separate NFL teams: the Rams and the Broncos.[68]

The Waltons have poured a lot of that money into the town that their company calls home. The Walton name features prominently on the terminal of the region's main airport as well as on a new medical school that is set to welcome its first students in 2025.[69] The family also backs several restaurants and hotels, along with owning the local bank.[70]

Alice Walton, Sam's daughter, built the Crystal Bridges Museum of American Art, a world-class facility with a renowned collection featuring artists Andy Warhol, Norman Rockwell, and Georgia O'Keefe, among many others.[71] The museum forms a nearly 360,000-square-foot complex with a satellite facility recently completed and an expansion underway.[72]

Sam's grandchildren have made their own contributions to Bentonville's cityscape. Steuart and Tom Walton financed a new art and music festival modeled after *Austin City Limits*.[73] Both heirs also have a keen interest in biking.[74] With their influence, the family has pushed to rebrand the town as the "mountain biking capital of the world."[75] To claim that title, the family and the company have poured over $85 million into the region's trails, hosted an international cycling event, and even convinced the national governing body of cycling to open a branch office in town.[76]

But there's a dark current running underneath that perfect cookie-cutter image. I've traveled to Bentonville a number of times since, and the town has felt a bit more eerie on each visit. I first noticed this odd vibe when visiting the recently renovated museum that Walmart built for itself on Bentonville's town square. The museum suggests that the building housed the first Walmart, but that's not entirely right. The first Walmart actually opened in nearby Rogers and is now a rundown building that's only partly occupied by an antique mall. It's fitting that the museum celebrating Walmart is situated in what's basically a movie set even as the company's actual birthplace illustrates the destruction that Sam Walton left behind.

The symbolism is telling, but I think the town's underbelly is best captured in its inequality statistics. When one thinks of systemic poverty in America, the portion of Arkansas that's located within the Mississippi

Delta comes to mind. But a 2018 investigation by the Arkansas Advocates for Children and Families found that the number of children living in poverty in the Bentonville region was actually higher than in any county in eastern Arkansas along the Mississippi River. "Almost half of children in Northwest Arkansas—48 percent—are growing up in families with low incomes, or combined incomes that aren't more than $41,560 for a family of three."

The idyllic town square may reflect the success of the other end of the income spectrum; the top 1 percent of households in the region earned an average of $2 million annually. But this income disparity makes the region one of the most unequal in America. In fact, the Economic Policy Institute ranked it 15th out of 916 metro areas in terms of inequality.[77]

Like the broader Gilded Age economy that Walmart exemplifies and has played a role in shaping, the wealth in Bentonville obscures the hardship surrounding it. After all, the Walton family has so much money to spend on museums and bike trails because they have extracted it from the communities in which Walmart operates—from shoppers but also from the company's employees, the towns themselves, and even from taxpayers through a series of hidden government subsidies.

For example, as Walmart expanded its traditional stores into Supercenters, it would often construct a new, larger building nearby instead of simply adding on to the existing one. Those old stores frequently sat empty or underused, just like the original Walmart in Rogers. That may be why Walmart openings have been linked to declines in nearby home values.[78]

Walmart and other major retailers have made the situation even worse by including restrictive covenants in the deeds of old buildings, which prevent other retailers from using the space for competitive purposes.[79] These provisions perpetuate food deserts and tie the hands of communities struggling to figure out what to do with these ghost buildings.[80] After all, it's not easy to find a use for an old Walmart that doesn't involve grocery or retail. One former Walmart Supercenter in Brownsville, Texas, became the center of a national debate when it was bought by a firm detaining migrant children.[81]

Limiting competition is apparently not enough for Walmart. The company understands what happens to communities when its stores are abandoned, and it uses this knowledge to leverage a tax break. The company often engages in what is known as the "dark stores" loophole, a tax dodge that lets it evade millions in property taxes by valuing its stores as if they were closed.[82]

These shenanigans further tilt the scales in Walmart's favor and deprive local communities of needed tax revenue. They are particularly egregious in light of the fact that many of their stores were built with massive taxpayer subsidies in the first place.[83] Of course, this isn't the only tax loophole the family has exploited. In 2013, Bloomberg reported that the family pioneered an estate tax loophole that is now widely used by American billionaires.[84]

As bad as Walmart is for communities as a whole, it creates conditions that are particularly damaging for workers. As labor historian Nelson Lichtenstein noted, Sam Walton built a company rooted in a "southernized, deunionized post-New Deal America." Walmart has long been defined by transnational commerce, employment insecurity, and poverty-level wages, which is an ironic geographic twist on history given that the region was at the heart of the New Deal and the anti-chain movement.[85]

Walmart employs about 1.6 million people in the United States alone, making it the nation's largest private employer.[86] In fact, more people are on the company's payroll than the populations of eleven states.[87] The company's impact on the labor market is so big that it drives down wages in the areas in which it builds Supercenters.[88] In the words of one academic, Walmart effectively "determine[s] the real minimum wage" in the country.[89] That's why it's national news when the company decides to raise wages.[90]

From its founding, Walmart has been notorious for its poverty-level wages; in its early years, the company exploited a loophole in order to pay the mostly female store employees half of the federal minimum wage.[91] It took a federal court battle for the workers to receive the minimum wage.[92] In 2021, Walmart employees' median income was about $25,000, whereas CEO Doug McMillon took home $25.7 million that year.[93]

Given this history, it should come as no surprise that Sam Walton hated unions. "I have always believed strongly that we don't need unions at Wal-Mart," he stated in his memoir.[94] Over the years, the company has aggressively fought efforts to unionize, and it seemingly closes stores whenever they gain traction. For example, after deli counter workers in a Texas Walmart Supercenter voted to unionize in 2000, the company switched to prepackaged meat and closed the department.[95] In 2015, Walmart suddenly closed five stores to deal with what it said were extensive plumbing issues, which it said would take six months to fix. Some speculated that the real reason it closed the stores was to let the employees go as retaliation for labor activism.[96]

And it's not just labor laws that the company has eluded. A 2017 report based on a survey of over one thousand Walmart employees found that the company was likely violating worker protections such as the Americans with Disabilities Act and the Family and Medical Leave Act, among others. According to the *New York Times*, the company "routinely refuses to accept doctors' notes, penalizes workers who need to take care of a sick family member and otherwise punishes employees for lawful absences."[97]

As the company's power grew, it reshaped labor options and norms for millions of Americans. Gary Chaison, a labor expert, told the *New York Times* in 2015, "What you're increasingly finding is that it's the primary wage earners who work at Walmart, because a lot of workers have more or less given up on getting middle-class jobs."[98] Meanwhile, many older Americans are working at the store past the normal retirement age because of their financial insecurity, a sad reality reflected by the recent TikTok trend of elderly Walmart employees asking for donations.[99]

This power imbalance between Walmart and its employees explains the poverty-level wages for many of Walmart's 1.6 million workers but also for employees of its competitors. Some unionized grocery stores have even used the opening of a Supercenter as an excuse to demand cuts to their own employees' wages and benefits.[100]

These low wages also obscure a generous hidden subsidy that the company receives from taxpayers. Many Walmart workers depend on government public assistance programs such as Medicaid (health care), the Earned Income Tax Credit (a low-wage tax subsidy), Section 8 vouchers (housing assistance), LIHEAP (energy assistance), and SNAP (food assistance), among others. In 2013, one estimate by congressional House Democrats found that taxpayers subsidized Walmart to the tune of more than $5,000 per employee each year through all of the government assistance programs that its workers need.[101]

In effect, instead of paying a living wage to these employees, the Walton family shifts the burden onto taxpayers. Although many people may recoil at the idea of the public filling the gap between Walmart's pay and the income its workers need to survive, not all policymakers see an issue with this sort of billionaire welfare. Jason Furman, former chair of the Council of Economic Advisers under President Obama, wrote a paper before joining the administration titled "Wal-Mart: A Progressive Success Story" that called for even more of these subsidies to Walmart's bottom line.[102]

There is, of course, another way to address the issue. Walmart failed to establish dominance in Germany because of the country's strong labor protections and antitrust guardrails.[103] These market protections may explain why the company eventually threw in the towel and sold off its operations there.[104]

In some instances, Walmart even receives a double subsidy. Its workers and shoppers frequently rely on SNAP, the Supplemental Nutrition Assistance Program, formerly known as "food stamps." The program originated as part of the New Deal as a temporary measure and was made permanent by President Lyndon Johnson in a bill signed in 1964.[105] This program and several smaller food assistance programs are now part of the Farm Bill. In fact, these food assistance programs make up more than 75 percent of the most recent Farm Bill.[106]

SNAP is in many ways a triumph of progressive social policy, with an average of 41.2 million people participating in the program each month in 2022.[107] The use rate is so high because, unlike many other programs, SNAP was structured by the US Congress so that anyone who qualifies is guaranteed to receive assistance. As a result, the program is a lifeline for millions of Americans who might otherwise struggle to put food on the table.

But because of Walmart's dominance of the grocery sector, a very large portion of SNAP dollars now run through the company's cash registers. In 2013, the company received $13 billion in sales from shoppers using SNAP.[108] By comparison, farmers markets took in only $17.4 million of all SNAP spending that same year.[109] The amount of SNAP money received by the company surged with the expansion of SNAP benefits in response to the COVID-19 pandemic. With some back-of-the-envelope math, I came up with a rough estimate that Walmart now receives somewhere around $26.8 billion each year from SNAP.[110]

Unfortunately, more concrete numbers are not available because the US Supreme Court has ruled that the amount of taxpayer money that the company receives from SNAP can be kept secret. In 2019, the Court heard a case involving the USDA's decision to deny a request by a South Dakota newspaper for this information. "Most of the time, the government tells the public which companies benefit from federal dollars earmarked for taxpayer-funded public assistance programs," agriculture and food reporter Claire Brown noted. "We know which insurance companies make the highest profits from Medicare and Medicaid, for example, and those figures have been used to pressure them to offer better options to their clients."[111] But in this instance, the Court rejected this level of transparency, with Justice Elena Kagan joining the Republican-appointed members of the Court to uphold the USDA decision under the notion that it was "confidential" business information.[112]

The program is important enough that it factors into Walmart's operational decision-making. Many Americans enrolled in SNAP schedule their trips to the grocery store around the days when their funds get deposited. In fact, the company factors this bump into its ordering system. One Arkansas reporter noted that sales of Hot Pockets triple on these days. Accordingly, Walmart worked with the company to ensure that its stores would not run out of these highly demanded items on cash infusion days.[113]

Both Walmart and Amazon are working hard to increase their share of SNAP dollars. Echoing the company's pivot to omnichannel sales, Walmart was one of the first retailers to begin taking part in the USDA's online SNAP program.[114] With the onset of the COVID-19 pandemic, online SNAP purchases increased twentyfold, and unfortunately, Walmart and Amazon hold a virtual duopoly on those sales.[115]

As a result, these programs end up subsidizing the fortunes of the Walton family and, by extension, Bentonville. Like barons of past eras, the Waltons have spent at least a chunk of their wealth on charity and public works. These contributions, of course, have aligned with the family's personal interests, such as fine art and bike riding.

Journalist Jeffrey Goldberg illustrated this point when he traveled to Bentonville for the opening of Crystal Bridges. After touring the museum, he went to one of the Walmart locations in town to ask employees what they thought of it, but he couldn't find a single one even contemplating a visit. "One worker I met in the parking lot said that the museum wasn't meant for Wal-Mart workers," Goldberg wrote. "Others were resentful. One middle-aged woman noted how odd it was that the Wal-Mart heirs could spend so much on paintings, but Wal-Mart workers couldn't get health-care benefits. 'Merry Christmas,' she said."[116]

Alice Walton, the daughter who led the charge to build Crystal Bridges, has now focused her energy on health care.[117] Her efforts led to the construction of the new medical school campus in Bentonville. In 2021, she told the Arkansas business publication *Talk Business & Politics*, "We have a health industry that does not produce healthy outcomes because we do not have a system that addresses behavior change."[118]

Meanwhile, the company she controls alongside her family is the country's largest seller of junk food and continues to sell cigarettes and guns. In Walmart stores alone, there were 363 gun-related incidents resulting in 112 deaths between 2020 and the end of November 2022.[119] And in 2022, Walmart agreed to pay over $3 billion to settle thousands of lawsuits over its pharmacies' role in the opioid crisis.[120]

The family also created a think tank called Heartland Forward with the stated goal of working to "unleash the Heartland's potential and improve the economic performance in the center of the United States."[121] The think tank hosts an annual extravaganza known as the Heartland Summit, which features thought leaders and celebrities engaging in "participatory conversations that explore topics important to the Heartland's future."[122] "This is a very powerful room," famed singer, songwriter, and producer Pharrell Williams said at a recent iteration of the Heartland Summit. "There's a lot of energy in here tonight."[123]

Meanwhile, the family has harnessed this energy to spend over a billion dollars undermining public schools by underwriting academics and policy organizations that advocate for charter schools. As one national reporter noted, the Waltons have "subsidized an entire charter school system in the nation's capital, helping to fuel enrollment growth so that close to half of all public school students in the city now attend charters, which receive taxpayer dollars but are privately operated."[124]

And both the Waltons and Walmart itself have long made significant political contributions. Walmart promised after the January 6 riot at the US Capitol that it would indefinitely suspend donations to members of Congress who opposed the Electoral College certification of President-elect Joe Biden.[125] But the following year, it contributed to sixty election deniers.[126]

The Waltons have, without a doubt, brought wealth and prosperity to their company's hometown. Between the high-paying jobs at the headquarters of a massive global corporation and the family's significant contributions to the community, it's very clear when you visit Bentonville that the city is having a moment.

But so much of this wealth has been built on the backs of workers, supercharged by taxpayer-funded subsidies and, ultimately, extracted from the communities in which the company operates. As Stacy Mitchell, co-executive director of the Institute for Local Self-Reliance, argued, "Communities dominated by global retail chains function in many respects like the colonial economies of the European superpowers, which were organized not to foster local development and prosperity but to enrich the colonizers."[127]

Steuart Walton, during a panel discussion on the future of Arkansas, recently remarked that "the communities that outperform are inevitably communities where resources are being reinvested."[128] Perhaps, then, every decaying heartland town just needs to recruit its own barons.

America's Politburo

When I set out to write this book, I had no plans to include a chapter about Walmart. The topic has been well covered in the past, and I was also wary because so many diatribes against the company are rooted in an undercurrent of classism. I didn't want to be one more critic with a smug sense of moral superiority toward its customers.

But I knew that I wanted to include a chapter about grocery stores. After all, they're the one place where all the other barons portrayed in this book intersect, not to mention the fundamental way in which most people interact with the food system. I knew that I couldn't tell the story about the concentration of power without talking about grocery.

On an even more basic level, I truly love grocery stores. When I travel, I feel compelled to visit every new supermarket that I haven't been to before. I enjoy walking the aisles, spotting products that I've never seen, and observing how the selection varies by store and region. Ironically, it's an interest that Sam Walton shared. In his memoir, Walton wrote about how he visited competitors during family vacations. In fact, he came up with the original idea for the Hypermart when visiting Carrefour on one of those trips.[129]

But as I tried to find a vehicle to talk about grocery, I kept coming back to Walmart. Nearly one of every three dollars that Americans spend at the grocery store goes through Walmart's registers.[130] "No other corporation in history has ever amassed this degree of control over the U.S. food system," one report concluded. "The closest comparison, the A&P grocery store, accounted for 16 percent of U.S. grocery sales at its peak in 1933" before triggering a reform movement to rein in its anti-competitive practices.[131] The more I tried to avoid the subject, the more it became clear that it would be impossible to talk about grocery without acknowledging the central role of Walmart.

In theory, shopping at a grocery store is capitalism at its finest. You have only so much space in your shopping cart, and each company is trying to earn a spot in that cart by constantly fine-tuning its products to find that right mix of price and quality.

But alas, true competition is largely a mirage. To start off, a grocery store is a privatized marketplace. A century ago, most Americans did their grocery shopping in public markets or bought food at individual stores (e.g., a bakery for bread or a butcher for meat). The notion of going to a private, for-profit space to buy all their groceries is largely a recent phenomenon, and that privatization fundamentally altered the retail incentive structure.[132] Unlike public markets, a grocery store is both a marketplace and a retailer in its own right. This shift, coupled with a consolidation of power in the space, unleashed a rampant game of legalized kickbacks and bribery centered on the grocery shelf.[133]

You can think of a grocery shelf as like a movie theater. There's a sweet spot right in the middle of a theater that most people consider to be the best spot to watch a movie. On the other hand, most people avoid the sides and front row. Shelving space in grocery stores functions the same way. Placement goes a long way in determining which product sells best.

Consequently, grocery stores can extort companies to sell access to their shelves and particularly the best spots. It's a classic example of pay to play. It becomes particularly problematic as the grocery chain gets bigger and bigger. Large grocery chains can sell access not just to an individual shelf but to a whole network of shelves. They use this leverage to extract concessions from suppliers, giving them both control over producers and a massive competitive advantage over their smaller rivals. A portion of the concessions can be passed on to consumers via discounts, leading to even greater market share, leading to even more concessions. As a result, the market power of grocery stores compounds as they grow.

In a fervor that's hard to imagine today, a backlash to this type of retail power swept America nearly a century ago, spurred in part by the market power of A&P. According to historian Bethany Moreton, state legislators introduced nearly a thousand bills between 1925 and 1937 grappling with this issue. Fifty of those bills were eventually enacted into law.[134] These laws echoed Justice Louis Brandeis's framework of attacking concentrated market power by attempting to preserve competition in retail. Many of them centered on giving producers a right to set a minimum or maximum price for wholesalers, which gave them bargaining leverage in their negotiations with retailers.

Congress strengthened these state efforts when it passed the Robinson-Patman Act of 1936. This federal legislation built on state actions by prohibiting certain price discrimination and other practices that favored preferred retailers. The goal of the law was to ensure that competition was based on price and service rather than bargaining strength, size, and raw financial muscle, which its authors understood would inevitably neuter competition. Accordingly, the law tried to prevent large retailers from using market power to coerce suppliers into preferential treatment.

For example, the law once prohibited suppliers from offering preferential terms such as promotional packaging or limiting access to scarce inventory to select retailers. As originally understood, the law required that special sizes offered to warehouse stores like Sam's Club or dollar stores like Dollar General would have to be offered to all retailers. Likewise, discounts for large orders would have to be extended to all retailers.[135]

But a law on the books is only as good as its enforcement. In 1977, around the time that the Bork anti-antitrust framework was taking hold, the US Department of Justice announced that it would effectively cease enforcement of the Robinson-Patman Act.[136] The law used to prohibit the sort of predatory pricing that Walmart engages in when it opens a new store or a new line of business to drive a competitor out of business.[137] That protection seems like a commonsense way to maintain competitive markets, but Robert Bork and his acolytes long opposed it. Partially because of their efforts, the Republican-appointed Supreme Court judges joined together to essentially neutralize this protection in a 1993 ruling.[138] One academic argued that the collapse of these types of competition guardrails played a major role in the death of downtowns of most American towns and cities.[139]

Walton built his retail empire just as these competition protections were neutered. Without stringent limits on its ability to exercise market power, Walmart and other dominant businesses engaged in exactly the sort of practices that lawmakers feared decades earlier. In fact, the company seemingly violated the Robinson-Patman Act and Arkansas state law with impunity.[140]

Because of its size and market share, Walmart can extract concessions in almost any dimension, which only further entrenches its dominance. These practices are so numerous that it's difficult to capture them all in a single list. Walmart contractually requires suppliers to offer it the lowest prices.[141] It adds on various charges called "warehousing allowance" and "margin audits" to its suppliers.[142]

Walmart even demanded the delivery of scarce inventory ahead of other retailers as shortages roiled the industry when COVID-19 started spreading in the United States. It also required suppliers to fulfill 98 percent of orders on time and in full or pay a 3 percent penalty. This command effectively forced suppliers to prioritize Walmart's order over everybody else's.[143] But because Walmart is the largest buyer for many suppliers, they were at the company's mercy.

One industry expert referred to these demands as examples of "mafioso capitalism": glorified shakedowns that companies engage in simply because they can. Collectively, these sorts of mandates create an abusive power dynamic that only compounds the company's market power, with the cost of the concessions passed on to the supplier's other clients.

It's an example of what is known as the waterbed effect. "If you push down on one side of a water bed, and the other side goes up, it doesn't necessarily mean that because there was rising on one side that there's more water in the bed. It's just shifting," Michael Needler, CEO of a regional grocery retailer, testified to Congress. "So if you have market power in a few that pushes the cost to the rest, it's zero-sum but makes an unfair advantage for the long run."[144]

The company is very cognizant of the power asymmetry between it and its suppliers. It requires that no more than 30 percent of their sales come from Walmart.[145] This rule may seem counterintuitive at first, but an industry expert told me that Walmart implemented it to manage its own supply chain risk. It knows that if suppliers cross that threshold, they are at risk of going out of business because Walmart is such an unprofitable and difficult client.

None of these strategies are entirely bad, but together they create an abusive power dynamic that only compounds itself. Although these sorts of tactics are nothing new, the company's unprecedented scale and power in the grocery industry give it a unique ability to shape the grocery marketplace that couldn't even have been imagined when the Robinson-Patman Act was enacted.

And with this power, the company shapes how we all eat. Decisions made in Bentonville ripple not only across America but globally. As one retail analyst commented, "Walmart lives in a world of supply and command."[146] Another critic noted that this power lets them shape what "goods the global economy produces, how they're made, and by whom."[147]

This command by America's largest retailer and grocer has altered America and the world in ways that are truly hard to grasp. First and foremost, the company has triggered a race to the bottom in every way imaginable. It practices what is known as Plus One policy, under which it demands that a supplier decrease the price or improve the quality of an item each year.[148] There is only so much a supplier can do to improve a can of green beans, so in practice the focus tends to be on finding new ways to lower the price.

Walmart does not need to tell the Berry Barons to shift their production offshore, nor does it need to demand that the Hog Barons or Dairy Barons stuff their animals into metal sheds. It does not have to. It tells its suppliers the price it wants and lets them figure out what corners to cut to get there. For example, in 2005 Walmart wanted its beef providers to fit four steaks into a package instead of three. In response, beef suppliers started to breed smaller cows that would yield smaller steaks to fit into the packages.[149]

This Plus One command goes a long way toward explaining why food and other goods are of such low quality these days—and why they are produced at such a high social and environmental cost. Stacy Mitchell echoed this sentiment back in 2011, calling the company out for greenwashing. Although the company makes pronouncements about greening its supply chain, it doesn't acknowledge the environmental toll caused by "the durability of products or the pace at which households burn through the stuff its stores sell."

As Mitchell put it, "Walmart has a powerful incentive to increase the scale of consumption. Sustainability will never be more than a modest sideshow to this larger endeavor."[150] Mitchell has since argued that the company mostly made these hollow pledges for show. Its game plan is to "announce an initiative that the media is sure to (mis)interpret as a game-changer and then quietly fail to deliver anything close to the promise."[151] Simply put, the company deflects, sets the terms of the conversation, and normalizes its behavior.

The Plus One edict has also intensified the offshoring of the American supply chain. "Twenty years ago, if you were a factory trying to sell a product to Walmart to put on their shelves, and you weren't making it in China, they pretty much didn't want to talk to you," Peter Goodman recently reported on the podcast *The Daily*. Neglecting to offshore was an "indication that you weren't producing at the lowest possible cost."[152] This command might explain why Walmart is the largest importer of goods from China.[153]

Sure, Walmart's Plus One command wrung efficiencies out of food supply chains, but eventually there is no fat left to cut. Workers tend to bear the brunt of this system through poverty-level wages and unsafe working conditions. It leads companies to engage in practices that would be considered illegal within US borders.[154] The Plus One directive is received by the Berry Barons, who pass the cost along to approved suppliers, which in turn pass the cost along to workers.

This race to the bottom has led to some truly horrific tragedies. In 2012, an apparel factory in Bangladesh that supplied Walmart caught fire. Two officials told the *New York Times* that, months earlier, Walmart officials had blocked an effort to improve electrical and fire safety at plants over cost concerns.[155] One hundred twelve workers died in the fire. The following year, a building housing an apparel factory that supplied Walmart collapsed, killing 1,134 workers.[156]

In response to these tragedies, a group of retailers, trade unions, and factory owners reached an agreement to improve conditions for workers in Bangladesh. It required independent inspections at the factories, legally binding safety commitments, and contributions for safety training and factory improvements. Many global retailers signed on, but Walmart refused to do so.[157]

Walmart's tremendous power allows the company to act as a gatekeeper for food not just on its own shelves but across the food system. It also locks in the dominant suppliers. "The slotting, the ad fees, the high-lows, the promotions, it really limits the ability for small startups to compete in almost every level, at any retailer," one food consultant told researchers. "The system is geared to support the big companies."[158]

The way Walmart exercises its market power makes it prohibitively expensive for smaller manufacturers to get products on supermarket shelves. That explains why the little guys often fail and why most new items in the grocery store are just a big brand's latest variation on one of its previous products, like yet another new Oreo flavor.

Even when you think you've found a new local food company, it may just be an illusion, like the one performed by the Coffee Barons with their multitude of local-seeming brands such as Stumptown and Intelligentsia. A recent article in *Grub Street* noted this rise of "small-washing"—the idea of marketing a product so that it feels local every-where.[159] Although shoppers like the idea of buying local, Walmart's scale makes it impracticable for the company to find an individual sup-plier for each store.

On a similar note, Walmart's unprecedented control over the supply chain has encouraged the near total takeover of our grocery shelves by unhealthy processed foods. Walmart's distribution centers are designed to handle processed foods instead of fresh ones because of their longer shelf lives. That may explain why obesity rates increase when Supercen-ters come to town.[160]

In many of the interviews I did for this book, I kept hearing about the "Walmart effect." The definition varied slightly from person to person. One person used the term to illustrate the death of local businesses after Walmart came to town. Others used it to talk about the degradation of product quality as Walmart squeezed suppliers. Another used it to describe the proliferation of low-wage, low-benefit jobs in the American economy.

Although the consequences differ in each of these examples, all used "Walmart effect" to comment on the power of one single family. And that power affects all of us more than we realize. One hidden effect of this power is the control that a single company has over the options available to all of us. Through its control over suppliers, Walmart makes product decisions that reverberate across the food supply chain. You may not shop at Walmart, but that doesn't mean that its decisions don't affect the options available on your grocery shelves.

Godzilla versus Mothra

"Walmart has not only survived 'Amazon-geddon,' it is firing on all cyl-inders," exclaimed the *Financial Times* in a recent article.[161] Amazon still dominates online purchases, but Walmart is catching up quickly.[162] In 2022, one-eighth of its sales came online, more than doubling the percentage from 2019.[163] Although the company reportedly loses money in e-commerce, CEO Doug McMillon views those losses as a short-term cost to maintain its dominance, similar to how it sold goods at a loss decades earlier to drive competitors out of business.[164]

Moreover, McMillon's thesis that online business would boost sales in the store seems to be paying off. As McMillon pivoted the company to his omnichannel strategy, the company discovered that a customer who shops only in-store spends an average of $1,400 per year with Walmart. On the other hand, a customer who shops both in-store and online spends about $2,500 per year.[165] It seems that the omnichannel approach creates more loyal shoppers.

So, just as with the company's pivot to Supercenters, Walmart dove into this new era headfirst. Copying the Amazon playbook, Walmart launched its own version of Prime called Walmart+. Grocery delivery options are a core component of a subscription in the program. For an additional fee, Walmart will even deliver your groceries right to your fridge in some areas.[166]

Meanwhile, the company spent billions on new warehouses and on increasing automation at existing ones.[167] In 2021, the company invested $7.2 billion in these systems.[168] Building on the idea that it is a distribution company at its core, Walmart is increasingly treating its Supercenters as distribution centers too. In 2022, the *Wall Street Journal* reported that the company was building automated fulfillment centers attached to existing stores.[169]

Automation is a central component of this strategy. According to the *Wall Street Journal*, "the backroom robots could help Walmart cut labor costs and fill orders faster and more accurately. It also could address another problem: unclogging aisles that these days can get crowded with clerks picking products for online orders." It's been reported that a store worker can collect 80 items per hour, whereas this robotic system is meant to handle 800 items per hour. The system can handle refrigerated and frozen foods, but fresh produce still needs to be collected by hand in the store.[170]

This omnichannel strategy proved to be perfectly timed when the COVID-19 pandemic hit. "Big-box retailers were among the early retail winners during the pandemic," the *Financial Times* stated in late 2020. "Big-box stores can partly attribute their success to their one-stop shopping advantage."[171] Another lasting effect of the pandemic was that it drove more shopping online. By late 2022, more than half of shoppers said they bought groceries online occasionally.[172]

The company's bet on the omnichannel strategy explains why the number of physical store locations hasn't changed much since 2018.[173] The era of the big-box expansion is over. Now the company is focused on growing orders that originate online and getting shoppers in the door of one of the thousands of stores that already exist.

Walmart has still been able to apply many of the lessons of the grocery space to its new online presence. Like shelf space, placement is everything in digital commerce. When you search for an item to buy on your phone or computer, Walmart could show you the bestseller, the best-reviewed option, the cheapest option, a local option, or a random option. Instead, it takes advantage of another revenue stream: digital slotting fees.

Like Amazon, Walmart now sells spots in your search query to suppliers. In a 2020 press release, the company announced that it was investing in an in-house advertising offering known as the Walmart Media Group, later renamed Walmart Connect.[174] The company plans to sell ad space in-store and online, with the aim of being a top ten ad company within only a few years.[175] To grow this line of business, it has acquired existing digital ad-tech firms.[176] The company appears to be on track to meet its lofty goals. Its global ad sales were up nearly 30 percent in 2022, generating $2.7 billion.[177]

But even with this focus on the omnichannel strategy, Walmart has continued to expand in several other directions. The company has even made moves into the actual production of food. In 2016, it announced its plans to open a milk-bottling plant in Indiana, said to be one of the largest in the industry.[178] The factory is located just a few hours' drive due east of the Dairy Barons' operation. Walmart also recently invested in a vertical farm company.[179]

But its biggest move has been into meat production, including a plan, announced in 2019, to develop an end-to-end supply chain for Angus beef.[180] Scott Neal, who at the time ran Walmart's meat business, told Bloomberg that "a retailer is judged in terms of how good they are at meat."[181] According to the publication, "the meat aisle has become a key element in Walmart's efforts to boost its grocery business."

Concerns over the increasing power of the Slaughter Barons and their ilk may have contributed to this push. "What drives a decision like that is if we start to see a consolidation in supply," Walmart US chief Greg Foran told analysts in 2019, according to CNN Business. As Foran put it, moving into the supply chain "gives us some leverage" when the company negotiates contracts with its suppliers.[182]

Yet the quest for dominance isn't limited to food. Since it's already bringing shoppers into the store with groceries, the company might as well also provide banking and health care—particularly targeting the millions of Americans without good-quality credit or health insurance. These moves bring a whole new meaning to the term "one-stop shop." "Foot traffic is the lifeblood of any brick-and-mortar retailer, and health services could give more shoppers a reason to visit stores in an era when shopping is increasingly done online," noted one Bloomberg reporter.[183]

Walmart is already one of the largest retail pharmacy players in America.[184] But the company doubled down on its health-care services when it opened its first Walmart Health center in 2019. These centers offer primary care services; lab tests, x-rays, and EKGs; dental, optical, and hearing services; counseling; nutrition and fitness advice; and health insurance education and enrollment.[185] Some of my sources have speculated that the company is aiming these centers at the millions of Americans who are uninsured or underinsured.

The company plans to install health centers in four thousand Supercenters by 2029.[186] The press release announcing the opening of the first center broadcast the company's intentions: "Our goal of becoming America's neighborhood health destination: introducing the Walmart Health center."[187] Walmart also recently purchased a telehealth provider, registered a health insurance company, and signed a ten-year partnership with UnitedHealth Group to deliver care to seniors enrolled in Medicare Advantage.[188] In September 2023, it even opened a pet services center that offers routine veterinary care and grooming services.[189]

The company has also gotten into banking, albeit through workarounds after facing significant political blowback in its attempt to get a bank license in 2007. At the front of most Supercenters, the company operates what it calls Walmart MoneyCenters, where shoppers can cash checks and pay bills. In 2013, it partnered with American Express to offer prepaid cards aimed at customers "unbanked, underbanked, or unhappily banked." They essentially operate as debit cards by allowing customers to set up direct deposit.[190] Then, in 2022, Walmart backed a financial service smartphone app that strives to be a "one-stop shop for a range of mobile-based financial services."[191]

But Walmart's move into banking hasn't been without problems. Regulators have dinged its MoneyCenters for poor oversight, and the Federal Trade Commission has accused the company of repeatedly failing to protect its customers from fraudsters.[192]

Nevertheless, when you serve as America's bank, health-care provider, retailer, grocer, and, increasingly, food producer, not to mention employer, you create a powerful force to be reckoned with. To the shock of many analysts who were giving Walmart little chance to compete with Amazon just a few years ago, the company somehow seems to have the upper hand in this clash of titans. In 2021, Walmart took in $459.51 billion in retail sales domestically, compared with $217.79 billion by Amazon.[193]

Meanwhile, Amazon's move into grocery has been largely a dud, perhaps because many shoppers perceive Whole Foods as too expensive. In response, Amazon launched its own branded grocery store called Amazon Fresh in 2020. Like Walmart, the company plans to use the stores as micro-fulfillment centers for orders.[194] But Amazon recently announced plans to put a pause on Amazon Fresh stores.[195] "If you would have asked me three years ago, where they would have been today in grocery, I would have expected a much bigger buildout, much more aggressive advancement," Matt Sargent, a consumer trends analyst, told Bloomberg in 2021.[196]

And even with its successes, Walmart has avoided the same level of antitrust scrutiny that Amazon has faced. In recent years, a bipartisan chorus has emerged calling on Congress to regulate Amazon's monopoly. Congress has held hearings, and several bills have been proposed that would reduce the company's market power.

Much of the justified criticism levied at Amazon could apply just as easily to Walmart. Yet unlike Amazon, Walmart has managed to avoid being drawn into these battles, though the company seems to understand that the issue could become a liability in the future. It recently created a new position for an antitrust attorney. The person that it ultimately hired as its chief antitrust counsel has served in an active leadership role in the Antitrust Law Section of the American Bar Association.[197]

But that hasn't stopped it from helping to stir the pot against its chief rival. In 2019, the *Wall Street Journal* reported that Walmart secretly funded a nonprofit called the Free and Fair Markets Initiative, which has criticized Amazon's practices, accusing it of stifling competition and mistreating its workers.[198] The former CEO of Walmart US even called for Congress to split up Amazon, arguing that "they're putting retailers out of business."[199]

I don't mean to imply by any means that Walmart is on the verge of sending Amazon to bankruptcy court. Amazon is still enormously profitable and is one of the five most valuable companies in the world. It has real advantages over Walmart, including in its lucrative cloud computing business, known as Amazon Web Services. Like Godzilla and Mothra, the two companies appear destined to be locked in a high-stakes struggle for the foreseeable future. It's far too early to predict which company will come out ahead.

But Walmart has won the first battle. So far, it has been far more successful in moving into online sales and distribution than Amazon has been in moving into grocery and physical store locations. Against all odds, it's accomplished this feat with the same vision, ingenuity, and organization that has defined the company ever since Sam Walton spotted an opportunity to move the five-and-dime concept to the edge of town back in 1962.

If anything, this clash of titans will just cement Walmart and Amazon as the only players in town, with each continuing to grow its share of the pie at the expense of everyone else. "What they do is conquest," Errol Schweizer, a grocery industry veteran, told me.

The most likely outcome is that this battle for supremacy will result in more consolidation and bankruptcies. It's not hard to imagine a wave of foreclosures and a surge of empty big-box stores sitting idle or underused in the middle of a massive parking lot, like the original Walmart location in Rogers or the Hypermart outside Dallas.

As with Godzilla and Mothra, it's fun to gawk at these two titans scratching and clawing in an all-out battle for supremacy. After all, it's rare to see corporations of this size and power stare each other down. But amid the spectacle, it's easy to overlook the destruction underneath.

Conclusion

I STARTED THE LONG PROCESS OF WRITING this book back in the spring of 2018. Over cheap beers in a dive bar in Des Moines, an Iowa political operative told me about a couple who had recently donated $300,000 to Kim Reynolds, the state's Republican governor, in support of her campaign for reelection in a hotly contested race. According to the operative, the donors were hog farmers who owned a private jet emblazoned with the phrase "When Pigs Fly."

I loved this detail, which I found to be juicy and, frankly, hilarious. Even beyond the tagline, the fact that hog farmers had the type of money to make six-figure political donations and buy a private jet ran directly counter to the image of independent family farmers that most people have in mind. The donors, of course, turned out to be Jeff and Deb Hansen.

The rumor led me down a rabbit hole on the Hansens and their hog empire. I ended up publishing a story in Vox with a friend, journalist Charlie Hope-D'Anieri, about how they built their business and the impact it was having on my home state. Unfortunately, despite my best efforts, including tracking the plane's movements and even hiring a local photographer to stake out the Des Moines airport, I was never able to confirm the rumor.

But as I wrote this article, it became clear to me that barons like the Hansens are the norm, not the exception. In fact, the American food supply chain—everything from seeds to baby formula—has fallen under the control of a narrow group of individuals, leaving family farmers and local businesses fighting an uphill battle just to stay in business.[1] Although economic concentration affects many industries, there are few areas where it is more prevalent, or where it more directly affects people, than the food system.

I realized that the Hog Barons were just a small piece of a much bigger story about the corruption of America's food industry. I ultimately decided to profile seven robber barons, with the goal of using each one as a window into how power has consolidated and our food system has been fundamentally transformed.

One point that became clear as I wrote this book is how recently this transformation occurred. Each of the barons portrayed in these pages experienced a dramatic breakthrough during the past forty years. The Slaughter Barons, for example, were a regional footnote at the turn of the twenty-first century, and the Coffee Barons didn't even enter the market until 2012. Even the Grain Barons, the longest-tenured barons portrayed in this group, saw their revenues nearly quadruple in the past two decades.[2]

This situation has been possible only because of a laissez-faire framework that has taken hold in American politics. Rather than working to limit concentrated power, politicians in both parties have either helped entrench powerful interests or attempted to conduct policy in a manner that is agnostic to power. For example, rather than acting to limit the market power of the Slaughter Barons, the US Department of Agriculture tried to address the problem by throwing money at a new entrant in the hope that doing so would somehow alter the underlying competitive dynamics of the industry. The inability to challenge power has meant that even the most well-intentioned policies have done nothing to prevent these markets from becoming increasingly broken and concentrated.

As this new framework took hold, competition laws and other rules that limit the power of large corporations were rolled back or eliminated. Previously, antitrust and competition policy was characterized by Louis Brandeis's emphasis on structural rules that directly attack the power of the largest corporations. These sorts of barriers might have prevented the Slaughter Barons and the Coffee Barons from going on spending sprees to acquire so much control over their industries. Laws like the Robinson-Patman Act limited the ability of the Grocery Barons to use their market share as a means of exerting power over suppliers and entrenching their dominance over competitors.

But because of the influence of a controversial academic named Robert Bork, the US Supreme Court adopted a radical new approach that dramatically restricted the government's ability to prevent the biggest companies from accumulating power. Meanwhile, rules that supported balance in our food system and that gave a leg up to family farmers slowly eroded, culminating in the adoption of a Farm Bill built for Wall Street.

Today, American food policy functions to subsidize a handful of commodity crops, which are often processed and transported by the Grain Barons. Diversified family farms raising a variety of crops and livestock have been replaced by large-scale industrial operations exclusively growing corn and soy, which provide the cheap feed necessary for the inhumane confinements operated by the Hog Barons and the Dairy Barons to be economically viable.

The impact on the food we eat and on the communities we live in has been profound. The relative cost of fresh fruits and vegetables has spiked by 40 percent since the 1980s, while the price of processed foods has decreased by a similar amount.[3] It's no wonder that the country has experienced an explosion in obesity over the same period, particularly among Americans with lower incomes.[4] Although wealthier folks can afford to opt out of this system, most Americans' choices are shaped by these incentives, as well as by the purchasing power of the Grocery Barons.

As American production has shifted almost entirely to corn and soy, other crops are increasingly imported to replace what is no longer grown locally on family farms. Robust regional food supply chains have been destroyed and replaced with national and international ones. The Berry Barons have taken advantage of this offshoring of production, as well as a business model that removes them from the actual farming of the crops they sell, to initiate a race to the bottom while absolving themselves from the harm that they cause.

These changes in the way we grow and transport food have inflicted serious damage on the environment. The increasing distance that agricultural products travel means that the industry uses more fossil fuels and produces more carbon emissions than ever before. Likewise, industrial facilities like the ones operated by the Dairy Barons process manure in ways that are much worse for climate change than traditional methods of raising cows who get to roam on pasture.

On a more local level, the manure produced by confinements operated by the Hog Barons is polluting the water in my home state of Iowa, making it a hazard even to go swimming in many lakes and rivers across the state. Meanwhile, producers growing crops for the Berry Barons are using too much water in areas such as Baja California, where the supply is shrinking.

If the environment is a casualty of the barons' rise, so too are family farms and local businesses. National chain restaurants and big-box stores like the ones operated by the Coffee Barons and the Grocery Barons have proliferated, and the local ones that remain face an uphill battle to survive. As local operations fade away, a sense of a distinct regional and local identity disappears with them. Unlike the barons, the owners of local businesses live in the communities they serve and are stakeholders in their success. Losing them means losing the glue that binds communities together.

The titans that remain are notorious for squeezing their workers. Company towns have reemerged in rural America, and workers throughout the country have seen their wages stagnate. Many workers increasingly feel that they are not respected or valued by their employer, which is likely headquartered across the country or even the world. Because of the sheer number of people employed in the food system, and because these jobs have traditionally played a critical role in driving upward mobility, this trend has contributed to the explosion of inequality in our country.

This inequality is not just a problem on an individual level; there is a strong regional component as well. The loss of family farms and local businesses means that the wealth produced in a community often no longer stays there. A handful of superstar metropolitan cities have experienced incredible growth, but rural areas and many other cities are being left behind. The Grocery Barons' hometown of Bentonville is booming, at least for those at the top of the economic ladder, but it is doing so at the expense of the many communities that the company operates in.

Entrenched interests have been able to convert their economic power into political power, which they have used to further stack the deck in their favor. The Dairy Barons have benefited greatly from the explosion of organizations called checkoffs, which are funded by a tax on all farmers growing a certain crop. Checkoffs are supposed to broadly benefit the entire industry, but they have been subject to little oversight and have tended to support the largest producers. Meanwhile, despite repeatedly engaging in potentially illegal conduct, the Slaughter Barons have escaped severe consequences and have even continued to benefit from federal largesse.

All of these factors have combined to produce a profound sense of dissatisfaction with our political system. There are a number of reasons for the increasing polarization and radicalization that have come to define our politics, including a media environment that has seen local papers built on trust put out of business by social media behemoths that push divisive, and often inaccurate, information. But a lack of economic balance has certainly been a contributing factor.

A culture of family farms and local businesses brings both economic and political balance. Local business owners live alongside their customers and employees and have a stake in the places they serve. Independence also gives people more control over their lives and the economic security to contribute to their community. Family farms and local businesses cultivate a healthy society in a way that outside investors and multinational conglomerates cannot.

That's why concentration of economic power has long been closely associated with a rise in extremist politics. Authoritarians prey on people who see their communities crumbling and feel that they are losing power over their lives and their financial future. But one of the great paradoxes of authoritarians is that they often are closely aligned with the same powerful interests that are causing this state of affairs, as the history of the Coffee Barons shows. It's not a coincidence that as economic balance is disappearing, political balance is fading with it.

It might be easy to read this book and conclude that the American food system is broken. But a friend and mentor once admonished me for calling the food system broken because, as he put it, "broken implies it once worked." Thomas Jefferson's "yeoman farmer" built his independence on the backs of enslaved men and women. The idyllic midwestern family farm was possible only because the Homestead Act parceled out land stolen from American Indians in the midst of a genocidal frenzy.

Even the New Deal Farm Bill, for all that it did to support economic and ecological balance, operated to benefit White farmers, who pocketed the New Deal farm supports and used them to push Black farmers off their land. White landowners got wealthier, and Black people got displaced. The consolidation of power in the American food system is tragic, and the current situation may feel hopeless, but the solution is not to return to some mythic past that never existed.

Yet the history of the American food system does reveal that it has always been shaped by societal decisions about who benefits from it and who does not. Nothing illustrates this point better than the trajectory of slaughterhouse workers during the past century. When Upton Sinclair wrote *The Jungle*, slaughterhouses employed some of the most exploited and poorly paid workers in the American economy. Working in the slaughterhouse became a pathway to the middle class only because the federal government challenged the power of the Beef Trust and put rules in place to ensure that workers were fairly compensated and protected in the workplace. A robust middle class has always been the product of conscious political decisions.

We previously made a choice that slaughterhouse workers deserve to be part of the middle class, and it's within our power to make this choice again for workers throughout the food system. As depressing as it is to acknowledge that we've chosen to build a food system dominated by a handful of barons, it's also freeing because it means that it's within our power to build it differently.

If there's anything to take away from this book, it's that the idea of a free market, unshaped by politics, our institutions, and other societal forces, is a myth. After all, the overproduction of corn and soy did not arise naturally. It's the result of the massive government subsidies that underpin the American agricultural economy. And it's not just the government that shapes markets. Market power compounds itself, making competition as much about size, power, and access to capital as it is about offering a better product at a lower price. The Grocery Barons, for instance, are able to use their size to coerce their suppliers and gain a competitive advantage over their smaller rivals.

Healthy markets are not a natural phenomenon. As a society, we make decisions about how markets are structured, about the rules that govern them and what constitutes fair play, about who holds power and who does not. Once we acknowledge how these decisions have shaped the food system we have now, we can opt to create a different system that better reflects our values.

Here are a few ideas about how to start.

First and foremost, we need to reorient our policies away from the broken laissez-faire approach that has reigned for the past forty years. That includes implementing pro-competition measures that limit giant corporations' ability to leverage their market power to exploit workers, farmers, and local businesses. Reinvigorating the Robinson-Patman Act would be a great start, and banning anti-competitive practices such as slotting fees—the amounts that large retailers like the Grocery Barons charge suppliers for a position on their shelves—is a no-brainer.

We also need to do a better job of stopping barons from rising to power in the first place. That means ending the consumer welfare standard, a failed approach that is inconsistent with the purpose of antitrust laws and that makes it nearly impossible to halt a large company's accumulation of power.

Rather than relying on esoteric mathematical formulas to determine when a company's market share is too big, we need to enact bright-line rules that prevent barons from using their dominance to establish control of one sector or to expand into others. One example of such a rule is a ban against meatpackers raising the animals they slaughter. We should also prohibit meatpackers from competing in more than one line of protein. These sorts of restrictions would disperse the power of the Slaughter Barons and protect employees in the sector as well as the ranchers and farmers who sell to the meatpackers.

We should also make it more difficult for large firms to engage in mergers and acquisitions. No company buys another company in order to increase competition. Once a company reaches a certain threshold, it should be incumbent on it to prove the necessity of the deal, rather than on the government to prove that it is problematic. Given the consolidation that has taken place over the past forty years, it's also clear that some trust-busting is necessary to restore competition and provide some oxygen in these calcified spaces.

Moving beyond antitrust and competition policy, it's time to sunset the Farm Bill as we know it. Congress should, of course, carve out and fully fund food assistance programs, but it's time to retire the Farm Bill's massive subsidies for a handful of commodity crops. Rather than paying farmers to grow corn and soy, we should use those funds to reward farmers for conservation and other sustainable practices.

Speaking of programs that have run their course, we need to retire the checkoffs. Although the original purpose of these programs was admirable, the history of checkoffs illustrates the limits of an approach that is not cognizant of power dynamics. The checkoffs have become a tool that protects the interests of the largest and most powerful actors in the industry. Short of eliminating them entirely, we should at least significantly increase oversight of these entities to ensure that their money is spent fairly and appropriately.

It's also time to put animals back on the land and aggressively phase out industrial animal operations like the ones operated by the Hog Barons and the Dairy Barons. Much attention has been paid to the abhorrent treatment of animals, especially hogs, in these facilities, but these metal sheds have also polluted the water and air of their surroundings, undermined family farmers, and destroyed the communities they operate in. It's time for them to go.

Beyond these sorts of restrictions, we should use the power of institutional buyers to drive the development of the sort of food system we want to see. Schools in particular spend a lot of money on food, much of which goes toward unhealthy options purchased from huge corporations. The substantial dollars and reliable contracts that schools and other institutions provide would be a game changer for many local and sustainable producers who are struggling to compete with the big boys.

And though the federal government can play a role in making the economics more favorable, the great thing about this approach is that state and local governments can pursue it on their own. If you're looking for a way to make a difference personally, pushing your local school or another institution to buy locally is a great way to do that.

By the same token, we should ensure that government money does not go toward bad actors or serial lawbreakers in the industry like the Slaughter Barons. Likewise, we should require that any recipient of government aid for agriculture be the person actually working the land, not some absentee owner. The best definition of a family farm I've seen comes from the Wisconsin Farmers Union's policy platform: "those farm economic units in which the family provides the significant majority of labor and management for the enterprise and receives a significant amount of its gross income."[5] Limiting government aid using this simple definition would exclude all of the barons in this book. Exploitive farming arrangements like the Southern Model should be banned too. Farmers are nothing more than low-wage workers under those power dynamics.

Speaking of which, we need to have a conversation about the US Department of Agriculture. Laws and policies are only as good as the enforcers. Through administrations of both parties, the USDA increasingly seems to serve the interest of the barons and Wall Street. We need to push for a reform-minded secretary of agriculture who is deeply committed to addressing these issues and who would breathe new life into the agency. Congress should also consider transferring some of the USDA's responsibilities to other government agencies, such as having the US Department of Health and Human Services oversee the nutritional assistance programs or giving the USDA's antitrust authority to the US Department of Justice.

Finally, we need to ensure that workers are fairly paid and are shielded from unsafe or exploitive working conditions. On a basic level, we should not be subsidizing behemoths like the Grocery Barons for failing to pay their employees a fair wage. Instead of shifting this cost onto the taxpayer, we should require these companies to pay a living wage.

It's also important to enact rules to protect the safety of workers, such as restoring limits on the speed of kill lines. The emphasis should be on the well-being of the people who feed the nation, not on what's best for the corporate bottom line. This type of repositioning is key for building a long-term political coalition for all of the reforms described here.

But these are just examples of a broader approach to fixing our food system. I'm certainly not the first person to point out many of the problems outlined in this book. Folks have been ringing the alarm about our food system for a while now. But the solutions to these problems always seem to focus on the choices of the consumer: opt out of the system, shop at a co-op, buy organic.

Here's the thing: the multinational corporations co-opted the alternative system. Stonyfield Farm and Siggi's Dairy are now owned by Lactalis, a French yogurt giant with annual revenues in the tens of billions.[6] Annie's Homegrown was acquired by General Mills.[7] The theory of alternative consumption ultimately just created a bifurcated system, with healthy options at a higher price point for a few and the same unhealthy processed foods for everyone else.[8] It didn't do anything for workers or local businesses or family farms.

The reality is that any solution to these problems that does not directly challenge power is doomed to failure. This isn't a utopian vision, nor does it require radical change. In fact, our current system—where one company controls more than one-third of the grocery market, where school districts in rural Iowa surrounded by some of the world's best farmland have sky-high rates of free or reduced-price lunch, and where workers considered "essential" don't even earn a living wage—is what's truly radical.[9]

We have an opportunity to turn the corner and build a better food system. But we cannot bring about this change without restructuring who has power. Only by challenging power can we restore balance in our food system and in our broader economy.

That's why we need to elect politicians willing to directly address concentrated power. As I've engaged in this work, I've been surprised how much this sentiment is shared across the political spectrum. Americans of all political stripes increasingly agree that big corporations have too much power over their families, communities, and government.[10] That may be why an article of mine published in the *American Conservative*, of all places, arguing for many of the ideas contained in this book resonated so much with that publication's audience. Although our political system may feel stuck in the mud, fighting for a more locally oriented food system might be an off-ramp that can appeal to folks on both sides of the aisle.

The consequences of continuing down our current path are increasingly clear. More and more power will flow into the hands of fewer and fewer of these barons. The family farms that have survived will continue to disappear, replaced by empires built by the likes of the Hog Barons and the Dairy Barons, who are raising animals that never see a blade of grass.

More of our produce will be offshored to developing countries that are willing to look the other way on labor and environmental exploitation. The offshore produce picked by middle schoolers will look appealing in American grocery stores, but long gone will be the taste, nutrition, and decency.

As local businesses are replaced by cookie-cutter stores owned by multinational corporations based in tax havens, cities and towns across the country will continue to rust away. The people living in them will work for lower wages in grimmer conditions that increasingly resemble those in *The Jungle*. Shrinking paychecks will mean that more Americans will rely on food made in the Grain Barons' factories instead of fields. One's income will increasingly be reflected in one's waistline. Another marker of haves and have-nots.

And my home state will continue down its current spiral. Iowa's water will grow more and more toxic, matched only by the state's political climate. The balanced economy that once defined it will be replaced with one that resembles an extraction colony. The countryside of my youth that was filled with family farms and apple orchards and old barns and fields dotted with cows and hogs will continue to fade away until it's only a distant memory.

But it doesn't have to be this way. My vision for the American food system is simple. It's one in which any American can sit down in a locally owned restaurant or go to a neighborhood grocery store and buy affordable, local food that was grown, picked, processed, transported, cooked, and served by folks earning a fair wage.

I hope you will join me in trying to build that system.

Acknowledgments

Like a good winter stew, this book was made by pulling together a lot of different ingredients and letting them simmer. I've relied on the advice of many people, from the academics and experts who graciously took my calls and answered my questions to the farmers who let me visit their farms. All of these conversations and the feedback people offered shaped the words of this book.

I want to give special thanks to the team at Island Press, including my editor, Emily Turner; my fact-checker, Leslie Nemo; my copy editor, Pat Harris; and my research assistants, Kody Craddick and David Townley. Thank you as well to reporter Clint Rainey for his research assistance in the dairy chapter. I want to thank all my friends and family for reviewing drafts of this book, especially Charlie Hope-D'Anieri, whose feedback helped me understand the importance of good storycraft. I also want to thank the Economic Security Project and Fiona Scott Morton for their support.

I am forever grateful to Grinnell College, where many of the ideas expressed in this book germinated. I really started getting interested in the food system when I wrote my senior thesis on slaughterhouse towns in Iowa, advised by Timothy Werner and the late Jean Ketter, and I haven't looked back since.

I also want to thank the organizations that let me present versions of this book to them, including the Illinois Farmers Union, the Iowa Farmers Union, the Kansas Farmers Union, Marbleseed, the University of Wisconsin–Madison, the Yale School of the Environment, and Yale Law School. I want to give special thanks to the Wisconsin Farmers Union for giving me the opportunity to serve as its first writer in residence. I cherished my time in Chippewa Falls and am continuously inspired by the work the organization does.

I am forever grateful for all the sacrifices and unconditional love my parents, Scott and Katherine, have shown me over the years. My mom fostered my love of reading by taking me to the library on a near-daily basis every summer and buying me a few treats anytime the book fair came to my school. One of the unexpected joys of adulthood has been appreciating the sacrifices my parents made for me and my siblings, as well as their cultivation of our passions. Thank you, Mom and Dad. I also want to thank my grandparents Geraldine and Ronald Frerick, who instilled in me a love for agriculture during all those weekends helping out on their plot. Without my family, this book would not exist.

And finally, I want to thank my husband, Daniel Honberg. His fingerprints are all over this text, but just as important, his support enabled me to write this book. I appreciate all the listening he did these past few years as I rambled on about some new tidbit I discovered while researching these barons. Without him, this book would not have been possible. As I told him in my wedding vows, he is the best thing that has ever happened to me.

Notes

Foreword

1. Adam Smith, *The Wealth of Nations*, ed. Charles J. Bullock (1776; repr., New York: Cosimo Classics, 2007), 447, Google Play Books.
2. Smith, *Wealth of Nations*, 358.
3. Smith, *Wealth of Nations*, 220.
4. Smith, *Wealth of Nations*, 220.
5. Smith, *Wealth of Nations*, 466.
6. Thomas Jefferson, letter to Alexander Donald, February 7, 1788, Volume 4, Article 7, Document 12 in *The Founders' Constitution*, ed. Philip B. Kurland and Ralph Lerner (Web Edition, University of Chicago Press and Liberty Fund), http://press-pubs.uchicago.edu/founders/documents/a7s12.html.
7. James Madison, letter to Thomas Jefferson, October 17, 1788, *Founders Online*, National Archives, https://founders.archives.gov/documents/Jefferson/01-14-02-0018.
8. Henry Demarest Lloyd, *Wealth against Commonwealth* (New York: Harper & Brothers, 1894), 297.
9. Lloyd, *Wealth against Commonwealth*, 298.

Introduction

1. Kathleen Kassel, "Agriculture and Its Related Industries Provide 10.5 Percent of U.S. Employment," US Department of Agriculture, Economic Research Service, last updated January 6, 2023, https://www.ers.usda.gov/data-products/chart-gallery/gallery/chart-detail/?chartId=58282.
2. Kathryn Schulz, "Eat Your Words: Anthony Bourdain on Being Wrong," Slate, May 31, 2010, https://slate.com/news-and-politics/2010/06/eat-your-words-anthony-bourdain-on-being-wrong.html.

Chapter 1: The Hog Barons

1. Charles D. Ikenberry, "Water Quality Improvement Plan for Upper Pine Lake, Hardin

County, Iowa," Iowa Department of Natural Resources, Watershed Improvement Section, 2014, https://www.epa.gov/sites/default/files/2015-03/documents/ia-upper-pine-lake -tmdl.pdf.

2. Scott E. Rupp, "Death Rates Rise, Environmental Challenges Grow at Large US Pig Farms," MultiBriefs: Exclusive, October 12, 2018, https://exclusive.multibriefs.com /content/death-rates-rise-environmental-challenges-grow-at-large-us-pig-farms/waste -management-environmental.

3. Kim Norvell, "Iowa Farm Forced to Euthanize Pigs Was 'Infiltrated' by Animal Activists," *Des Moines Register*, May 21, 2020, https://www.desmoinesregister.com/story/news /2020/05/20/iowa-farm-forced-euthanize-pigs-infiltrated-animal-activists/5232631002/.

4. Donnelle Eller, "Iowa Could Support 45,700 Livestock Confinements, but Should It?," *Des Moines Register*, March 12, 2018, https://www.desmoinesregister.com/story/money /agriculture/2018/03/08/iowa-can-support-47-500-cafos-but-should/371440002/.

5. Stephen Braun, "Iowa Turns Pigs into a Political Football," *Los Angeles Times*, February 2, 1996, https://www.latimes.com/archives/la-xpm-1996-02-02-mn-31555-story.html; Staci Hupp, "Study Says Hog Lots Hurt Value of Property," *Des Moines Register*, August 28, 2003; Duke Health, "N.C. Residents Living Near Large Hog Farms Have Elevated Disease, Death Risks," Duke Health News & Media, September 18, 2018, https://corporate .dukehealth.org/news/nc-residents-living-near-large-hog-farms-have-elevated-disease -death-risks.

6. Iowa Pork Producers Association, "2020 Iowa Pork Industry Facts," accessed December 16, 2022, https://www.iowapork.org/newsroom/facts-about-iowa-pork-production; M. Shahbandeh, Statista, "Top 10 U.S. States by Inventory of Hogs and Pigs as of March 2022 (in 1,000s)," May 18, 2022, https://www.statista.com/statistics/194371/top-10-us -states-by-number-of-hogs-and-pigs/.

7. US Department of Agriculture, National Agricultural Statistics Service, "Table 17. Milk Cow Herd Size by Inventory and Sales: 2017," 2017 Census of Agriculture—United States Data, https://www.nass.usda.gov/Publications/AgCensus/2017/Full_Report/Volume_1, _Chapter_1_US/st99_1_0017_0019.pdf; US Department of Agriculture, National Agricultural Statistics Service, "Table 31. Hogs and Pigs—Inventory: 1992 and 1987," 1992 Census of Agriculture—State Data, https://agcensus.library.cornell.edu/wp-content /uploads/1992-Virginia-CHAPTER_1_State_Data-1569-Table-31.pdf.

8. Chris Jones, "Iowa's Real Population," University of Iowa, IIHR—Hydroscience & Engineering, March 14, 2019, https://web.archive.org/web/20210801145507/https://www .iihr.uiowa.edu/cjones/iowas-real-population/?doing_wp_cron=1617366873.7112309932 708740234375.

9. "Residents Awarded $33 Million from Hog Producer," Associated Press, October 9, 2002.

10. Jones, "Iowa's Real Population."

11. Jared Strong, "Two-Thirds of State Beaches Had Swim Advisories This Year, Group Says," *Iowa Capital Dispatch*, September 29, 2022, https://iowacapitaldispatch.com/2022/09/29 /two-thirds-of-state-beaches-had-swim-advisories-this-year-group-says/; Tom Cullen and Karina Guerrero, "Rising Livestock Numbers Feed Nitrate Load," *Storm Lake (IA) Times*, March 25, 2021, https://www.stormlake.com/articles/rising-livestock-numbers-feed-nitrate -load/.

12. Edward Walsh, "Corporate Pork Worries Iowa Family Farmers," *Washington Post*, October 19, 1994.

13. Charlie Mitchell and Austin Frerick, "The Hog Barons," Vox and Food & Environment

Reporting Network, April 19, 2021, https://www.vox.com/the-highlight/22344953/iowa -select-jeff-hansen-pork-farming.

14. Mitchell and Frerick, "Hog Barons"; Kyle Bagenstose, Sky Chadde, and Rachel Axon, "COVID-19 Deaths Go Uninvestigated as OSHA Takes a Hands-Off Approach to Meat-packing Plants," *USA Today*, January 11, 2021, https://www.usatoday.com/in-depth/news /2021/01/11/covid-19-deaths-not-investigated-osha-meatpacking-plants/6537524002/; Leah Douglas, "Mapping Covid-19 Outbreaks in the Food System," Food & Environment Reporting Network, April 22, 2020, https://thefern.org/2020/04/mapping-covid-19-in -meat-and-food-processing-plants/.

15. Betsy Freese, "Pork Powerhouses 2020: Backing Up," *Successful Farming*, October 7, 2020, https://www.agriculture.com/livestock/pork-powerhouses/pork-powerhouses-2020 -backing-up.

16. Mitchell and Frerick, "Hog Barons."

17. Dale Miller, "2013 Master of the Pork Industry Jeff Hansen," *National Hog Farmer*, May 14, 2013, https://www.nationalhogfarmer.com/pork-market-news/2013-master-of-the -pork-industry-jeff-hansen.

18. Miller, "Jeff Hansen."

19. Christopher Leonard, *The Meat Racket: The Secret Takeover of America's Food Business* (New York: Simon & Schuster, 2014).

20. Michael D. Thompson, "This Little Piggy Went to Market: The Commercialization of Hog Production in Eastern North Carolina from William Shay to Wendell Murphy," *Agricultural History* 74, no. 2 (Spring 2000): 569–84, https://doi.org/10.1215/00021482 -74.2.569.

21. David Barboza, "America's Cheese State Fights to Stay That Way; Wisconsin Struggles to Keep Pace with West," *New York Times*, June 28, 2001, https://nyti.ms/3EiUpP2.

22. US Department of Agriculture, National Agricultural Statistics Service, "Table 20. Hogs and Pigs—Sales: 2017 and 2012," 2017 Census of Agriculture—United States Data, https://www.nass.usda.gov/Publications/AgCensus/2017/Full_Report/Volume_1,_Chap ter_1_US/st99_1_0020_0023.pdf.

23. Scott Kilman, "Iowans Can Handle Pig Smells, but This Is Something Else—Giant Hog 'Factories' Strain Inherent Neighborliness of a Rural Community," *Wall Street Journal*, May 4, 1995.

24. Donnelle Eller, "Nearly 60 Percent of Iowa Farmland Owners Don't Farm; One-Third Have No Ag Experience," *Des Moines Register*, June 28, 2018, https://www.desmoines register.com/story/money/agriculture/2018/06/28/iowa-state-isu-farmland-farm-facts -ownership-tenure-survey-owners-debt-land-rent-family-income/742159002/; Jean C. Prior, "Des Moines Lobe," University of Iowa, Iowa Geological Survey, June 19, 2017, https://web.archive.org/web/20170702151013/https://www.iihr.uiowa.edu/igs/des-moines -lobe/.

25. Glen W. Almond, "How Much Water Do Pigs Need?," *Proceedings of the North Carolina Healthy Hogs Seminar*, accessed December 17, 2022, https://web.archive.org/web/20211 216023311/https://projects.ncsu.edu/project/swine_extension/healthyhogs/book1995 /almond.htm.

26. Miller, "Jeff Hansen."

27. Mitchell and Frerick, "Hog Barons."

28. "The Nation's Largest Hog Owners," Associated Press, April 20, 1997.

29. Jerry Perkins, "Pork Producer List Has Smithfield No. 1," *Des Moines Register*, October 17, 1999; Jerry Perkins, "Hog Giant Seeks Debt Revision," *Des Moines Register*, June 8, 2000.

30. Freese, "Pork Powerhouses 2020."

31. Kevin Baskins, "Power Loss Leads to Hog Kill," *Globe Gazette* (Mason City, IA), March 13, 1997; Matt Johnson, "Factory Farming Model Incorporates Abuses, So We Need to Adopt Something Radically New," *Des Moines Register*, March 1, 2021, https://www.des moinesregister.com/story/opinion/columnists/iowa-view/2021/03/01/iowa-agriculture -systemic-animal-abuse-new-approach-iowa-select-farms/4454798001/.

32. Braun, "Iowa Turns Pigs into a Political Football"; Thomas O'Donnell, "Living with Big Pork," *Des Moines Register*, August 23, 1998; Kathy Dobie, "One Woman Takes a Brave Stand against Factory Farming," *O, The Oprah Magazine*, November 2011, https://www .oprah.com/world/health-risks-that-large-factory-farming-leaves-behind/all.

33. Julia Kravchenko et al., "Mortality and Health Outcomes in North Carolina Communities Located in Close Proximity to Hog Concentrated Animal Feeding Operations," *North Carolina Medical Journal* 79, no. 5 (September–October 2018): 278–88, https://doi.org /10.18043/ncm.79.5.278.

34. Rekha Basu, "More Protections for Polluters," *Des Moines Register*, May 18, 2003; Carrie Hribar, "Understanding Concentrated Animal Feeding Operations and Their Impact on Communities," National Association of Local Boards of Health, 2010, https://www.cdc .gov/nceh/ehs/docs/understanding_cafos_nalboh.pdf.

35. Kaye H. Kilburn, "Human Impairment from Living near Confined Animal (Hog) Feeding Operations," *Incorporating Environmental Health in Clinical Medicine* (2012), article 565690, https://doi.org/10.1155/2012/565690.

36. Richard Jones et al., "Eleven Years after Agreement, EPA Has Not Developed Reliable Emission Estimation Methods to Determine Whether Animal Feeding Operations Comply with Clean Air Act and Other Statutes," US Environmental Protection Agency, Office of Inspector General, Report No. 17-P-0396, September 19, 2017, https://www.epa.gov /sites/production/files/2017-09/documents/_epaoig_20170919-17-p-0396.pdf; Grant Rodgers and Donnelle Eller, "Iowa Father, Son Die from Manure Pit Fumes," *Des Moines Register*, July 30, 2015, https://www.desmoinesregister.com/story/money/agriculture/2015 /07/28/iowa-father-son-die-manure-pit-fumes/30809037/.

37. Darcy Dougherty-Maulsby, "Dust Busters: Trees, Technology Help Iowa Select Farms Control Odors," *Fort Dodge (IA) Messenger*, June 3, 2018, https://www.messengernews .net/news/local-business/2018/06/dust-busters-trees-technology-help-iowa-select-farms -control-odors/.

38. Brian Thiede et al., "6 Charts That Illustrate the Divide between Rural and Urban America," *PBS NewsHour*, March 17, 2017, https://www.pbs.org/newshour/nation/six-charts -illustrate-divide-rural-urban-america.

39. Eller, "Iowa Could Support 45,700 Livestock Confinements"; Iowa Select Farms, "Pork Production Growth Boosts Rural Iowa Economy," *Homegrown Iowa*, no. 4 (February 2017), https://www.iowaselect.com/webres/File/Homegrown Iowa/Iowa's Hometown Hero--How Pork Production Boosts Our Rural Economy.pdf; Iowa Select Farms, "Growing Rural Communities, Growing Iowa," accessed December 17, 2022, https://www .iowaselect.com/webres/File/Homegrown%20Iowa/Dermot%20Hayes%20ISU%20Eco nomic%20Impact%20Report_Iowa%20Select%20Farms%202019.pdf; Supreme Court of Iowa, *Jerry Dovico, et al., v. Valley View Swine, LLC, et al.* (Wapello County Case No. LALA105144—Division A), June 8, 2016, https://www.iowacourts.gov/courtcases/408 /briefs/649/embedBrief; Summit Agricultural Group, "Our Team," accessed December 17, 2022, https://www.summitag.com/our-team.

40. Kate M. Conlow, "Digging In: Ethics, Disclosure, and Conflicts of Interest in Academic Agricultural Economic Publishing," in *Reforming America's Food Retail Markets*, Yale University conference compendium edited by Austin Frerick, 126–32, June 2022, https://law

.yale.edu/sites/default/files/area/center/isp/documents/grocery-compendium_may2023
.pdf.

41. Mitchell and Frerick, "Hog Barons."

42. Chris McGreal, "How America's Food Giants Swallowed the Family Farms," *Guardian*, March 9, 2019, https://www.theguardian.com/environment/2019/mar/09/american-food -giants-swallow-the-family-farms-iowa.

43. "Immigration Agents Arrest 7 Alleged Fugitives near Hampton," Associated Press, July 22, 2009.

44. David Wallinga, "Better Bacon: Why It's High Time the U.S. Pork Industry Stopped Pigging Out on Antibiotics," Natural Resources Defense Council, May 2018, https:// www.nrdc.org/sites/default/files/better-bacon-pork-industry-antibiotics-ib.pdf.

45. Danny Hakim and Matt Richtel, "Warning of 'Pig Zero': One Drugmaker's Push to Sell More Antibiotics," *New York Times*, June 7, 2019, https://www.nytimes.com/2019/06/07 /health/drug-companies-antibiotics-resistance.html.

46. Centers for Disease Control and Prevention, "More People in the United States Dying from Antibiotic-Resistant Infections than Previously Estimated," press release, November 13, 2019, https://www.cdc.gov/media/releases/2019/p1113-antibiotic-resistant.html.

47. Anna Jones, "'What They Put on the Fields Contaminates Our Water': Iowa's Pollution Problem," *Guardian*, September 26, 2019, https://www.theguardian.com/environment /2019/sep/26/nitrate-problem-iowa-dont-use-the-tap-water-for-babies.

48. Mitchell and Frerick, "Hog Barons."

49. Erin Jordan, "Overflowing Manure Tanks Reported in Western Iowa, Eastern Iowa on Alert," *Cedar Rapids (IA) Gazette*, March 25, 2019, https://www.thegazette.com/crime -courts/overflowing-manure-tanks-reported-in-western-iowa-eastern-iowa-on-alert/.

50. Wynne Davis, "Overflowing Hog Lagoons Raise Environmental Concerns in North Caro-lina," *Weekend Edition Saturday*, NPR, September 22, 2018, https://www.npr.org/2018 /09/22/650698240/hurricane-s-aftermath-floods-hog-lagoons-in-north-carolina.

51. Iowa Environmental Council (IEC) and Environmental Law and Policy Center (ELPC), "Animal Feeding Operations in Iowa's Floodplain: A Risk to Iowa's Waters," June 25, 2023, https://elpc.org/wp-content/uploads/2023/06/IEC_AFO_floodplain_report_FINAL.pdf.

52. Des Moines Water Works, "Des Moines Water Works Begins Operation of Nitrate Removal Facility Because of Nutrient Spikes in Raw Source Water," news release, June 9, 2022, https://www.dmww.com/news_detail_T37_R328.php.

53. Marc Ribaudo et al., "Nitrogen in Agricultural Systems: Implications for Conservation Policy," US Department of Agriculture, Economic Research Service, Report No. 127, September 2011, https://www.ers.usda.gov/webdocs/publications/44918/6767_err127 .pdf?v=1049.

54. Alan Guebert, "Dirty Secrets, Dirty Water," *Farm & Food File*, March 9, 2016, https:// farmandfoodfile.com/2016/03/09/dirty-secrets-dirty-water/.

55. Clay Masters, "Iowa's Nasty Water War: Des Moines' Lawsuit against Farming Counties Is about More than Just Pollution," *Politico*, January 21, 2016, https://www.politico.com /magazine/story/2016/01/iowas-nasty-water-war-213551/.

56. Dirck Steimel, "Wetlands, Not Hog Lot, Set for Hamilton County," *Des Moines Register*, March 20, 1994.

57. Braun, "Iowa Turns Pigs into a Political Football."

58. Richard L. Berke, "Dole Tops the Field in Iowa Caucuses," *New York Times*, February 13, 1996, https://nyti.ms/44ySlwV.

59. Miller, "Jeff Hansen."

60. Jay P. Wagner, Dirck Steimel, and Jerry Perkins, "A Furor over Big Hog Farms," *Des Moines Register*, May 22, 1994; O'Donnell, "Living with Big Pork."

61. Rogers Worthington, "Iowa Hog Industry Fighting Its Sweet Smell of Success," *Chicago Tribune*, June 25, 1994; Kilman, "Iowans Can Handle Pig Smells"; Walsh, "Corporate Pork"; Braun, "Iowa Turns Pigs into a Political Football."

62. Jay P. Wagner, "County: Slow Down on Hog Lots," *Des Moines Register*, August 5, 1995.

63. Eller, "Iowa Could Support 45,700 Livestock Confinements."

64. Johns Hopkins Center for a Livable Future, "CAFO Moratorium Poll Results 2019," Johns Hopkins Bloomberg School of Public Health, December 10, 2019, https://clf.jhsph.edu/projects/food-citizen/cafo-moratorium-poll-results-2019.

65. Dermot J. Hayes, Daniel M. Otto, and John D. Lawrence, "Iowa's Enormous Livestock Potential," *Des Moines Register*, May 26, 1996.

66. Veronica Fowler, "A Blunt Analysis of D.M.'s Future," *Des Moines Register*, July 1, 1993.

67. Wagner, Steimel, and Perkins, "Furor over Big Hog Farms."

68. Walsh, "Corporate Pork."

69. Bruce Williams, "Hot Lot Operators: Regulations Will Force Us to Leave," *Des Moines Register*, October 14, 1994; Jay P. Wagner, "Big Pork Heeds Call to Go West," *Des Moines Register*, March 26, 1995.

70. Todd Dorman, "Hog Producer Dismisses Charges as 'Unfounded'; Says Branstad's Appearance in Video Is Inconsequential," *Fort Dodge (IA) Messenger*, October 29, 1994; Mike Glover, "Vilsack, Gross Clash in Final Campaign Debate," Associated Press, October 12, 2002.

71. David Yepsen, "Branstad, Campbell Trade Barbs over Big Hog Facilities," *Des Moines Register*, October 28, 1994.

72. Jay P. Wagner and Jerry Perkins, "Plan a 'Good Compromise,'" *Des Moines Register*, May 3, 1995.

73. Dave Murphy, "Coming Together to Work toward a Sustainable Food and Farm Future," Grist, January 15, 2009, https://grist.org/article/hope-and-the-new-usda-chief/; Erin Jordan, "Large-Scale Pork Production May Push Farther into Eastern Iowa," *Cedar Rapids (IA) Gazette*, May 6, 2018, https://www.thegazette.com/business/large-scale-pork-production-may-push-farther-into-eastern-iowa/.

74. Joe Benedict, "Application for 'Twister' House-Adjacent CAFO Withdrawn," *Iowa Falls Times Citizen*, February 7, 2018, https://www.timescitizen.com/news/application-for-twister-house-adjacent-cafo-withdrawn/article_464d762e-0c13-11e8-a107-cbc025497577.html.

75. Josh Funk, "Auditor Says Iowa Livestock Farm Fund Was Mishandled," Associated Press, November 20, 2018, https://apnews.com/09270f6875074e8f91563526747a8f65.

76. Donnelle Eller, "Cuts Threaten Iowa DNR's Ability to 'Carry Out Its Mission,' Commission Tells Lawmakers," *Des Moines Register*, January 22, 2018, https://www.desmoinesregister.com/story/news/2018/01/19/budget-cuts-threaten-iowa-dnr-mission-lawmakers-told/1040946001/.

77. Iowa Department of Natural Resources, "2020 305(b) Assessment Summary: 2020 Integrated Report including the 2020 Impaired Waters List; Approved by U.S. EPA on May 14, 2021,"https://programs.iowadnr.gov/adbnet/Assessments/Summary/2020.

78. Mitchell and Frerick, "Hog Barons."

79. Alan Guebert, "Big Ag's Weak Hand in Nitrate Fight," *Farm & Food File*, February 25, 2015, https://farmandfoodfile.com/2015/02/25/big-ags-weak-hand-nitrate-fight/.

80. Chris Jones, "Iowa Is Hemorrhaging Nitrogen," University of Iowa, IIHR—Hydroscience

& Engineering, November 7, 2019, https://web.archive.org/web/20201127060245/
https://www.iihr.uiowa.edu/cjones/iowa-is-hemorrhaging-nitrogen/.

81. Kristine A. Tidgren, "Des Moines Board of Water Works Trustees Files Lawsuit," Iowa
State University, Center for Agricultural Law and Taxation, March 16, 2015, https://www
.calt.iastate.edu/article/des-moines-board-water-works-trustees-files-lawsuit.

82. Art Cullen, *Storm Lake: A Chronicle of Change, Resilience, and Hope from a Heartland
Newspaper* (New York: Viking, 2018), 75.

83. William Petroski and Brianne Pfannenstiel, "D.M. Water Works Dismantling Bill Still
Alive in Iowa Legislature," *Des Moines Register*, March 30, 2017, https://www.desmoines
register.com/story/news/politics/2017/03/30/des-moines-water-works-dismantling-bill
-still-alive-iowa-legislature/99819416/.

84. Maura Allaire, Haowei Wu, and Upmanu Lall, "National Trends in Drinking Water Quality Violations," *Proceedings of the National Academy of Sciences* 115, no. 9 (February 2018):
2078–83, https://doi.org/10.1073/pnas.1719805115.

85. Jason Noble and Brianne Pfannenstiel, "'Biggest and Boldest' Water Quality Plan Gets
Mixed Reception," *Des Moines Register*, January 5, 2016, https://www.desmoinesregister
.com/story/news/politics/2016/01/05/water-quality-would-get-47b-school-tax-diversion
/78305186/; William Petroski and Brianne Pfannenstiel, "Branstad Weighs School Tax
Diversion for Water Quality," *Des Moines Register*, January 4, 2016, https://www.des
moinesregister.com/story/news/politics/2016/01/04/branstad-weighs-school-tax-diversion
-water-quality/78282150/; Donnelle Eller, "Branstad Offers a Twist on His Controversial
Water Quality Plan," *Des Moines Register*, July 28, 2016, https://www.desmoinesregister
.com/story/money/agriculture/2016/07/28/branstad-offers-twist-his-controversial-water
-quality-plan/87668762/.

86. Art Cullen, editorial, *Storm Lake (IA) Times*, March 2, 2016.

87. George Goehl, "Here's One Thing Democrats Can Do to Win Rural Voters: Fight Factory
Farms," *Guardian*, April 26, 2019, https://www.theguardian./commentisfree/2019/apr/26
/factory-farms-are-polluting-our-water-with-hog-manure-democrats-should-take-note.

88. Art Cullen, "BV Is Losing the Public," *Storm Lake (IA) Times*, March 2, 2016, https://
www.stormlake.com/articles/bv-is-losing-the-public/.

89. Donnelle Eller, "Exclusive: Des Moines Partnership Hopes to Broker Water Agreement,"
Des Moines Register, July 20, 2015, https://www.desmoinesregister.com/story/money
/agriculture/2015/07/20/water-works-nitrates-lawsuit-settlement/30440159/.

90. Tom Cullen, "Final Legal Bills Paid Off in Water Works Case," *Storm Lake (IA) Times*,
December 1, 2017, https://www.stormlake.com/articles/final-legal-bills-paid-off-in-water
-works-case/.

91. Tom Cullen, "County Clears Out Legal Fees from Water Lawsuit," *Storm Lake (IA) Times*,
June 9, 2017, https://www.stormlake.com/articles/county-clears-out-legal-fees-from-water
-lawsuit/.

92. Art Cullen, "Settle Now," *Storm Lake (IA) Times*, April 27, 2016.

93. MacKenzie Elmer, "Sides Clash over Water Works Bill in Radio Ads," *Des Moines Register*,
March 28, 2017, https://www.desmoinesregister.com/story/news/2017/03/28/radio-ads
-des-moines-water-works-lawsuit-iowa-legislature/99528876/.

94. Kim Norvell, "'We're All Lucky to Have Been Able to Know Him': Bill Stowe, Water
Works CEO, Has Died," *Des Moines Register*, April 14, 2019, https://www.desmoines
register.com/story/news/2019/04/14/des-moines-water-works-ceo-bill-stowe-pancreatic
-cancer-obituary-iowa-nevada-grinnell-midamerican/3363533002/.

95. Art Cullen, "Bill Stowe Started an Honest Conversation about Our State," *Des Moines
Register*, March 22, 2019, https://www.desmoinesregister.com/story/opinion/columnists

/iowa-view/2019/03/20/bill-stowe-started-honest-conversation-our-state-water-lawsuit
-environment-pollution-art-cullen/3225416002/.

96. Mitchell and Frerick, "Hog Barons."

97. Jordan, "Large-Scale Pork Production May Push Farther"; Tom Cullen, "More Hogs Coming to Northwest Iowa," *Storm Lake (IA) Times*, November 30, 2020, https://www.storm lake.com/articles/more-hogs-coming-to-northwest-iowa/.

98. Kristin Guess, "Demands for CAFO Regulation Increasing," *Waterloo–Cedar Falls (IA) Courier*, July 29, 2018, https://wcfcourier.com/news/local/govt-and-politics/demands-for -cafo-regulation-increasing/article_57d53625-ff6b-5c94-ae82-be3b990c1081.html.

99. Mitchell and Frerick, "Hog Barons."

100. Mitchell and Frerick, "Hog Barons."

101. Iowa State University, College of Agriculture and Life Sciences, "Dedication Held for ISU's Jeff and Deb Hansen Agriculture Student Learning Center," press release, September 2, 2014, https://www.cals.iastate.edu/news/2014/dedication-held-isus-jeff-and-deb-hansen -agriculture-student-learning-center.

102. Ryan J. Foley, "Iowa Governor Auctioned Off Access for Pork Barons' Charity," Associated Press, February 8, 2021, https://apnews.com/1cf07b143b8f528d68dbaf9a8ec4ec19.

103. Caroline Cummings, "Gov. Reynolds Says Meatpacking Plants, Sites of COVID-19 Outbreaks, Need to Remain Open," KGAN, April 20, 2020, https://cbs2iowa.com/news/local /gov-reynolds-says-meatpacking-plants-will-stay-open-even-as-hundreds-of-workers -infected; Erin Murphy, "Iowa Governor's Race: Unions, Big-Money Donors and Multimillion-Dollar Hauls," *Cedar Rapids (IA) Gazette*, January 25, 2018, https://www.the gazette.com/government-politics/iowa-governors-race-unions-big-money-donors-and -multimillion-dollar-hauls/.

104. David Pitt and Ryan J. Foley, "Iowa Arranged COVID-19 Tests at Office of Governor's Donors," Associated Press, January 27, 2021, https://apnews.com/article/public-health -iowa-kim-reynolds-des-moines-coronavirus-pandemic-639cc1c485701ce6eef074a34577 d8e2.

105. Pitt and Foley, "COVID-19 Tests."

Chapter 2: The Grain Barons

1. "W. Duncan MacMillan," *Minneapolis Star Tribune*, November 2, 2006, https://www .startribune.com/obituaries/detail/8861738/; Wayne G. Broehl Jr., *Cargill: Trading the World's Grain* (Hanover, NH: Dartmouth College Press, 1992); Wayne G. Broehl Jr., *Cargill: Going Global* (Hanover, NH: Dartmouth College Press, 1998); Wayne G. Broehl Jr., *Cargill: From Commodities to Customers* (Hanover, NH: Dartmouth College Press, 2008).

2. Sarah Reid, "Inside the Cargill Family," Creaghan McConnell Group, June 14, 2019, https://cmgpartners.ca/cargill/.

3. Andrea Murphy, "America's Largest Private Companies 2022: Twitter and Continental Resources Join the Ranks," *Forbes*, December 1, 2022, https://www.forbes.com/sites /andreamurphy/2022/12/01/americas-largest-private-companies-2022-twitter-and -continental-resources-join-the-ranks/?sh=1c28b3ca34c7.

4. Statista, "State Government Tax Revenue in the United States in the Fiscal Year of 2021, by State (in Billion U.S. Dollars)," April 2022, https://web.archive.org/web/2022072001 4457/https://www.statista.com/statistics/248932/us-state-government-tax-revenue-by -state/; Cargill, Inc., "Cargill at a Glance," accessed May 31, 2021, https://www.cargill .com/about/cargill-at-a-glance.

5. Seth S. King, "It's Said, 'The Sun Never Sets on Cargill,'" *New York Times*, September 25,

1972, https://nyti.ms/3Ek4Y48, https://timesmachine.nytimes.com/svc/tmach/v1/refer?
pdf=true&res=9A0DEED6133FE73ABC4D51DFBF668389669EDE.

6. Patrick Thomas, "Cargill Names Brian Sikes as Chief Executive," *Wall Street Journal*,
November 21, 2022, https://www.wsj.com/articles/cargill-names-brian-sikes-as-chief
-executive-11669036029.

7. Brewster Kneen, *Invisible Giant: Cargill and Its Transnational Strategies*, 2nd ed. (London:
Pluto Press, 2002), 2.

8. US Department of Agriculture, Risk Management Agency, "Coarse Grains: Corn, Grain
Sorghum, and Soybeans," November 2021, https://www.rma.usda.gov/en/Fact-Sheets
/National-Fact-Sheets/Coarse-Grains.

9. Yale University, "Whitney MacMillan, Longtime Friend of Yale, and Namesake of the
Whitney and Betty Macmillan Center for International and Area Studies, Dies at the Age
of 90," April 1, 2020, https://macmillan.yale.edu/news/whitney-macmillan-longtime
-friend-yale-and-namesake-whitney-and-betty-macmillan-center.

10. Austin Frerick, "To Save Rural Iowa, We Need to Make Healthy Food a Right," Slow Food
USA, March 9, 2018, https://slowfoodusa.org/to-save-rural-iowa-we-need-to-make
-healthy-food-a-right/.

11. Cargill, Inc., "A History of Nourishing the World," accessed March 30, 2023, https://
www.cargill.com/about/cargill-history-timeline; US Department of Agriculture, "About
the U.S. Department of Agriculture," accessed March 30, 2023, https://www.usda.gov/our
-agency/about-usda.

12. Robert Lee and Tristan Ahtone, "Land-Grab Universities," *High Country News*, March 30,
2020, https://www.hcn.org/issues/52.4/indigenous-affairs-education-land-grab-universities.

13. Robert Fink, "Homestead Act of 1862," *Encyclopedia Britannica*, accessed June 30, 2020,
https://www.britannica.com/topic/Homestead-Act.

14. Stephanie A. Mercier and Steve A. Halbrook, *Agricultural Policy of the United States: Historic Foundations and 21st Century Issues* (Cham, Switzerland: Palgrave Macmillan, 2021),
45; State of Delaware, "Facts & Symbols," accessed May 28, 2023, https://delaware.gov
/guides/facts/.

15. National Park Service, "Homesteading Significance," July 10, 2019, https://web.archive
.org/web/20190710160343/https://www.nps.gov/home/learn/historyculture/homestead
ing-significance.htm.

16. Cargill, Inc., "History of Nourishing the World."

17. Cargill, Inc., "History of Nourishing the World."

18. Cargill, Inc., "Planting the Seeds of Cargill's Global Business," accessed March 30, 2023,
https://www.cargill.com/history-story/en/seeds-as-gateway.jsp.

19. Bill Winders, *The Politics of Food Supply: U.S. Agricultural Policy in the World Economy*
(New Haven, CT: Yale University Press, 2009), 32.

20. R. Douglas Hurt, *Problems of Plenty: The American Farmer in the Twentieth Century* (Chicago: Ivan R. Dee, 2002), 36.

21. Ken Burns, *The Dust Bowl* (Florentine Films and WETA Television, 2012), https://kenburns
.com/films/dust-bowl/.

22. Hurt, *Problems of Plenty*, 37.

23. Hurt, *Problems of Plenty*, 43.

24. John C. Culver and John Hyde, *American Dreamer: A Life of Henry Wallace* (New York: W.
W. Norton, 2000), 72.

25. Broehl, *Cargill: Trading the World's Grain*, 613.

26. Broehl, *Cargill: Trading the World's Grain*, 370, 455.

27. Broehl, *Cargill: Trading the World's Grain*, 284.

28. Cargill, Inc., "Finding Stability in the Great Depression," January 1, 2015, https://www
.cargill.com/history-story/en/gain-farm-community-trust.jsp.

29. Broehl, *Cargill: Trading the World's Grain*, 414, 556, 582.

30. Dean Snyder, "Commercial Capital and the Political Economy of Agricultural Overproduction" (PhD diss., Syracuse University, 2015), 129.

31. Snyder, "Commercial Capital," 558.

32. Snyder, "Commercial Capital," 556, 561, 564–66.

33. Cargill, Inc., "Grain Flows Down the Mississippi," January 1, 2015, https://www.cargill
.com/history-story/en/grain-down-mississippi.jsp.

34. Cargill, Inc., "Building Ships to Provide Wartime Resources," January 1, 2015, https://
www.cargill.com/history-story/en/port-cargill-est.jsp.

35. "Chicago Board Expels Cargill Grain Co. for 'Squeeze' in Corn There Last Fall," *New York
Times*, March 26, 1938, https://nyti.ms/47Q1SCH.

36. Sidonie Devarenne and Bailey DeSimone, "History of the United States Farm Bill,"
Library of Congress, *In Custodia Legis* (blog), March 15, 2021, accessed May 28, 2023,
https://blogs.loc.gov/law/2021/03/history-of-the-united-states-farm-bill/.

37. Hurt, *Problems of Plenty*, 69.

38. Culver and Hyde, *American Dreamer*, 161.

39. Culver and Hyde, *American Dreamer*, 158.

40. Broehl, *Cargill: Trading the World's Grain*, 574.

41. Culver and Hyde, *American Dreamer*, 160.

42. Melissa Petruzzello, "Sharecropping," *Encyclopedia Britannica*, July 31, 2020, https://www
.britannica.com/topic/sharecropping.

43. Eric Foner, *Reconstruction: America's Unfinished Revolution, 1863–1877* (New York: Harp-
erCollins, 1988), 409.

44. Hurt, *Problems of Plenty*, 73–75; Louis Cantor, "A Prologue to the Protest Movement: The
Missouri Sharecropper Roadside Demonstration of 1939," *Journal of American History* 55,
no. 4 (March 1969): 804–22; Bruce J. Reynolds, "Black Farmers in America, 1865–2000:
The Pursuit of Independent Farming and the Role of Cooperatives," US Department of
Agriculture, Rural Business–Cooperative Service, RBS Research Report 194, October
2002, https://www.rd.usda.gov/files/RR194.pdf.

45. Harry S. Truman, "Address at Dexter, Iowa, on the Occasion of the National Plowing
Match," American Presidency Project, September 18, 1948, accessed July 1, 2020, https://
www.presidency.ucsb.edu/documents/address-dexter-iowa-the-occasion-the-national
-plowing-match.

46. Broehl, *Cargill: Trading the World's Grain*, 777.

47. Wolfgang Saxon, "Ezra Taft Benson Dies at 94; Was Head of Mormon Church," *New York
Times*, May 31, 1994, https://nyti.ms/3EfSOJE.

48. Ezra Taft Benson, *Cross Fire: The Eight Years with Eisenhower* (Westport, CT: Greenwood
Press, 1976), 68.

49. James E. Sherow, *The Grasslands of the United States: An Environmental History* (Santa
Barbara, CA: ABC-CLIO, 2007), 139.

50. University of Virginia, Miller Center, "Ezra Taft Benson (1953–1961)," accessed May 28,
2023, https://millercenter.org/president/eisenhower/essays/benson-1953-secretary-of
-agriculture.

51. Gary James Bergera, "'Weak-Kneed Republicans and Socialist Democrats': Ezra Taft

Benson as U.S. Secretary of Agriculture, 1953–61, Part 2," *Dialogue: A Journal of Mormon Thought* 41, no. 4 (Winter 2008): 64, https://www.dialoguejournal.com/articles/weak -kneed-republicans-and-socialist-democrats-ezra-taft-benson-as-u-s-secretary-of-agriculture -1953-61/.

52. Gary James Bergera, "'Rising above Principle': Ezra Taft Benson as U.S. Secretary of Agriculture, 1953–61, Part 1," *Dialogue: A Journal of Mormon Thought* 41, no. 3 (Fall 2008), https://www.dialoguejournal.com/articles/rising-above-principle-ezra-taft-benson-as-u-s -secretary-of-agriculture-1953-61-part-1/.

53. John D. Morris, "Minnesota Farm Disquiet Found Aiding Democrats," *New York Times*, October 19, 1958, https://nyti.ms/47Q3bBB.

54. "Republicans: Chance for Glory," *TIME*, March 10, 1958, https://content.time.com/time /subscriber/article/0,33009,863053,00.html.

55. Bergera, "'Weak-Kneed Republicans,'" 65–67.

56. Richard Goldstein, "Earl L. Butz, Secretary Felled by Racial Remark, Is Dead at 98," *New York Times*, February 4, 2008, https://www.nytimes.com/2008/02/04/washington/04butz .html.

57. Tom Philpott, "A Reflection on the Lasting Legacy of 1970s USDA Secretary Earl Butz," Grist, February 8, 2008, https://grist.org/article/the-butz-stops-here/.

58. Michael C. Jensen, "Soviet Grain Deal Is Called a Coup," *New York Times*, September 29, 1972, https://nyti.ms/44xGC1J; Elmer B. Staats, Comptroller General of the United States, "Exporters' Profits on Sales of U.S. Wheat to Russia," US General Accounting Office, 1974, https://www.gao.gov/assets/b-176943.pdf.

59. Jonathan Coppess, "A Brief Review of the Consequential Seventies," *farmdoc daily* 9, no. 99, University of Illinois Urbana-Champaign, Department of Agricultural and Consumer Economics, May 30, 2019, https://farmdocdaily.illinois.edu/2019/05/a-brief-review-of -the-consequential-seventies.html.

60. James Risser and George Anthan, "Why They Love Earl Butz," *New York Times*, June 13, 1976, https://nyti.ms/47Uhy7R.

61. Risser and Anthan, "Why They Love Earl Butz."

62. Broehl, *Cargill: From Commodities to Customers*, 61–62.

63. Warren Weaver Jr., "Farm Issues Seen as Likely to Play Key Role in Shaping the 1988 Campaign," *New York Times*, September 20, 1987, https://nyti.ms/3YUpphE.

64. Jon Lauck, "After Deregulation: Constructing Agricultural Policy in the Age of 'Freedom to Farm,'" *Drake Journal of Agricultural Law* 5, no. 1 (Spring 2000): 18, http://aglaw journal.wp.drake.edu/wp-content/uploads/sites/66/2016/09/agVol05No1-Luack.pdf.

65. David Burnham, "Questions Rising over U.S. Study and Role of Company Executives," *New York Times*, September 28, 1982, https://nyti.ms/3KYIQ36.

66. George Anthan, "Freedom to Farm, from Bill to Act," *Des Moines Register*, April 21, 1996; Barry Wilson, "Groups Jostle for Opportunity to Present Words of Wisdom," *Western Producer*, June 1, 1995, https://www.producer.com/news/groups-jostle-for-opportunity -to-present-words-of-wisdom/.

67. US Senate, "Roll Call Vote 104th Congress—2nd Session: On the Conference Report (H.R. 2854 Conference Report)," March 28, 1996, https://www.senate.gov/legislative /LIS/roll_call_votes/vote1042/vote_104_2_00057.htm.

68. Lauck, "After Deregulation," 22; Vann R. Newkirk II, "The Real Lessons from Bill Clinton's Welfare Reform," *Atlantic*, February 5, 2018, https://www.theatlantic.com/politics /archive/2018/02/welfare-reform-tanf-medicaid-food-stamps/552299/.

69. Hossein Ayazi and Elsadig Elsheikh, "The US Farm Bill: Corporate Power and Structural

Racialization in the US Food System," University of California, Berkeley, Haas Institute for a Fair and Inclusive Society, October 28, 2015, https://belonging.berkeley.edu/farm -bill-report-corporate-power-and-structural-racialization-us-food-system.

70. "Testimony of Neil E. Harl," United States Senate, September 15, 1998, http://www2 .econ.iastate.edu/faculty/harl/Senate_Testimony_Sept_15.html.

71. Dick Ziggers, "Cargill Acquires Ethanol Facilities," All About Feed, May 4, 2011, https:// www.allaboutfeed.net/home/cargill-acquires-ethanol-facilities/; Statista, "Leading Produc- ers of Ethanol by Capacity in the United States as of 2023," March 2023, https://www .statista.com/statistics/828532/largest-us-ethanol-producers-by-capacity/; Snyder, "Com- mercial Capital."

72. US Energy Information Administration, "Total Energy," accessed October 4, 2023, https://www.eia.gov/totalenergy/data/browser/index.php?tbl=T10.03#/?f=A&start=1981 &end=2022&charted=7-8.

73. US Department of Agriculture, Economic Research Service, "Feed Grains Sector at a Glance," accessed October 4, 2023, https://web.archive.org/web/20230130120841 /https://www.ers.usda.gov/topics/crops/corn-and-other-feed-grains/ feed-grains-sector-at-a-glance/.

74. C. Ford Runge, "The Case against More Ethanol: It's Simply Bad for Environment," Yale Environment 360, May 25, 2016, https://e360.yale.edu/features/the_case_against_ethanol _bad_for_environment; Noah Kaufman, "A Chance to Phase Out Support for Corn Ethanol in the Renewable Fuel Standard," Center on Global Energy Policy at Columbia University—School of International and Public Affairs, November 7, 2022, https://www .energypolicy.columbia.edu/publications/chance-phase-out-support-corn-ethanol -renewable-fuel-standard/.

75. Jesse Newman and Jacob Bunge, "The Transformation of the American Farm, in 18 Charts," Wall Street Journal, December 28, 2017, https://www.wsj.com/articles/the-trans formation-of-the-american-farm-in-18-charts-1514474480.

76. "The Economic Cost of Food Monopolies: The Dirty Dairy Racket," Food & Water Watch, January 2023, https://www.foodandwaterwatch.org/wp-content/uploads/2023/01 /RPT2_2301_EconomicCostofDairy-web.pdf.

77. James M. MacDonald, Robert A. Hoppe, and Doris Newton, "Three Decades of Consol- idation in U.S. Agriculture," US Department of Agriculture, Economic Research Service, Economic Information Bulletin No. EIB-189, March 2018, https://www.ers.usda.gov /webdocs/publications/88057/eib-189.pdf?v=3290.1.

78. Jennifer Fahy, "How Heirs' Property Fueled the 90 Percent Decline in Black-Owned Farm- land," Farm Aid, February 28, 2022, https://www.farmaid.org/blog/heirs-property-90 -percent-decline-black-owned-farmland/.

79. Osha Gray Davidson, Broken Heartland: The Rise of America's Rural Ghetto (Iowa City: University of Iowa Press, 1996).

80. Wendong Zhang, Alejandro Plastina, and Wendiam Sawadgo, "Iowa Farmland Ownership and Tenure Survey, 1982–2017: A Thirty-Five-Year Perspective," Iowa State University Extension and Outreach, August 2018, https://www2.econ.iastate.edu/faculty/zhang /publications/outreach-articles/FM1893_2017_Ownership_Survey.pdf.

81. Tom Harkin, "Opening Remarks," Folder 53, Grinnell Symposium on the Small Town, March 7, 1987, Thomas R. Harkin Collection: Speeches Series, 1972–2014, Drake Uni- versity, https://cowles-archon.drake.edu/index.php?p=collections/findingaid&id=315& rootcontentid=34615&q=Grinnell#id36731.

82. Mark Paul, "Community-Supported Agriculture in the United States: Social, Ecological, and Economic Benefits to Farming," Journal of Agrarian Change 19, no. 1 (January 2019): 162–80, https://doi.org/10.1111/joac.12280.

83. Tim Weiner, "The Nation: It's Raining Farm Subsidies," *New York Times*, August 8, 1999, https://nyti.ms/3OUeWy5.

84. Broehl, *Cargill: From Commodities to Customers*, 298.

85. "John D. Rockefeller: American Industrialist," *Encyclopedia Britannica*, https://www.britannica.com/biography/John-D-Rockefeller.

86. Steven Greenhouse, "For a Grain Giant, No Farm Crisis," *New York Times*, March 30, 1986, https://nyti.ms/3KY4BQH; Chloe Sorvino, "The Last Cargill Family Member to Run the Giant Agribusiness Company Has Died," *Forbes*, March 12, 2020, https://www.forbes.com/sites/chloesorvino/2020/03/12/the-last-cargill-family-member-to-run-the-giant-agribusiness-company-has-died/.

87. Allen R. Myerson, "Cargill Set to Buy Main Unit of Continental Grain, Its Chief Rival," *New York Times*, November 11, 1998, https://nyti.ms/3PgKxeJ.

88. "Grain Deal Gets DOJ Nod," CNN Money, July 8, 1999, https://money.cnn.com/1999/07/08/companies/cargill/.

89. "Series K 354–357. Farm-to-Retail Price Spreads of Farm Food Products: 1913 to 1970," in *Bicentennial Edition: Historical Statistics of the United States, Colonial Times to 1970* (Washington, DC: US Department of Commerce, Bureau of the Census, 1975), 489; US Department of Agriculture, Economic Research Service, "Food Dollar Series: Quick Facts," November 17, 2022, https://www.ers.usda.gov/data-products/food-dollar-series/quick-facts/.

90. Cargill, Inc., "Timeline," accessed March 31, 2023.

91. Greenhouse, "For a Grain Giant, No Farm Crisis."

92. Mary Hendrickson, Harvey S. James Jr., and William D. Heffernan, "Vertical Integration and Concentration in US Agriculture," in *Encyclopedia of Food and Agricultural Ethics*, edited by Paul B. Thompson and David M. Kaplan, 1799–1806 (Dordrecht: Springer, 2014).

93. "Cargill Denies It Manipulates Market in Grain," *New York Times*, June 25, 1976, https://nyti.ms/3suIhaR; Gregory Meyer, "Ohio Accuses Cargill and Morton of Salt Plot," *Financial Times*, March 21, 2012; Dave Yost, "Ohio Attorney General DeWine Announces $11.5 Million Settlement over Rock Salt Prices," news release, June 3, 2015, https://www.ohioattorneygeneral.gov/Media/News-Releases/June-2015/Ohio-Attorney-General-DeWine-Announces-$11-5-Milli; Mike Leonard, "Tyson, Cargill, Hormel, Butterball to Face Turkey Cartel Claims," Bloomberg Law, October 27, 2020, https://news.bloomberglaw.com/antitrust/tyson-cargill-hormel-butterball-to-face-turkey-cartel-claims.

94. Kurt Eichenwald, "Archer Daniels Settles Suit Accusing It of Price Fixing," *New York Times*, June 18, 2004, https://www.nytimes.com/2004/06/18/business/archer-daniels-settles-suit-accusing-it-of-price-fixing.html; Reuters, "Company News: Cargill to Pay $24 Million to Settle Class-Action Suit," *New York Times*, March 12, 2004, https://www.nytimes.com/2004/03/12/business/company-news-cargill-to-pay-24-million-to-settle-class-action-suit.html.

95. Dan Papscun, "Cargill, Sanderson, Wayne to Pay $85 Million in DOJ Settlement," Bloomberg Law, July 25, 2022, https://news.bloomberglaw.com/antitrust/cargill-wayne-farms-sued-by-doj-for-sharing-wage-benefits-data.

96. "Company News: Tyson to Acquire Chicken Operations of Cargill," *New York Times*, July 15, 1995, https://www.nytimes.com/1995/07/15/business/company-news-tyson-to-acquire-chicken-operations-of-cargill.html.

97. Christopher Doering and Chris Casey, "Cargill and Continental Grain Close $4.5B Purchase of Sanderson Farms," Food Dive, July 22, 2022, https://www.fooddive.com/news/cargill-and-continental-grain-complete-45b-sanderson-farms-purchase/627910/.

98. "The Biden Plan for Rural America," Biden President, December 6, 2019, https://web .archive.org/web/20191206205542/https://joebiden.com/rural/.

99. Nathaniel Popper, "You Call That Meat? Not So Fast, Cattle Ranchers Say," *New York Times*, February 9, 2019, https://www.nytimes.com/2019/02/09/technology/meat-veggie -burgers-lab-produced.html; Eduardo Garcia, "You Might Not Want to Eat Bugs. But Would You Eat Meat That Ate Bugs?," *New York Times*, September 21, 2019, https://www .nytimes.com/2019/09/21/climate/insects-animal-feed-climate-change.html.

100. Tom Philpott, "The Secret History of Why Soda Companies Switched from Sugar to High-Fructose Corn Syrup," *Mother Jones*, July 26, 2019, https://www.motherjones.com /food/2019/07/the-secret-history-of-why-soda-companies-switched-from-sugar-to-high -fructose-corn-syrup/.

101. Broehl, *Cargill: From Commodities to Customers*, 78.

102. Statista, "Average per Capita Consumption of Sugar as of 2016, by Country (in Grams)," March 2016, https://www.statista.com/statistics/535219/global-sugar-per-capita-consump tion-by-country/.

103. John C. Beghin and Helen H. Jensen, "Farm Policies and Added Sugars in US Diets," *Food Policy* 33, no. 6 (December 2008): 480–88, https://doi.org/10.1016/j.foodpol.2008.05 .007.

104. David S. Ludwig and Harold A. Pollack, "Obesity and the Economy: From Crisis to Opportunity," *Journal of the American Medical Association* 301, no. 5 (February 4, 2009): 533–35, https://doi.org/10.1001/jama.2009.52.

105. Anthony Rodgers et al., "Prevalence Trends Tell Us What Did Not Precipitate the US Obesity Epidemic," *Lancet* 3, no. 4 (February 28, 2018): E162–63, https://doi.org/10.1016 /S2468-2667(18)30021-5.

106. Karen R. Siegel et al., "Association of Higher Consumption of Foods Derived from Subsidized Commodities with Adverse Cardiometabolic Risk among US Adults," *JAMA Internal Medicine* 176, no. 8 (2016): 1124–32, https://doi.org/10.1001/jamainternmed .2016.2410; Filippa Juul et al., "Ultra-processed Food Consumption among US Adults from 2001 to 2018," *American Journal of Clinical Nutrition* 115, no. 1 (January 2022): 211–21, https://doi.org/10.1093/ajcn/nqab305.

107. Bryant Simon, *The Hamlet Fire: A Tragic Story of Cheap Food, Cheap Government, and Cheap Lives* (New York: New Press, 2017), 155; Kristi Jacobson and Lori Silverbush, *A Place at the Table* (Culver City, CA: Participant Media, 2012), https://participant.com /film/place-table.

108. Simon, *Hamlet Fire*, 151.

109. Zachary J. Ward et al., "Projected U.S. State-Level Prevalence of Adult Obesity and Severe Obesity," *New England Journal of Medicine* 381, no. 25 (December 19, 2019): 2440–50, https://doi.org/10.1056/NEJMsa1909301.

110. Julia Belluz, "Scientists Don't Agree on What Causes Obesity, but They Know What Doesn't," *New York Times*, November 21, 2022, https://www.nytimes.com/2022/11/21 /opinion/obesity-cause.html.

111. Dave Philipps, "Trouble for the Pentagon: The Troops Keep Packing On the Pounds," *New York Times*, September 4, 2019, https://www.nytimes.com/2019/09/04/us/military-obesity .html.

112. Melanie Warner, "Striking Back at the Food Police," *New York Times*, June 12, 2005, https://www.nytimes.com/2005/06/12/business/yourmoney/striking-back-at-the-food -police.html.

113. Andrew Jacobs and Matt Richtel, "How Big Business Got Brazil Hooked on Junk Food,"

New York Times, September 16, 2017, https://www.nytimes.com/interactive/2017/09/16/health/brazil-obesity-nestle.html.

114. Mark Bittman, "That Flawed Stanford Study," *New York Times*, October 2, 2012, https://archive.nytimes.com/opinionator.blogs.nytimes.com/2012/10/02/that-flawed-stanford-study/.

115. Eric Lipton, "Rival Industries Sweet-Talk the Public," *New York Times*, February 11, 2014, https://www.nytimes.com/2014/02/12/business/rival-industries-sweet-talk-the-public.html.

116. Somini Sengupta, "That Salmon on Your Plate Might Have Been a Vegetarian," *New York Times*, March 24, 2021, https://www.nytimes.com/2021/03/24/climate/salmon-vegetarian-fish.html.

117. Sengupta, "That Salmon on Your Plate"; Rosamond L. Naylor et al., "Author Correction: A 20-Year Retrospective Review of Global Aquaculture," *Nature* 593, no. E12 (April 2021), https://doi.org/10.1038/s41586-021-03508-0.

118. "Cargill Inc.: Annual Lobbying Totals: 1998–2022," OpenSecrets, accessed March 31, 2023, https://www.opensecrets.org/orgs/cargill-inc/lobbying?id=D000000511; Marshall Burke, "FSE Receives $3 Million from Cargill to Support Visiting Fellows, Program Activities," Stanford Center on Food Security and the Environment, June 17, 2008, https://fse.fsi.stanford.edu/news/fse_receives_3_million_from_cargill_to_support_visiting_fellows_program_activities_20080617; Ashley Dean, "Stanford-Cargill Partnership Strengthens to Address Food Security Issues," Stanford Center on Food Security and the Environment, November 27, 2011, https://fse.fsi.stanford.edu/news/stanfordcargill_partnership_strengthens_to_address_food_security_issues_20111127; Zach Boren, "Revealed: How the Livestock Industry Funds the 'Greenhouse Gas Guru,'" Unearthed, October 31, 2022, https://unearthed.greenpeace.org/2022/10/31/frank-mitloehner-uc-davis-climate-funding/.

119. Hiroko Tabuchi, "He's an Outspoken Defender of Meat. Industry Funds His Research, Files Show," *New York Times*, October 31, 2022, https://www.nytimes.com/2022/10/31/climate/frank-mitloehner-uc-davis.html.

120. North American Meat Institute, "Board of Directors," accessed March 31, 2023, https://meatinstitute.org/Board_of_Directors.

121. Oxfam International, "'Divide and Purchase': How Land Ownership Is Being Concentrated in Colombia," press release, September 27, 2013, https://www.oxfam.org/en/press-releases/divide-and-purchase-how-land-ownership-being-concentrated-colombia; Andres Schipani, "Colombia: Cargill Accused of Overbuying Land," *Financial Times*, October 2, 2013, https://www.ft.com/content/006ce00b-ff1b-38ce-a750-46b88dff068e.

122. Simon Romero, "Brazil's Spreading Exports Worry Minnesota Farmers," *New York Times*, June 22, 2004, https://www.nytimes.com/2004/06/22/business/brazil-s-spreading-exports-worry-minnesota-farmers.html; Nick Halter, "Cargill's Headquarters Complex Sells for $75M in Internal Deal," *Minneapolis/St. Paul Business Journal*, March 6, 2020, https://www.bizjournals.com/twincities/news/2020/03/06/cargill-s-headquarters-complex-sells-for-75m-in.html.

123. US Environmental Protection Agency, How's My Waterway?, "Minnehaha Creek," accessed March 31, 2023, https://mywaterway.epa.gov/community/minnehaha%20creek/overview.

Chapter 3: The Coffee Barons

1. Yasemin Craggs Mersinoglu et al., "Lipsticks, Lattes . . . and Now Labradors: JAB's Bet on Pets," *Financial Times*, July 11, 2022, https://www.ft.com/content/f32bee39-0ddf-47a3-8560-67838e7c9089.

2. Nick Brown, "JAB-Backed 'Trade' Selling Coffees from 50 Prominent US Roasters," *Daily Coffee News*, April 5, 2018, https://dailycoffeenews.com/2018/04/05/jab-backed-trade

-selling-coffees-from-50-prominent-us-roasters/; Zeke Turner and Julie Jargon, "The Secretive Company That Pours America's Coffee," *Wall Street Journal*, March 7, 2018, https://www.wsj.com/articles/the-secretive-company-that-pours-americas-coffee-1520440633; M. Ridder, "Market Share of Single-Cup Coffee in the United States in 2022, by Leading Brands," Statista, July 2022, https://www.statista.com/statistics/315036/market-share-of-single-cup-coffee-in-the-us-by-leading-brand/; Keurig Dr Pepper Inc., "Keurig Dr Pepper and La Colombe Announce Strategic Partnership," press release, July 20, 2023, https://news.keurigdrpepper.com/2023-07-20-keurig-dr-pepper-and-la-colombe-announce-strategic-partnership.

3. Katrin Bennhold, "Nazis Killed Her Father. Then She Fell in Love with One," *New York Times*, June 14, 2019, https://www.nytimes.com/2019/06/14/business/reimann-jab-nazi-keurig-krispy-kreme.html; Mersinoglu et al., "Lipsticks, Lattes"; Eric Sylvers, "Lavazza and Illy Say 'Basta' as Global Coffee Wars Come to Italy," *Wall Street Journal*, October 13, 2018, https://www.wsj.com/articles/lavazza-and-illy-say-basta-as-global-coffee-wars-come-to-italy-1539432052.

4. Michael J. de la Merced, "Joh. A. Benckiser to Buy Peet's Coffee & Tea for $974 Million," *New York Times*, July 23, 2012, https://archive.nytimes.com/dealbook.nytimes.com/2012/07/23/joh-a-benckiser-to-buy-peets-coffee-for-973-9-million/.

5. Sylvers, "Lavazza and Illy Say 'Basta.'"

6. "The Reimann Hypothesis," *Economist*, June 20, 2020; "Wolfgang Reimann," *Forbes*, accessed December 19, 2022, https://www.forbes.com/profile/wolfgang-reimann/.

7. "Reimann Hypothesis."

8. James Shotter, "Germany's Intensely Private and Immensely Wealthy Reimann Family," *Financial Times*, March 11, 2016, https://www.ft.com/content/242db7ea-d1a8-11e5-831d-09f7778e7377.

9. Bennhold, "Nazis Killed Her Father"; Katrin Bennhold, "Germany's Second-Richest Family Discovers a Dark Nazi Past," *New York Times*, March 25, 2019, https://www.nytimes.com/2019/03/25/world/europe/nazi-laborers-jab-holding.html.

10. Shotter, "Reimann Family."

11. Shotter, "Reimann Family."

12. Bennhold, "Nazis Killed Her Father."

13. Bennhold, "Nazis Killed Her Father."

14. Bennhold, "Nazis Killed Her Father."

15. Bennhold, "Nazis Killed Her Father."

16. David de Jong, *Nazi Billionaires: The Dark History of Germany's Wealthiest Dynasties* (New York: Mariner Books, 2022), 276.

17. Bennhold, "Nazis Killed Her Father."

18. Saabira Chaudhuri, "Why This Coffee Giant Is Staying Put in Russia," *Wall Street Journal*, updated August 18, 2023, https://www.wsj.com/business/retail/why-this-coffee-giant-is-staying-put-in-russia-1c7e9ffa.

19. Tim Wu, *The Curse of Bigness: Antitrust in the New Gilded Age* (New York: Columbia Global Reports, 2018), 80.

20. Diarmuid Jeffreys, *Hell's Cartel: IG Farben and the Making of Hitler's War Machine* (London: Bloomsbury, 2008), 6.

21. Jeffreys, *Hell's Cartel*, 6.

22. Library of Congress, Legislative Reference Service, "Fascism in Action: A Documented Study and Analysis of Fascism in Europe," 1947, https://stars.library.ucf.edu/cgi/viewcontent.cgi?article=1080&context=prism.

23. Jeffreys, *Hell's Cartel*, 143.

24. Ganesh Sitaraman, "Unchecked Power: How Monopolies Have Flourished—and Undermined Democracy," *New Republic*, November 29, 2018, https://newrepublic.com/article/152294/unchecked-power.

25. Bennhold, "Nazis Killed Her Father."

26. Joseph McAuley, "The Legacy of Louis Brandeis, 100 Years after His Historic Nomination," *America: The Jesuit Review*, January 27, 2016, https://www.americamagazine.org/content/all-things/justice-brandeis-and-right-be.

27. "John D. Rockefeller: American Industrialist," *Encyclopedia Britannica*, https://www.britannica.com/biography/John-D-Rockefeller.

28. Wu, *Curse of Bigness*, 36.

29. Wu, *Curse of Bigness*, 37.

30. Melvin I. Urofsky, *Louis D. Brandeis: A Life* (New York: Pantheon Books, 2009), 154.

31. Brian Duignan, "Muckraker," *Encyclopedia Britannica*, accessed October 8, 2019, https://www.britannica.com/topic/muckraker.

32. Binyamin Appelbaum, *The Economists' Hour: False Prophets, Free Markets, and the Fracture of Society* (New York: Little, Brown, 2019), 133.

33. Brian Duignan, "Sherman Antitrust Act," *Encyclopedia Britannica*, accessed June 4, 2020, https://www.britannica.com/event/Sherman-Antitrust-Act/additional-info#history.

34. US Department of Justice, "A Study of the Development of the Antitrust Laws and Current Problems of Antitrust Enforcement: Report of the Department of Justice to the Subcommittee on Monopoly of the Select Committee on Small Business, United States Senate" (Washington, DC: US Government Printing Office, May 23, 1952), https://babel.hathitrust.org/cgi/pt?id=uiug.30112064309583&seq=11.

35. US Department of Justice, "Study of the Development of the Antitrust Laws," 5.

36. David E. Sanger, "The Nation: Big Time; From Trustbusters to Trust Trusters," *New York Times*, December 6, 1998, https://nyti.ms/45xzSlG.

37. Jeffrey Rosen, *Louis D. Brandeis: American Prophet* (New Haven, CT: Yale University Press, 2017), 53; Lewis J. Paper, *Brandeis* (Englewood Cliffs, NJ: Prentice Hall, 1983), 101.

38. Rosen, *Louis D. Brandeis*, 192.

39. Rosen, *Louis D. Brandeis*, 98.

40. John C. Culver and John Hyde, *American Dreamer: A Life of Henry Wallace* (New York: W. W. Norton, 2000), 122.

41. Nelson L. Dawson, "Louis D. Brandeis, Felix Frankfurter, and Franklin D. Roosevelt: The Origins of a New Deal Relationship," *American Jewish History* 68, no. 1 (September 1978): 32–42, http://www.jstor.org/stable/23882047.

42. Jeffrey Rosen, "The Curse of Bigness," *Atlantic*, June 3, 2016, https://www.theatlantic.com/politics/archive/2016/06/the-forgotten-wisdom-of-louis-d-brandeis/485477/.

43. Jim Puzzanghera, "Something Trump and Elizabeth Warren Agree On: Bringing Back Glass-Steagall to Break Up Big Banks," *Los Angeles Times*, May 12, 2017, https://www.latimes.com/business/la-fi-glass-steagall-20170514-htmlstory.html.

44. "A Biography of Louis Brandeis: Let's Look at the Facts," *Economist*, September 24, 2009, https://www.economist.com/books-and-arts/2009/09/24/lets-look-at-the-facts.

45. Bennhold, "Nazis Killed Her Father."

46. Anupreeta Das and Emily Glazer, "Trio Builds Consumer-Goods Empire," *Wall Street Journal*, December 24, 2012, https://www.wsj.com/articles/SB10001424127887324731304578193380376860070.

47. Scheherazade Daneshkhu, "JAB Ready for More after Pret A Manger Deal," *Financial Times*, June 2, 2018.

48. "Keurig Green Mountain to Be Acquired by JAB Holding Company-Led Investor Group for $92 per Share in Cash," press release, Business Wire, December 7, 2015, https://www.businesswire.com/news/home/20151207005651/en/Keurig-Green-Mountain-to-be-Acquired-by-JAB-Holding-Company-Led-Investor-Group-for-92-Per-Share-in-Cash; David de Jong, "JAB's Billionaire Backers Want to Create a Global Coffee Empire," Bloomberg, December 7, 2015, https://www.bloomberg.com/news/articles/2015-12-07/jab-trio-creates-global-coffee-empire-for-billionaire-backers.

49. Thomas Heath, "Keurig Is Finally Designing a More Eco-Friendly K-Cup," *Washington Post*, May 19, 2017, https://www.washingtonpost.com/business/economy/keurig-is-finally-designing-a-more-eco-friendly-k-cup/2017/05/16/df76de2c-397c-11e7-9e48-c4f199710b69_story.html.

50. "Too Much of a Good Thing," *Economist*, March 26, 2016, https://www.economist.com/briefing/2016/03/26/too-much-of-a-good-thing.

51. Will Kenton, "Concentration Ratio," Investopedia, July 8, 2019.

52. "New Report Exposes Corporate Monopolies Driving U.S. Dairy Crisis," press release, January 31, 2023, Food & Water Watch, https://www.foodandwaterwatch.org/2023/01/31/new-report-exposes-corporate-monopolies-driving-u-s-dairy-crisis/.

53. IBISWorld, "Washer & Dryer Manufacturing Industry 2018," Open Markets Institute, n.d., accessed January 24, 2023, http://concentrationcrisis.openmarketsinstitute.org/industry/washer-dryer-manufacturing/.

54. IBISWorld, "Coffin & Casket Manufacturing Industry 2019," Open Markets Institute, n.d., accessed January 24, 2023, http://concentrationcrisis.openmarketsinstitute.org/industry/coffin-casket-manufacturing/.

55. Philip H. Howard, *Concentration and Power in the Food System: Who Controls What We Eat?* (London: Bloomsbury Academic, 2016).

56. EssilorLuxottica, "Brands," accessed July 1, 2020, https://www1.essilorluxottica.com/en/brands/.

57. "Grocery Goliaths: How Food Monopolies Impact Consumers," Food & Water Watch, December 2013, https://foodandwaterwatch.org/wp-content/uploads/2021/03/Grocery-Goliaths-Report-Dec-2013.pdf.

58. Austin Frerick, "To Revive Rural America, We Must Fix Our Broken Food System," *American Conservative*, February 27, 2019, https://www.theamericanconservative.com/to-revive-rural-america-we-must-fix-our-broken-food-system/.

59. IBISWorld, "Meat Processing Industry 2018," Open Markets Institute, n.d., accessed July 1, 2020, http://concentrationcrisis.openmarketsinstitute.org/industry/meat-processing/.

60. IBISWorld, "Peanut Butter Industry 2017," Open Markets Institute, n.d., accessed July 1, 2020, http://concentrationcrisis.openmarketsinstitute.org/industry/peanut-butter/.

61. Nathaniel Meyersohn, "The Hidden Makers of Costco's Kirkland Signature and Trader Joe's O's," CNN Business, August 6, 2022, https://www.cnn.com/2022/08/06/business/costco-kirkland-signature-trader-joes-store-brands/index.html.

62. Nick Brown, "Nearly Four of Every Five US Coffee Shops Are Now Starbucks, Dunkin' or JAB Brands," *Daily Coffee News*, October 25, 2019, https://dailycoffeenews.com/2019/10/25/nearly-four-of-every-five-us-coffee-shops-are-now-starbucks-dunkin-or-jab-brands/.

63. Mike Scarcella, "Amid Claim of Delay in Keurig Antitrust Case, U.S. Appeals Court Sets Clock," Reuters, November 16, 2022, https://www.reuters.com/legal/litigation/amid-claim-delay-keurig-antitrust-case-us-appeals-court-sets-clock-2022-11-16/.

64. Sarah Pringle, "JAB Investors' NVA Buys SAGE Vet for Some $1.25b, AKKR Scores 12x

Return on Seequent, CVC Buys ExamWorks for $4b-Plus," PE Hub, June 23, 2021, https://www.pehub.com/?s=JAB+Investors%E2%80%99+NVA+Buys+SAGE+Vet+for +Some+%241.25b; Sarah Pringle, "JAB Investors' NVA Buys Ethos Veterinary Health in $1.65bn Deal," PE Hub, August 16, 2021, https://www.pehub.com/jab-investors-nva -buys-ethos-veterinary-health-in-1-65bn-deal/; "Fairfax Completes $1.4bn Sale of US Pet Business," The Insurer, November 1, 2022, https://www.theinsurer.com/news/fairfax -completes-1-4bn-sale-of-us-pet-business/.

65. "Reimann Hypothesis."

66. Kerry A. Dolan and Chase Peterson-Withorn, eds., "Forbes World's Billionaires List: The Richest in 2022," *Forbes*, accessed January 11, 2023, https://www.forbes.com/billionaires/.

67. Dylan Matthews, "'Antitrust Was Defined by Robert Bork. I Cannot Overstate His Influence,'" *Washington Post*, December 20, 2012, https://www.washingtonpost.com/news/wonk /wp/2012/12/20/antitrust-was-defined-by-robert-bork-i-cannot-overstate-his-influence/.

68. Mark Sherman, "Bork: Nixon Offered Next High Court Vacancy in '73," Associated Press, February 25, 2013, https://apnews.com/article/d402250301744029826a4a99c41e35a4.

69. Milton Friedman, "Policy Forum: 'Milton Friedman on Business Suicide,'" CATO Institute, March/April 1999, https://www.cato.org/policy-report/march/april-1999/policy -forum-milton-friedman-business-suicide#.

70. Robert H. Bork, *The Antitrust Paradox: A Policy at War with Itself* (New York: Basic Books, 1978).

71. Wu, *Curse of Bigness*, 89.

72. Robert O'Harrow Jr. and Shawn Boburg, "A Conservative Activist's Behind-the-Scenes Campaign to Remake the Nation's Courts," *Washington Post*, May 21, 2019, https://www .washingtonpost.com/graphics/2019/investigations/leonard-leo-federalists-society-courts/.

73. Adam Cohen, *Supreme Inequality: The Supreme Court's Fifty-Year Battle for a More Unjust America* (New York: Penguin Press, 2020), xv–xvi.

74. Federal Trade Commission, "FTC Appropriation and Full-Time Equivalent (FTE) History," n.d., accessed January 11, 2023, https://www.ftc.gov/about-ftc/bureaus-offices/office -executive-director/financial-management-office/ftc-appropriation.

75. Eleanor M. Fox, "Modernization of Antitrust: A New Equilibrium," *Cornell Law Review* 66, no. 6 (August 1981): 1140–92, https://scholarship.law.cornell.edu/clr/vol66/iss6/3; Farm Action, "Re: Request for Information on Merger Enforcement," April 21, 2022, https://farmaction.us/wp-content/uploads/2022/04/Farm-Action-Merger-Guidelines-Com ment-4.21.22.pdf.

76. Jesse Eisinger and Justin Elliott, "These Professors Make More Than a Thousand Bucks an Hour Peddling Mega-Mergers," ProPublica, November 16, 2016, https://www.propublica .org/article/these-professors-make-more-than-thousand-bucks-hour-peddling-mega -mergers.

77. David Dayen, *Monopolized: Life in the Age of Corporate Power* (New York: New Press, 2020), 7.

78. Lisa L. Gill, "Shop Around for Lower Drug Prices," *Consumer Reports*, April 5, 2018, https://www.consumerreports.org/drug-prices/shop-around-for-better-drug-prices/.

79. Jessica Van Parys, "ACA Marketplace Premiums Grew More Rapidly in Areas with Monopoly Insurers than in Areas with More Competition," *Health Affairs* 37, no. 8 (August 2018): 1243–51, https://doi.org/10.1377/hlthaff.2018.0054.

80. Victoria Graham, "Turkey Remains Rare Meat Not Embroiled in Antitrust Probes," Bloomberg Law, November 26, 2019, https://news.bloomberglaw.com/antitrust/turkey -remains-rare-meat-not-embroiled-in-antitrust-probes.

81. Mike Leonard, "Agribusinesses, Facing Antitrust Wave, Hit with Turkey Suit," Bloomberg

Law, December 20, 2019, https://news.bloomberglaw.com/antitrust/agribusinesses-facing
-price-fixing-wave-hit-with-turkey-claims.

82. Ethan Miller, "The Consolidation of Coffee," *Global Coffee Report*, July 1, 2020, https://
www.gcrmag.com/the-consolidation-of-coffee/.

83. "JAB Holding Company Headquarters and Office Locations," Craft, n.d., accessed January 11, 2023, https://craft.co/jab-holding-company/locations.

84. "C.R. Contest Seeks Sweet Potato Pies," *Cedar Rapids (IA) Gazette*, November 7, 2000.

85. William Knoedelseder, *Bitter Brew: The Rise and Fall of Anheuser-Busch and America's Kings of Beer* (New York: Harper Business, 2012), 362.

86. Austin Frerick, "Rise of Majority-Minority Districts in Rural Iowa: How Changes in Meatpacking Impacted Rural Schooling" (thesis, Grinnell College, August 2011).

87. Charles M. Tolbert et al., "Civic Community in Small-Town America: How Civic Welfare Is Influenced by Local Capitalism and Civic Engagement," *Rural Sociology* 67, no. 1 (March 2002): 90–113, https://doi.org/10.1111/j.1549-0831.2002.tb00095.x; Charles M. Tolbert, Thomas A. Lyson, and Michael D. Irwin, "Local Capitalism, Civic Engagement, and Socioeconomic Well-Being," *Social Forces* 77, no. 2 (December 1998): 401–27, https://doi.org/10.2307/3005533.

88. Iowa Secretary of State, "2012 Election Results, Official Canvass by County," https://
sos.iowa.gov/elections/results/index.html#11; Blake McGhghy, "Interrogating 'Post-Fact' Populism: Voter Rationality in Southeast Iowa" (thesis, Harvard University, 2017).

89. Iowa Secretary of State, "2016 General Election Canvass Summary," https://sos.iowa.gov
/elections/pdf/2016/general/canvsummary.pdf; Iowa Secretary of State, "General Election—2020 Canvass Summary," https://sos.iowa.gov/elections/pdf/2020/general/canv
summary.pdf.

90. Nicholas Riccardi and Angeliki Kastanis, "Trump's Election Day Surge Powered by Small-Town America," Associated Press, November 4, 2020, https://apnews.com/article
/election-2020-donald-trump-elections-e915054734d4914d8f1f3c27b369c8af.

91. Danielle Kurtzleben, "Rural Voters Played a Big Part in Helping Trump Defeat Clinton," NPR, November 14, 2016, https://www.npr.org/2016/11/14/501737150/rural-voters
-played-a-big-part-in-helping-trump-defeat-clinton.

92. Bennhold, "Nazis Killed Her Father."

Chapter 4: The Dairy Barons

1. Jillian Kramer, "Why Sue McCloskey Started Fair Oaks Farms, the U.S.'s Largest Agritourism Attraction," *Food & Wine*, January 9, 2018, updated June 6, 2019, https://www.food
andwine.com/travel/united-states/fair-oaks-farms-visitors.

2. There are sixteen school milk servings in a gallon, and as of 2019, the farm pumped 250,000 gallons per day. Casey Smith, "I Took a Tour of Fair Oaks Farms. Here's What I Saw," *Indianapolis Star*, June 10, 2019, https://www.indystar.com/story/news/2019/06/10
/fair-oaks-farms-abuse-touring-indiana-dairy-hog-operation-experience/1381857001/;
Colleen Kottke, "Fair Oaks Farms Opens Robotic Milking Facility," *Wisconsin State Farmer*, February 5, 2020, https://www.wisfarmer.com/story/news/2020/02/05/fair-oaks-farms
-opens-robotic-milking-facility-and-visitors-center/4588680002/.

3. Gaby Vinick, "Wisconsin Loses More Dairy Farms in 2021, with the Total Down by a Third Since 2014," PBS Wisconsin, March 29, 2022, https://pbswisconsin.org/news-item
/wisconsin-loses-more-dairy-farms-in-2021-with-total-down-by-a-third-since-2014/.

4. Monte Reel, "Milk Money: The Dairy Farm of Your Imagination Is Disappearing," *Bloomberg Businessweek*, February 28, 2020, corrected March 2, 2020, https://www

.bloomberg.com/news/features/2020-02-28/the-dairy-farm-of-your-imagination-is
-disappearing#xj4y7vzkg.

5. Emily Moon, "Dairy Disneyland: One Farm's Quest to Save Industrial Agriculture," *Pacific Standard*, March 19, 2019, updated May 24, 2019, https://psmag.com/environment
/dairy-disneyland-one-farms-quest-to-save-industrial-agriculture; Conner Prairie, "Conner Prairie Expands and Enhances Visitor Experiences with Announcement of $24 Million in New Capital Projects," press release, August 12, 2022, https://www.connerprairie.org
/conner-prairie-expands-and-enhances-visitor-experiences-with-announcement-of-24
-million-in-new-capital-projects/; Domenica Bongiovanni, "As Museums Have Lost Millions, They Have Had to Re-engineer How They Reach Visitors and Kids," *Indiana-polis Star*, December 17, 2020, https://www.indystar.com/story/entertainment/arts/2020
/12/17/large-indianapolis-museums-see-revenue-losses-and-greater-need/3856878001/.

6. Moon, "Dairy Disneyland."

7. Correspondence with Darin Von Ruden, president, Wisconsin Farmers Union, December 16, 2022.

8. "Milk Prices by Year and Adjusted for Inflation," U.S. Inflation Calculator, n.d., accessed December 16, 2022, https://www.usinflationcalculator.com/inflation/milk-prices-adjusted
-for-inflation/.

9. Julie C. Keller, *Milking in the Shadows: Migrants and Mobility in America's Dairyland* (New Brunswick, NJ: Rutgers University Press, 2019).

10. Carly Fox et al., "Milked: Immigrant Dairy Farmworkers in New York State," Workers' Center of Central New York and Worker Justice Center of New York, 2017, https://
milkedny.files.wordpress.com/2017/05/milked_053017.pdf.

11. Zoe Chace and Ira Glass, "Same Bed, Different Dreams," WBEZ Chicago, *This American Life*, May 1, 2015, https://www.thisamericanlife.org/556/same-bed-different-dreams.

12. Records from Indiana Department of Labor—IOSHA Compliance, received January 9, 2023.

13. Records from "Denis Samuel Padilla Godoy, as Personal Representative of the Estate of Samuel Antonio Padilla Castro v. Prairies Edge Dairy Farms, LLC, Fair Oaks Farms, LLC, Fair Oaks Farms Management LLC et al.," January 9, 2023.

14. US Department of Labor, Occupational Safety and Health Administration, "Inspection Detail: Inspection 1509883.015—111599—Prairies Edge Dairy Farm LLC," accessed December 16, 2022, https://www.osha.gov/ords/imis/establishment.inspection_detail?id
=1509883.015.

15. Janice Lewandowski, "You Have Been Exposed!" letter to the editor, *Newton County (IN) Enterprise*, August 12, 2019, https://animalrecoverymission.org/wp-content/uploads/2019
/08/npd-Newton-County-Enterprise.pdf.

16. Christine Kopaczewski, "Meet 2017 Awesome Women Awards Honoree, Sue McCloskey," *Good Housekeeping*, August 14, 2017, https://www.goodhousekeeping.com/life/inspirational
-stories/a45431/awesome-women-awards-sue-mccloskey/; Kramer, "Why Sue McCloskey Started Fair Oaks Farms."

17. David Rogers, "GOP, Industry Rifts Spill Over," *Politico*, December 30, 2012, https://
www.politico.com/story/2012/12/gop-industry-rifts-bring-milk-imbroglio-to-a-head
-085589.

18. Will Gilmer, "Farmers: A Surprise Showing at South by Southwest Festival," *Progressive Dairy*, April 18, 2017, https://www.agproud.com/articles/18781-farmers-a-surprise
-showing-at-south-by-southwest-festival; Yale MacMillan Center Program in Agrarian Studies, "Industrial Livestock Production, Fish Farming, Global Climate Change, and

Global Health on October 23," October 16, 2020, https://agrarianstudies.macmillan.yale
.edu/news/2020-10.

19. LexisNexis Public Records, accessed May 28, 2021.

20. LexisNexis Public Records, accessed May 28, 2021; "Marion County Tax Warrant
11438284," August 22, 2017.

21. Dan Charles, "Chasing a Dream Built on Dairy, This Master of Milk Came Home," *The
Salt*, NPR, February 4, 2017, https://www.npr.org/sections/thesalt/2017/02/04/513091341
/chasing-a-dream-built-on-dairy-this-emperor-of-milk-came-home; Tony Cook, Sarah
Bowman, and Tim Evans, "It's Vigilante Activist vs. Politically Connected Farmer in Fair
Oaks Cruelty Controversy," *Indianapolis Star*, June 7, 2019, https://www.indystar.com
/story/news/politics/2019/06/07/fair-oaks-farms-abuse-vigilante-activist-vs-politically
-connected-farmer/1365849001/.

22. Courtney Love, "Fairlife Founder Tells Her Story," *Lancaster Farming*, February 13, 2020,
https://www.lancasterfarming.com/farming-news/news/fairlife-founder-tells-her-story
/article_96797fa5-d8ef-5fea-9127-c00ec32c05b8.html.

23. Beth Kowitt, "Big Agriculture Gets Its Sh*t Together," *Fortune*, February 1, 2016.

24. Kowitt, "Big Agriculture Gets Its Sh*t Together."

25. US Department of Agriculture, Agricultural Statistics Board, National Agricultural Statistics Service, "Milk Production," February 22, 2022, https://downloads.usda.library.cornell
.edu/usda-esmis/files/h989r321c/jh345531b/n8711359j/mkpr0223.pdf.

26. Hannah Himmelmann and Donna M. Amaral-Phillips, "Water Needs for the Dairy
Herd," University of Kentucky, Department of Animal & Food Sciences, Martin-Gatton
College of Agriculture, Food and Environment Cooperative Extension Service, n.d.,
accessed December 16, 2022, https://afs.ca.uky.edu/content/water-needs-dairy-herd.

27. "Big Ag, Big Oil and California's Big Water Problem," Food & Water Watch, October 12,
2021, https://www.foodandwaterwatch.org/wp-content/uploads/2021/10/CA-Water-White
-Paper.pdf.

28. Noah Gallagher Shannon, "The Water Wars of Arizona," *New York Times Magazine*, July
19, 2018, https://www.nytimes.com/2018/07/19/magazine/the-water-wars-of-arizona
.html.

29. Andrew Stern, "Draining Arizona: Residents Say Corporate Mega-Farms Are Drying Up
Their Wells," NBC News, September 17, 2019, https://www.nbcnews.com/news/us-news
draining-arizona-residents-say-corporate-mega-farms-are-drying-their-n1052551.

30. Mark Babineck, "Panhandle Becomes Promised Land for Dairymen," *Houston Chronicle*,
May 29, 2007, https://www.chron.com/news/houston-texas/article/Panhandle-becomes
-promised-land-for-dairymen-1829676.php.

31. Kowitt, "Big Agriculture Gets Its Sh*t Together."

32. "Grand Kankakee Marsh," Citizen Potawatomi Nation Cultural Heritage Center, n.d.,
accessed January 8, 2023, https://www.potawatomiheritage.com/encyclopedia/grand-kan
kakee-marsh/.

33. Elan Pochedley, "Restorative Cartography of the Theakiki Region: Mapping Potawatomi
Presences in Indiana," *Open Rivers: Rethinking Water, Place & Community*, no. 18 (Spring
2021), https://openrivers.lib.umn.edu/article/mapping-potawatomi-presences/.

34. *Everglades of the North: The Story of the Grand Kankakee Marsh*, directed by Brian Kallies
(Merrillville, IN: Lakeshore PBS, 2012), 42:00, https://lakeshorepbs.org/evergladesofthe
north/.

35. US Environmental Protection Agency, How's My Waterway?, "Curtis Creek—Unnamed
Tributary," accessed December 16, 2022, https://mywaterway.epa.gov/waterbody-report
/21IND/INK0241_T1005/2022.

36. US Department of the Interior, US Geological Survey, Water Science School, "Bacteria and E. Coli in Water," June 5, 2018, https://www.usgs.gov/special-topics/water-science -school/science/bacteria-and-e-coli-water.

37. Indiana Department of Natural Resources, Division of Water, "Water Resource Availability in the Kankakee River Basin, Indiana—Executive Summary," 1990, https://www.in.gov /dnr/water/files/kankakee_basinsums.pdf.

38. Sierra Club Grassroots Network, Food and Agriculture Team, "What Is a CAFO?," fact sheet, n.d., accessed January 8, 2023, https://www.sierraclub.org/sites/www.sierraclub.org /files/2022-10/What%20is%20a%20CAFO_0.pdf.

39. US Department of Agriculture, Agricultural Marketing Service, "2022 Class I Milk Price—Monthly and Year-to-Date," n.d., accessed January 17, 2023, https://www.ams .usda.gov/sites/default/files/media/ClassIPrices2022.pdf.

40. Thomas Quaife, "Market Connections Can Help Us Avoid Hog Producers' Fate," *Dairy Herd Management*, January 1999.

41. P. Kelly Smith, "Cow Speaks Up for H-E-B's MooTopia," *Adweek*, September 27, 2004, https://www.adweek.com/brand-marketing/cow-speaks-h-e-bs-mootopia-75110/.

42. Lorene Yue, "Dreaming of Milk and Honey," *Crain's Chicago Business*, October 15, 2011, https://www.chicagobusiness.com/article/20111015/ISSUE01/310159975/dreaming-of -milk-and-honey.

43. Donna Berry, "Fairlife's Journey from Startup to Scale," *Food Business News*, February 2, 2021, https://www.foodbusinessnews.net/articles/17839-fairlifes-journey-from-startup-to -scale.

44. James Carper, "2015 Processor of the Year Fairlife Aims for a Better Life," Dairy Foods, December 3, 2015, https://www.dairyfoods.com/articles/91483-processor-of-the-year -fairlife-aims-for-a-better-life; "Farm to Table: Fairlife's Office Reflects Relaxed Dairy Culture," *Chicago Tribune*, October 2, 2015, https://www.chicagotribune.com/business/blue -sky/ct-fairlife-office-tour-bsi-photos-20151002-photogallery.html.

45. Marian Bull, "The Milk Situation," *New York Times*, March 14, 2020, https://www .nytimes.com/2020/03/14/style/milk-dairy-marketing.html; Nicole Olynk Widmar, "Dairy and Milk Markets in 2021–2022," Purdue University, Agricultural Economics Department, January 13, 2022, https://ag.purdue.edu/commercialag/home/paer-article /dairy-and-milk-markets-in-2021-2022/.

46. Fairlife, "Fairlife 2% Ultra-Filtered Milk," accessed January 8, 2023, https://fairlife.com /ultra-filtered-milk-14oz/fairlife-2-milk-14oz/.

47. Fairlife, "FAQ: How Long Does Fairlife Last Unopened?," accessed January 8, 2023, https://web.archive.org/web/20230202180353/https://fairlife.com/faq/#faq-how-long -does-fairlife-last-unopened; US Department of Agriculture, AskUSDA, "How Long Can You Keep Dairy Products Like Yogurt, Milk, and Cheese in the Refrigerator?," March 22, 2023, accessed January 8, 2023, https://ask.usda.gov/s/article/How-long-can-you-keep -dairy-products-like-yogurt-milk-and-cheese-in-the-refrigerator.

48. Donna Berry, "Fairlife—the Story behind the Innovation," Food Business News, February 10, 2015, https://www.foodbusinessnews.net/articles/5596-fairlife-the-story-behind-the -innovation; Fairlife, "FAQ: How Long Does Fairlife Last Unopened?"; "Got Coke? Soda Maker Starts Selling 'Premium Milk,'" Associated Press, February 3, 2015.

49. Coca-Cola Company, "The Coca-Cola Company Acquires Remaining Stake in Fairlife LLC," press release, January 2, 2020, https://www.coca-colacompany.com/media-center /coca-cola-company-acquires-remaining-stake-in-fairlife-llc.

50. Comedy Central, *Colbert Report*, season 11, "Thought for Food—Fairlife Milk & Pizza

Hut's Subconscious Menu," aired December 3, 2014, https://www.cc.com/video/ziipwv/the-colbert-report-thought-for-food-fairlife-milk-pizza-hut-s-subconscious-menu.

51. Rachel Sanders, "We Tried Coca-Cola's New 'Premium' Milk So You Don't Have To," BuzzFeed, February 10, 2015, https://www.buzzfeed.com/rachelysanders/fairlife-milk-taste-test.

52. Eric Mandel, "Coca-Cola Buys Fairlife, Applauding the Brand's Response to Animal Abuse Video," *Atlanta Business Chronicle*, January 6, 2020, https://www.bizjournals.com/atlanta/news/2020/01/06/coca-cola-buys-fairlife-applauding-the-brands.html.

53. Yue, "Dreaming of Milk and Honey."

54. Seeking Alpha, "The Coca-Cola Company's (KO) Presents at Morgan Stanley Global Consumer Conference (Transcript)," November 19, 2014, https://seekingalpha.com/article/2695965-the-coca-cola-companys-ko-presents-at-morgan-stanley-global-consumer-conference-transcript.

55. Seeking Alpha, "Coca-Cola Presents."

56. Corey Geiger, "Dairy Imitators Don't Measure Up," *Hoard's Dairyman*, November 15, 2018, https://hoards.com/article-24384-dairy-imitators-dont-measure-up.html; "Coca-Cola Scouting Northeast for Fairlife Plant Site," *Milkweed*, December 2022.

57. Wyatt Bechtel, "$200 Million Dollar Fairlife Processing Plant to Be Built in Arizona," *Dairy Herd Management*, April 9, 2019, https://www.dairyherd.com/news/business/200-million-dollar-fairlife-processing-plant-be-built-arizona; Taylor Leach, "Fairlife Crosses the Canadian Border, Now Made from 100% Canadian Milk," *Dairy Herd Management*, November 13, 2020, https://www.dairyherd.com/news/new-products/fairlife-crosses-canadian-border-now-made-100-canadian-milk.

58. Leach, "Fairlife Crosses the Canadian Border."

59. US Department of Agriculture, National Institute of Food and Agriculture, Extension Foundation, Cooperative Extension, DAIReXNET, "How Many Pounds of Feed Does a Cow Eat in a Day?," August 16, 2019, accessed December 16, 2022, https://dairy-cattle.extension.org/how-many-pounds-of-feed-does-a-cow-eat-in-a-day/.

60. Kowitt, "Big Agriculture Gets Its Sh*t Together."

61. The average human produces 0.4 gallon of manure per day: Michael Van Amburgh and Karl Czymmek, "Series: Phosphorus and the Environment, 2. Setting the Record Straight: Comparing Bodily Waste between Dairy Cows and People," *Cornell Field Crops: What's Cropping Up?* (blog), June 21, 2017, https://blogs.cornell.edu/whatscroppingup/2017/06/21/series-phosphorus-and-the-environment-2-setting-the-record-straight-comparing-bodily-waste-between-dairy-cows-and-people/. This is equivalent to 1,075,000 people. William H. Frey, "2020 Census: Big Cities Grew and Became More Diverse, Especially among Their Youth," Brookings, October 28, 2021, https://www.brookings.edu/articles/2020-census-big-cities-grew-and-became-more-diverse-especially-among-their-youth/, https://www.brookings.edu/wp-content/uploads/2021/10/Big-cities-grew-and-became-more-diverse-Table-A.xlsx.

62. Environmental Defense Fund, "Methane: A Crucial Opportunity in the Climate Fight," n.d., accessed January 8, 2023, https://www.edf.org/climate/methane-crucial-opportunity-climate-fight.

63. Fiona MacKay, "Looking for a Solution to Cows' Climate Problem," *New York Times*, November 16, 2009, https://www.nytimes.com/2009/11/17/business/global/17iht-rbofcows.html.

64. PennState Extension, "Biogas from Manure," March 5, 2012, https://extension.psu.edu/biogas-from-manure.

65. US Environmental Protection Agency, AgSTAR, "How Does Anaerobic Digestion Work?,"

March 2, 2022, updated February 9, 2023, https://www.epa.gov/agstar/how-does-anae robic-digestion-work.

66. Kowitt, "How a Huge Dairy Is Solving a Major Pollution Problem."

67. Kevin T. Higgins, "Food Automation & Manufacturing Conference Report," *Food Engineering*, June 8, 2012, https://www.foodengineeringmag.com/articles/89417-food -automation-manufacturing-conference-report.

68. Kowitt, "How a Huge Dairy Is Solving a Major Pollution Problem."

69. Robert Holly, "Chicago's AMP Americas Gets $47M to Turn More Cow Manure into Natural Gas," *Chicago Tribune*, August 10, 2017, https://www.chicagotribune.com/business /blue-sky/ct-bsi-amp-americas-investment-20170810-story.html; Ally Marotti, "Farm to Fleets: Manure Helps Chicago Startup Build Natural Gas Network," *Chicago Tribune*, March 17, 2016, https://www.chicagotribune.com/business/blue-sky/ct-ampcng-opens -more-filling-stations-20160317-story.html.

70. "Dairy Cow Midwife," *Dirty Jobs*, season 4, episode 11, aired April 28, 2008.

71. Hyunok Lee and Daniel A. Sumner, "Dependence on Policy Revenue Poses Risks for Investments in Dairy Digesters," *California Agriculture* 72, no. 4 (December 2018): 226–35, https://doi.org/10.3733/ca.2018a0037.

72. "Written Testimony of Dr. Mike McCloskey," House Committee on Agriculture, Subcommittee on Commodity Exchanges, Energy, and Credit, July 23, 2020, https://docs.house .gov/meetings/AG/AG22/20200723/110928/HHRG-116-AG22-Wstate-McCloskeyM -20200723.pdf.

73. Riley M. Duren et al., "California's Methane Super-Emitters," *Nature* 575 (November 2019): 180–84, https://doi.org/10.1038/s41586-019-1720-3; Liza Gross, "Can California Reduce Dairy Methane Emissions Equitably?" Inside Climate News, August 9, 2021, https://insideclimatenews.org/news/09082021/california-dairy-methane-emissions/.

74. State of Indiana, County of Marion, *Commissioner of the Department of Environmental Management v. Prairies Edge Dairy Farms, LLC*, Case No. 2017-24978-A, 2018, https:// www.in.gov/idem/oe/cause/AO/24978-A.htm.

75. Joseph Fanelli, "Methane Fueled Explosion at Aumsville Dairy Farm Causes Fire," *Oregonian*, July 25, 2012, https://www.oregonlive.com/pacific-northwest-news/2012/07 /methane_fueled_explosion_at_au.html; "Wisconsin Manure Digester Explosion Sparks Fire," *St. Paul Pioneer Press*, August 7, 2014, https://www.twincities.com/2014/08/07 /wisconsin-manure-digester-explosion-sparks-fire-4/.

76. Vermont Department of Environmental Conservation, "Anaerobic Digesters," accessed January 8, 2023, https://dec.vermont.gov/air-quality/permits/source-categories/anae robic-digesters.

77. Jessica McKenzie, "The Misbegotten Promise of Anaerobic Digesters," The Counter, December 3, 2019, https://thecounter.org/misbegotten-promise-anaerobic-digesters-cafo/.

78. White House, "Fact Sheet: Biden Administration Tackles Super-Polluting Methane Emissions," January 31, 2022, https://www.whitehouse.gov/briefing-room/statements-releases /2022/01/31/fact-sheet-biden-administration-tackles-super-polluting-methane-emissions/.

79. Kevin Hall, "Under Guise of Climate Benefit, Manure Is More Valuable than Milk at California Dairies," *Fresno Bee*, October 16, 2021, https://www.fresnobee.com/opinion /readers-opinion/article255037057.html.

80. Sarah Milov, "Promoting Agriculture: Farmers, the State, and Checkoff Marketing, 1935–2005," *Business History Review* 90, no. 3 (Autumn 2016): 515, http://www.jstor.org /stable/26290955.

81. Milov, "Promoting Agriculture," 516.

82. Milov, "Promoting Agriculture," 519.

83. John M. Crespi and Richard J. Sexton, "US Generic Advertising and Promotion Programs," in *US Programs Affecting Food and Agricultural Marketing*, edited by Walter J. Armbruster and Ronald D. Knutson, 171–94 (New York: Springer, 2013).

84. Geoffrey S. Becker, "Federal Farm Promotion ('Check-Off') Programs," Library of Congress, Congressional Research Service, March 25, 2004, https://www.everycrsreport.com /files/20040325_95-353_20ad110e0587662af94c6b3c0d38d0446a32da7b.pdf.

85. National Agricultural Law Center, "Checkoff Programs—an Overview," accessed January 4, 2021, https://nationalaglawcenter.org/overview/checkoff/.

86. US Government Accountability Office (GAO), "Agricultural Promotion Programs: USDA Could Build on Existing Efforts to Further Strengthen Its Oversight," GAO-18-54, November 2017, https://www.gao.gov/assets/690/689213.pdf.

87. GAO, "Agricultural Promotion Programs."

88. Sarah Milov, *The Cigarette: A Political History* (Cambridge, MA: Harvard University Press, 2019).

89. Parke E. Wilde, "Federal Communication about Obesity in the Dietary Guidelines and Checkoff Programs," *Obesity (Silver Spring)* 14, no. 6 (June 2006): 968, https://doi.org/10 .1038/oby.2006.110.

90. Herbert Baum, *Quest for the Perfect Strawberry: A Case Study of the California Strawberry Commission and the Strawberry Industry; A Descriptive Model for Marketing Order Evaluation* (Lincoln, NE: iUniverse, 2005), 52.

91. World Dairy Expo, "How the Dairy Checkoff Is Driving Demand for You," YouTube video, 53:31, October 7, 2016, https://www.youtube.com/watch?v=eur3H3Gaml0.

92. Joe Fassler, "Inside Big Beef's Climate Messaging Machine: Confuse, Defend, and Downplay," *Guardian*, May 3, 2023, https://www.theguardian.com/environment/2023/may/03 /beef-industry-public-relations-messaging-machine.

93. Karen McMahon, "Pork Powerhouses 2021: Bouncing Back from COVID-19," *Successful Farming*, October 6, 2021, https://www.agriculture.com/livestock/pork-powerhouses /pork-powerhouses-2021-bouncing-back-from-covid-19; Caroline Christen, "Top Pork Producing States: Who Is the Largest Pork Producer in the U.S.?," Sentient Media, January 29, 2021, https://sentientmedia.org/top-pork-producing-states/.

94. National Pork Board, "Pork Checkoff Names 2019–20 Officers," *National Hog Farmer*, June 5, 2019, https://www.nationalhogfarmer.com/pork-market-news/pork-checkoff -names-2019-20-officers.

95. Cary Spivak, "A Nonprofit That's Supposed to Promote Dairy Pays Its Leaders Millions— While the Farmers Who Fund It Are Going Out of Business," *Milwaukee Journal Sentinel*, September 4, 2019, updated February 18, 2020, https://www.jsonline.com/in-depth /news/special-reports/dairy-crisis/2019/09/04/dairy-management-inc-pays-execs-salaries -millions-farmer-checkoff-program-got-milk-prices-fall/1884361001/.

96. Milov, "Promoting Agriculture," 528–29.

97. "The Other Political Pork," *New York Times*, November 10, 2002, https://nyti.ms/3PjpSHd.

98. Parke Wilde, "Do Pork Producers Want the Right to Vote on Their Checkoff Program?," *U.S. Food Policy* (blog), November 30, 2008, https://usfoodpolicy.blogspot.com/2008/11/.

99. "Pork Producers Dismiss Referendum on the Checkoff," *National Hog Farmer*, February 24, 2009.

100. Spivak, "Nonprofit That's Supposed to Promote Dairy."

101. US Department of Agriculture (USDA), Office of Inspector General (OIG), "Agricultural Marketing Service's Oversight of Federally Authorized Research & Promotion Board Activities," March 2012; US Department of Agriculture, Office of Inspector General,

"Agricultural Marketing Service Oversight of the Beef Promotion and Research Board's Activities," January 2014; US Government Accountability Office, "Agricultural Promotion Programs: USDA Could Build on Existing Efforts to Further Strengthen Its Oversight," GAO-18-54, November 2017, https://www.gao.gov/pdf/product/688519.

102. Danny Vinik, "A $60 Million Pork Kickback?," *Politico*, August 30, 2015, https://www.politico.com/agenda/story/2015/08/a-60-million-pork-kickback-000210/; Sam Thielman, "USDA Scrambles to Investigate Egg Lobby as CEO Resigns," *Guardian*, October 23, 2015, https://www.theguardian.com/business/2015/oct/23/usda-investigate-american-egg-board-hampton-creek-just-mayo.

103. Alan Guebert, "Checkoff Oversight Virtually Nil," *Tri-State Livestock News*, April 16, 2012, https://www.tsln.com/news/alan-guebert-checkoff-oversight-virtually-nil/.

104. Dan Nosowitz, "USDA Secretary Tom Vilsack Abruptly Quits. What the Heck Is Going On over There?," *Modern Farmer*, January 13, 2017, https://modernfarmer.com/2017/01/usda-secretary-tom-vilsack-abruptly-quits-heck-going/; U.S. Dairy Export Council, "Tom Vilsack to Take Helm of U.S. Dairy Export Council," news release, January 17, 2017, https://www.usdec.org/newsroom/news-releases/news-releases-archives/news-release-01/17/2017.

105. Andrea Zippay, "Pa. Couple Sues over Milk Checkoff," *Farm and Dairy*, April 11, 2002; "Benjamin F "Ben" Yale (1951–2012)," Find a Grave, accessed March 29, 2023, https://www.findagrave.com/memorial/91919583/benjamin-f-yale.

106. Yoni Brook and Nicholas Bruckman, directors, untitled dairy documentary, forthcoming.

107. John Kramer, "U.S. Supreme Court Vacates 'Got Milk?' Decision; Remands to 3rd U.S. Circuit for Further Proceedings," Institute for Justice, May 31, 2005, https://ij.org/press-release/qgot-milkq-ad-campaign-release-5-31-2005/.

108. ProPublica, Nonprofit Explorer, "Dairy Management Inc, Form 990-O for period ending December 2018," https://projects.propublica.org/nonprofits/display_990/363992031/06_2020_prefixes_31-36%2F363992031_201812_990O_2020060917183102.

109. ProPublica, Nonprofit Explorer, "Dairy Management Inc, full text of 'Full Filing' for fiscal year ending Dec. 2019," https://projects.propublica.org/nonprofits/organizations/363992031/202013179349308981/full.

110. US Department of Agriculture, Agricultural Marketing Service, "Report to Congress on the National Dairy Promotion and Research Program and the National Fluid Milk Processor Promotion Program 2012 Program Activities," https://www.ams.usda.gov/sites/default/files/media/2012%20-%20Dairy%20Report%20to%20Congress.pdf; US Department of Agriculture, Agricultural Marketing Service, "Report to Congress on the Dairy Promotion and Research Program and the Fluid Milk Processor Promotion Program 2013 and 2014 Program Activities," https://www.ams.usda.gov/sites/default/files/media/2013%20-%20 2014%20Dairy%20Report%20To%20Congress.pdf; US Department of Agriculture, "Memorandum of Understanding between United States Department of Agriculture and the Innovation Center for U.S. Dairy," April 24, 2013, https://www.usda.gov/sites/default/files/documents/usda-mou-innovation-center-us-dairy.pdf.

111. Editorial Board, "An Animal Abuse Video Destroys Fair Oaks Farms' Charming Facade," *Chicago Tribune*, June 6, 2019, https://www.chicagotribune.com/opinion/editorials/ct-edit-fair-oaks-animal-abuse-20190607-story.html.

112. Gabrielle Canon, "Secret Footage Exposes Abuse of Calves at Coca-Cola Affiliated Dairy Farm," *Guardian*, June 6, 2019, https://www.theguardian.com/environment/2019/jun/06/secret-footage-calves-fair-oaks-farms-illinois.

113. Editorial Board, "Animal Abuse Video."

114. Editorial Board, "Animal Abuse Video."

115. Robert Channick, "2-Year-Old Animal Abuse Video Goes Viral Again, Renewing Calls to Boycott Fairlife, though Brand Has Cut Ties with Dairy Farm," *Chicago Tribune*, May 28, 2021, https://www.chicagotribune.com/business/ct-biz-fairlife-fair-oaks-dairy-animal -abuse-video-20210528-nuapaswfergpzfy4gxc2yjlete-story.html.

116. Amy Lavalley, "Fair Oaks Founder: Animal Rights Group's Video 'Goes against Everything We Stand For,'" *Chicago Tribune*, June 5, 2019, https://www.chicagotribune.com/suburbs /post-tribune/ct-ptb-fair-oaks-video-st-0606-story.html; Alexia Elejalde-Ruiz, "Fair Oaks Farms under Investigation for Alleged Abuse," *Chicago Tribune*, June 6, 2019; Alexia Ele-jalde-Ruiz, "Fair Oaks Farms Owner Says Video of Alleged Cow Abuse 'Broke My Heart,' Vows to Add Cameras, Animal Welfare Audits," *Chicago Tribune*, June 7, 2019, https:// www.chicagotribune.com/business/ct-biz-fair-oaks-farms-animal-abuse-mccloskey -20190607-story.html.

117. Lavalley, "Fair Oaks Founder."

118. Elejalde-Ruiz, "Fair Oaks Farms under Investigation for Alleged Abuse"; "Fairlife Milk Ultra-Filtered Reduced Fat 2%," Jewel Osco, accessed December 16, 2022, https://www .jewelosco.com/shop/product-details.960127167.html; "Fairlife Milk—2% Reduced Fat," Tony's Fresh Market, accessed December 16, 2022, https://www.tonysfreshmarket.com /shop/dairy/milk_and_cream/milk/2_milk/fairlife_milk_2_reduced_fat_ultra_filtered_52 _fluid_ounce_bottle/p/2044549.

119. National Dairy FARM Program, "Mike McCloskey," accessed December 16, 2022, https://nationaldairyfarm.com/staff/mike-mccloskey/.

120. Interview with Andrew deCoriolis, June 1, 2021.

121. Nielsen Company, "Fairlife Brand Sales," August 16, 2021.

122. Mike Curley, "$21M Deal Gets Go-ahead in Coca-Cola Milk False Ad MDL," Law360, April 28, 2022, https://www.law360.com/articles/1488236.

123. Sue McCloskey, "The Innovation of Milk," TEDxWillowCreek, March 2018, https:// www.ted.com/talks/sue_mccloskey_the_innovation_of_milk.

124. Author's correspondence.

125. "Meet the Influential People in Dairy," *Progressive Dairy*, January 19, 2023, https://www .agproud.com/articles/56678-meet-the-influential-people-in-dairy.

126. Federal Election Commission, "Individual Contributions," accessed May 29, 2021.

127. Jose A. DelReal, "Several Members of Trump's Agriculture Committee Have Supported Legal Status for Undocumented Workers," *Washington Post*, August 16, 2016, https://www .washingtonpost.com/news/post-politics/wp/2016/08/16/several-members-of-trumps -agriculture-committee-have-supported-legal-status-for-undocumented-workers/; Nancy Cook and Andrew Restuccia, "Meet Trump's Cabinet-in-Waiting," *Politico*, November 9, 2016, https://www.politico.com/story/2016/11/who-is-in-president-trump-cabinet -231071.

128. Cook, Bowman, and Evans, "Vigilante Activist"; author's Freedom of Information Act (FOIA) request to the US Department of Agriculture.

129. Indiana Economic Development Corporation, "About Us," accessed December 16, 2022, https://www.iedc.in.gov/about; Defense Business Board, "Meeting Minutes, May 6, 2020," accessed December 16, 2022, https://dbb.defense.gov/Portals/35/Documents /Meetings/2020/May%202020/DBB%20Meeting%20Minutes%20-%20May%206%20 2020%20-%20signed%20w_addendum.pdf.

130. Gregory Myers, "Pence Speaks with Community at Fair Oaks Farms," *Rensselaer Republi-can*, November 11, 2015, https://www.newsbug.info/rensselaer_republican/pence-speaks -with-community-at-fair-oaks-farms/article_2d089ef6-88d4-11e5-976e-ab74865a3d4c .html.

131. Maureen Groppe, "Fair Oaks Farms Wants to Make Ag Careers Exciting," *Indianapolis Star*, June 15, 2016, updated June 16, 2016, https://www.indystar.com/story/news /politics/2016/06/15/vilsack-hopes-indiana-farm-inspires-future-farmers/85943586/.

132. Consulting & Ancillary Services of Puerto Rico, joincaspr.com, mobile version, accessed June 2, 2021.

133. Jesse Barron, "How Puerto Rico Became the Newest Tax Haven for the Super Rich," *GQ*, September 18, 2018, https://www.gq.com/story/how-puerto-rico-became-tax-haven-for -super-rich.

134. *Lake States Dairy Center, Inc., v. Newton County Assessor*, Petition No. 56-003-08-2-8 -00001, Final Determination, September 14, 2009, https://www.in.gov/ibtr/files/Lake _States_Dairy_56-003-08-2-8-00001.pdf.

135. US Securities and Exchange Commission, "*Securities and Exchange Commission v. Michael J. McCloskey, Rance C. Miles, Luis E. Vallejo, and Daniel Harris*, Case No. 1:04CV01294," https://www.sec.gov/litigation/litreleases/lr-18819, August 3, 2004.

136. Charles, "Chasing a Dream"; "US Dairy Farmer Eager to Take Milk Products to China," *Global Times*, May 20, 2018, https://www.globaltimes.cn/page/201805/1103148.shtml.

137. US Department of Agriculture, "USDA Announces Details of Direct Assistance to Farm-ers through the Coronavirus Food Assistance Program," press release no. 0266.20, May 19, 2020, https://www.usda.gov/media/press-releases/2020/05/19/usda-announces-details -direct-assistance-farmers-through; David Yaffe-Bellany and Michael Corkery, "Dumped Milk, Smashed Eggs, Plowed Vegetables: Food Waste of the Pandemic," *New York Times*, April 11, 2020, https://www.nytimes.com/2020/04/11/business/coronavirus-destroying -food.html.

138. ProPublica, Tracking PPP, "Prairie's Edge Dairy Farms, LLC," accessed December 16, 2022, https://projects.propublica.org/coronavirus/bailouts/loans/prairie-s-edge-dairy -farms-llc-2376527201.

139. "Coca-Cola Scouting Northeast for Fairlife Plant Site"; Coca-Cola Company, "Raising Animal Welfare Standards across Our Supply Chain," press release, August 28, 2019, https://www.coca-colacompany.com/media-center/fair-oaks-farms.

140. Andrea Deckert, "Coca-Cola Chooses Webster Site for $650M Fairlife Production Facil-ity," *Rochester Business Journal*, May 9, 2023, https://rbj.net/2023/05/09/coca-cola -chooses-webster-site-for-650-million-fairlife-production-facility/.

Chapter 5: The Berry Barons

1. "Tenerife Airline Disaster," *Encyclopedia Britannica*, accessed September 20, 2022, https:// www.britannica.com/event/Tenerife-airline-disaster.

2. "The Collision at Tenerife," *New York Times*, April 3, 1977, https://nyti.ms/3OOvabW; "KLM Pilot in Collision Reportedly Didn't Hear Controller's 'Stand By,'" *New York Times*, April 9, 1977, https://nyti.ms/3EjffOa; Karl E. Weick, "The Vulnerable System: An Analy-sis of the Tenerife Air Disaster," *Journal of Management* 16, no. 3 (1990): 571–93, https:// doi.org/10.1177/014920639001600304.

3. "The Deadliest Plane Crash," *NOVA*, PBS, October 17, 2006, accessed January 29, 2023, https://www.pbs.org/wgbh/nova/planecrash/.

4. "Memorial Services Set for Plane Crash Victims," *Santa Cruz Sentinel*, March 30, 1977.

5. "Joseph Reiter and Glovie Reiter," obituary, *Santa Cruz Sentinel*, March 30, 1977.

6. Dana Goodyear, "How Driscoll's Reinvented the Strawberry," *New Yorker*, August 14, 2017, https://www.newyorker.com/magazine/2017/08/21/how-driscolls-reinvented-the -strawberry.

7. Dvera I. Saxton, *The Devil's Fruit: Farmworkers, Health, and Environmental Justice* (New Brunswick, NJ: Rutgers University Press, 2021), 57.

8. Goodyear, "How Driscoll's Reinvented the Strawberry."

9. David Karp, "For Raspberries, Ubiquity (at a Price)," *New York Times*, July 7, 2004, https://www.nytimes.com/2004/07/07/dining/for-raspberries-ubiquity-at-a-price.html.

10. Christina Babbitt, "How Driscoll's, The World's Largest Berry Company, Is Becoming a Leader in Water Conservation," Environmental Defense Fund, January 23, 2019, https://blogs.edf.org/growingreturns/2019/01/23/driscolls-berry-company-water-conservation/.

11. Pajaro Valley Historical Association, "Driscoll Strawberry Associate's, Inc.," July 14, 1993.

12. Goodyear, "How Driscoll's Reinvented the Strawberry."

13. Goodyear, "How Driscoll's Reinvented the Strawberry"; Allison Balogh, "The Rise and Fall of Monoculture Farming," *Horizon: The EU Research & Innovation Magazine*, December 13, 2021, https://ec.europa.eu/research-and-innovation/en/horizon-magazine/rise-and-fall -monoculture-farming.

14. Pat Bailey, "Public Strawberry Breeding Program Backgrounder: Frequently Asked Questions," University of California, Davis, May 8, 2017, https://www.ucdavis.edu/news /strawberry-breeding-program-backgrounder-frequently-asked-questions.

15. Goodyear, "How Driscoll's Reinvented the Strawberry."

16. Goodyear, "How Driscoll's Reinvented the Strawberry."

17. Goodyear, "How Driscoll's Reinvented the Strawberry."

18. Driscoll's, Inc., "Our Story: 1872–Now," accessed March 10, 2023, https://www.driscolls .com/about/heritage.

19. Driscoll's, "Our Story."

20. Jaclyn Kramer, "U.S. Fresh Strawberry Production Expands with Newer Varieties," US Department of Agriculture, Economic Research Service, May 19, 2021, https://www.ers .usda.gov/data-products/chart-gallery/gallery/chart-detail/?chartId=101156.

21. US Department of Agriculture, Bureau of Agricultural Economics, "Commercial Vegetables for Fresh Market, Revised Estimates, 1939–50," May 1953, 139, https://ageconsearch .umn.edu/record/153251/files/sb126.pdf?ln=en&withWatermark=1.

22. Naomi Klein, *No Logo: Taking Aim at the Brand Bullies* (New York: Picador, 1999).

23. Goodyear, "How Driscoll's Reinvented the Strawberry."

24. Douglas H. Constance, "The Southern Model of Broiler Production and Its Global Implications," *Culture & Agriculture* 30, nos. 1–2 (November 2008): 17–31, https://doi.org/10 .1111/j.1556-486X.2008.00004.x.

25. Rachel Luban, "Alleging Labor Abuses, U.S. and Mexican Workers Call for Boycott of Driscoll's Berries," *In These Times*, April 18, 2015, https://inthesetimes.com/article/alleging -labor-abuses-u-s-and-mexican-workers-call-for-boycott-of-driscoll.

26. Dune Lawrence, "How Driscoll's Is Hacking the Strawberry of the Future," *Bloomberg Businessweek*, July 29, 2015, https://www.bloomberg.com/news/features/2015-07-29/how -driscoll-s-is-hacking-the-strawberry-of-the-future#xj4y7vzkg.

27. Goodyear, "How Driscoll's Reinvented the Strawberry."

28. J. Miles Reiter, "Driscoll's Family Heritage—Pursuit of Flavor—Fresh Berries," YouTube video, 03:00, April 5, 2018, https://www.youtube.com/watch?v=VYSyPDgIIis.

29. Herbert Baum, *Quest for the Perfect Strawberry: A Case Study of the California Strawberry Commission and the Strawberry Industry; A Descriptive Model for Marketing Order Evaluation* (Lincoln, NE: iUniverse, 2005), 14.

30. City of Watsonville, California, "Economic Profile," accessed January 29, 2023, https://www.watsonville.gov/932/Economic-Profile.

31. Julie Guthman and Estelí Jiménez-Soto, "Socioeconomic Challenges of California Strawberry Production and Disease Resistant Cultivars," *Frontiers in Sustainable Food Systems,* sec. Agroecology and Ecosystem Services, 5, article 764743 (2021), https://doi.org/10.3389/fsufs.2021.764743.

32. Nathanael Johnson, "How Strawberry Farmers Got Themselves (and the Ozone Layer) Out of a Jam," Grist, September 10, 2019, https://grist.org/article/how-strawberry-farmers-got-themselves-and-the-ozone-layer-out-of-a-jam/.

33. U.S. Climate Data, "Climate Watsonville—California," accessed January 29, 2023, https://www.usclimatedata.com/climate/watsonville/california/united-states/usca1215.

34. Brianna Elliott, "19 Water-Rich Foods That Help You Stay Hydrated," Healthline, August 9, 2017, updated February 7, 2023, https://www.healthline.com/nutrition/19-hydrating-foods.

35. Justin T. Brandt et al., "Detection and Measurement of Land-Surface Deformation, Pajaro Valley, Santa Cruz and Monterey Counties, California, 2015–18," Open-File Report 2021-1101, US Department of the Interior, US Geological Survey, October 22, 2021, https://doi.org/10.3133/ofr20211101.

36. Debra Kahn, "State's Farmers Begin to Confront Their Ominous Groundwater Shortage," ClimateWire, March 6, 2015, https://www.eenews.net/articles/states-farmers-begin-to-confront-their-ominous-groundwater-shortage/.

37. Joshua Partlow, "As California's Wells Dry Up, Residents Rely on Bottled Water to Survive," *Washington Post,* November 14, 2022, https://www.washingtonpost.com/climate-environment/2022/11/14/california-drought-bottled-water/.

38. Kahn, "State's Farmers Begin to Confront."

39. Josh Harkinson, "Meet the California Couple Who Uses More Water than Every Home in Los Angeles Combined," *Mother Jones,* August 9, 2016, https://www.motherjones.com/environment/2016/08/lynda-stewart-resnick-california-water/; Sammy Roth, "In the California Desert, a Farm Baron Is Building a Water and Energy Empire," *Palm Springs Desert Sun,* August 1, 2018, https://www.desertsun.com/in-depth/tech/science/energy/2018/08/01/california-desert-farm-baron-builds-water-and-energy-empire/636894002/; "Desert Summary," *Encyclopedia Britannica,* accessed March 10, 2013, https://www.britannica.com/summary/desert.

40. Jeffrey Mount and Ellen Hanak, "Water Use in California," Public Policy Institute of California, PPIC Water Policy Center, May 2019, https://cwc.ca.gov/-/media/CWC-Website/Files/Documents/2019/06_June/June2019_Item_12_Attach_2_PPICFactSheets.pdf?la=en&hash=E233EA870DFB826F235B258177849300179E1B64.

41. Julia Lurie, "California's Almonds Suck as Much Water Annually as Los Angeles Uses in Three Years," *Mother Jones,* January 12, 2015, https://www.motherjones.com/environment/2015/01/almonds-nuts-crazy-stats-charts/.

42. Tom Philpott, *Perilous Bounty: The Looming Collapse of American Farming and How We Can Prevent It* (New York: Bloomsbury, 2020), 27.

43. Mark Arax, "A Kingdom from Dust," *California Sunday Magazine,* January 31, 2018, https://story.californiasunday.com/resnick-a-kingdom-from-dust/.

44. J. Miles Reiter, "Guest Commentary: Protecting Our Groundwater, and Our Future," *Santa Cruz Sentinel,* October 6, 2019, https://www.santacruzsentinel.com/2019/10/06/guest-commentary-protecting-our-groundwater-and-our-future/; Kahn, "State's Farmers Begin to Confront."

45. Timm Herdt, "Brown Signs Historic Laws to Regulate Groundwater Pumping," *Ventura*

County Star, September 16, 2014; US Department of the Interior, US Geological Survey, California Water Science Center, "Sustainable Groundwater Management," accessed March 20, 2023, https://www.usgs.gov/centers/california-water-science-center/science /sustainable-groundwater-management.

46. Community Water Dialogue of the Pajaro Valley, "About the CWD," accessed March 10, 2023, http://www.communitywaterdialogue.org/about-the-cwd.

47. Babbitt, "How Driscoll's."

48. Susie Cagle, "Everything You Need to Know about California's Historic Water Law," *Guardian*, February 27, 2020, https://www.theguardian.com/environment/2020/feb/27 /california-groundwater-sgma-law-what-does-it-mean; Nick Bowlin, "How 'Sustainable' Is California's Groundwater Sustainability Act?," *High Country News*, May 10, 2021, https://www.hcn.org/issues/53.6/south-water-how-sustainable-is-californias-groundwater -sustainability-act.

49. Sam Bloch, "California Must Abandon 535,000 Acres of Prized Farmland to Meet Water Conservation Goals," The Counter, February 28, 2019, https://thecounter.org/california -san-joaquin-valley-farmland-groundwater-aquifer-drought/.

50. California Department of Food and Agriculture, "California Agricultural Production Statistics," accessed January 29, 2023, https://www.cdfa.ca.gov/statistics/; Guthman and Jiménez-Soto, "Socioeconomic Challenges."

51. Liza Gross, "Farmworkers at Driscoll's Supplier Demand Fair Pay, Safe Conditions amid Pandemic," *FERN's Ag Insider*, May 28, 2020, https://thefern.org/ag_insider/farmworkers -at-driscolls-supplier-demand-fair-pay-safe-conditions-amid-pandemic/.

52. Gross, "Farmworkers at Driscoll's Supplier Demand Fair Pay."

53. Nick Martin, "American Farming Runs on Exploitation," *New Republic*, October 17, 2019, https://newrepublic.com/article/155403/american-farming-runs-exploitation.

54. James Gilbert Cassedy, "African Americans and the American Labor Movement," *Federal Records and African American History* 29, no. 2 (Summer 1997), https://www.archives.gov /publications/prologue/1997/summer/american-labor-movement.html.

55. Don Villarejo et al., "The Health of California's Immigrant Hired Farmworkers," *American Journal of Industrial Medicine* 53, no. 4 (April 2010): 387–97, https://doi.org/10.1002 /ajim.20796.

56. Bracero History Archive, accessed January 29, 2023, https://braceroarchive.org/.

57. "Ten Thousand Farm Workers on Strike in California," *El Malcriado*, September 1, 1970; Carey Goldberg, "The Battle of the Strawberry Fields," *New York Times*, July 3, 1996, https://nyti.ms/47VHUpW.

58. Frank Bardacke, *Trampling Out the Vintage: Cesar Chavez and the Two Souls of the United Farm Workers* (London: Verso, 2011).

59. Eric Schlosser, "Testimony: Ending Abuses and Improving Working Conditions for Tomato Workers," US Senate Committee on Health, Education, Labor and Pensions, April 15, 2008, https://www.help.senate.gov/hearings/ending-abuses-and-improving-working -conditions-for-tomato-workers.

60. Martin, "American Farming Runs on Exploitation."

61. Philip Martin, "The H-2A Farm Guestworker Program Is Expanding Rapidly," Economic Policy Institute, *Working Economics Blog*, April 13, 2017, https://www.epi.org/blog/h-2a -farm-guestworker-program-expanding-rapidly/.

62. Kyd D. Brenner, "NAFTA and U.S. Agriculture," *Environmental Health Perspectives* 101, no. 7 (December 1993): 565, https://doi.org/10.1289/ehp.93101565; Elizabeth Becker, "U.S. Corn Subsidies Said to Damage Mexico," *New York Times*, August 27, 2003, https:// www.nytimes.com/2003/08/27/business/us-corn-subsidies-said-to-damage-mexico.html;

Lesley Ahmed, "U.S. Corn Exports to Mexico and the North American Free Trade Agreement," US International Trade Commission, Office of Industries, May 2018, https://www.usitc.gov/publications/332/working_papers/ahmed.htm.

63. Alison Hope Alkon and Julie Guthman, eds., *The New Food Activism: Opposition, Cooperation, and Collective Action* (Oakland: University of California Press, 2017), 293.

64. Becker, "U.S. Corn Subsidies Said to Damage Mexico"; Oxfam International, "Dumping without Borders: How US Agricultural Policies Are Destroying the Livelihoods of Mexican Corn Farmers," Oxfam briefing paper, August 2003, https://oxfamilibrary.openrepository.com/bitstream/10546/114471/1/bp50-dumping-without-borders-010803-en.pdf.

65. Mark Weisbrot, Stephan Lefebvre, and Joseph Sammut, "Did NAFTA Help Mexico? An Assessment after 20 Years," Center for Economic and Policy Research, February 2014, https://cepr.net/documents/nafta-20-years-2014-02.pdf.

66. Eric Schlosser, "In the Strawberry Fields," *Atlantic*, November 1, 1995, https://www.theatlantic.com/magazine/archive/1995/11/in-the-strawberry-fields/305754/.

67. Rachel Nolan, "A Translation Crisis at the Border," *New Yorker*, December 30, 2019, https://www.newyorker.com/magazine/2020/01/06/a-translation-crisis-at-the-border.

68. Jelena Jezdimirovic, "California Farmers Face Labor Drought," Public Policy Institute of California, blog post, May 23, 2017, https://www.ppic.org/blog/california-farmers-face-labor-drought/.

69. Gross, "Farmworkers at Driscoll's Supplier Demand Fair Pay."

70. Schlosser, "In the Strawberry Fields."

71. Mary Bauer and Meredith Stewart, "Close to Slavery: Guestworker Programs in the United States," Southern Poverty Law Center, February 19, 2013, https://www.splcenter.org/20130218/close-slavery-guestworker-programs-united-states.

72. US Department of Agriculture, Economic Research Service, "Farm Labor," March 15, 2022, https://web.archive.org/web/20220317170154/https://www.ers.usda.gov/topics/farm-economy/farm-labor/; Marcelo Castillo, Philip Martin, and Zachariah Rutledge, "The H-2A Temporary Agricultural Worker Program in 2020," US Department of Agriculture, Economic Research Service, Economic Information Bulletin No. EIB-238, August 2022, https://www.ers.usda.gov/publications/pub-details/?pubid=104605.

73. Bauer and Stewart, "Close to Slavery."

74. Philip L. Martin, Suzanne Vaupel, and Daniel Egan, "Farmworker Unions: Status and Wage Impacts," *California Agriculture* (July–August 1986): 11–13, https://hilgardia.ucanr.edu/fileaccess.cfm?article=171797&p=QPVEWQ; Melissa Montalvo and Nigel Duara, "In Familiar Refrain, United Farm Workers Grapples with How to Grow," Cal Matters, January 18, 2022, https://calmatters.org/projects/united-farm-workers-union/.

75. US Bureau of Labor Statistics, "Occupational Employment and Wages, May 2022: 45-2092 Farmworkers and Laborers, Crop, Nursery, and Greenhouse," https://www.bls.gov/oes/current/oes452092.htm.

76. Linda Geist, "Farming: The Most Dangerous Job in the U.S.," University of Missouri Extension, September 19, 2022, https://extension.missouri.edu/news/farming-the-most-dangerous-job-in-the-u.s.-5785.

77. Matt McConnell, "'When We're Dead and Buried, Our Bones Will Keep Hurting': Workers' Rights under Threat in US Meat and Poultry Plants," Human Rights Watch, September 4, 2019, https://www.hrw.org/report/2019/09/04/when-were-dead-and-buried-our-bones-will-keep-hurting/workers-rights-under-threat.

78. Bauer and Stewart, "Close to Slavery."

79. David Bacon, "The Pacific Coast Farm-Worker Rebellion," *Nation*, August 28, 2015.

80. Malea Martin, "Rancho Laguna Farms Workers Allegedly Faced Retaliation for Striking," *Santa Maria Sun*, June 3, 2020, https://www.santamariasun.com/news/rancho-laguna-farms-workers-allegedly-faced-retaliation-for-striking-14795074.

81. Driscoll's, Inc., "Rancho Laguna Farms Update," accessed January 30, 2023, https://www.driscolls.com/Rancho-Laguna-Farms-Update.

82. Gerald F. Davis, *Managed by the Markets: How Finance Re-shaped America* (Oxford: Oxford University Press, 2009), 94.

83. Tony Nuñez, "The Fight against Pesticides in the Pajaro Valley," *Good Times* (Santa Cruz, CA), October 25, 2022, https://www.goodtimes.sc/how-pesticides-are-impacting-the-pajaro-valley/.

84. Bernice Yeung, Kendall Taggart, and Andrew Donohue, "California's Strawberry Industry Is Hooked on Dangerous Pesticides," *Guardian*, November 10, 2014, https://www.theguardian.com/us-news/2014/nov/10/-sp-california-strawberry-industry-pesticides.

85. Yeung, Taggart, and Donohue, "California's Strawberry Industry."

86. Dan Charles, "The Secret Life of California's World-Class Strawberries," *The Salt / All Things Considered*, NPR, May 17, 2012, https://www.npr.org/sections/thesalt/2012/05/17/152522900/the-secret-life-of-californias-world-class-strawberries.

87. Charles, "Secret Life of California's World-Class Strawberries."

88. Goodyear, "How Driscoll's Reinvented the Strawberry."

89. Johnson, "How Strawberry Farmers Got Themselves Out of a Jam."

90. Environmental Working Group, "Pesticides + Poison Gases = Cheap, Year-Round Strawberries," March 20, 2019, https://www.ewg.org/foodnews/strawberries.php.

91. Daryl Kelley, "Teachers Protest Use of Pesticides Near Schools," *Los Angeles Times*, May 3, 1998; Nathan Rice, "The Fight over a Much-Needed Pesticide: Methyl Iodide," *High Country News*, July 25, 2011, https://www.hcn.org/issues/43.12/the-fight-over-a-much-needed-pesticide-methyl-iodide.

92. Mark Conley, "Pressure Building on Pesticides, Driscoll's Says It Will Consider Organic-Only by Schools," Lookout Santa Cruz, October 3, 2022, https://lookout.co/santacruz/civic-life/story/2022-10-03/driscolls-berries-organic-pesticides-watsonville-reiter-farming.

93. Robert B. Gunier et al., "Residential Proximity to Agricultural Fumigant Use and IQ, Attention and Hyperactivity in 7-Year-Old Children," *Environmental Research* 158 (October 2017): 358–65, https://doi.org/10.1016/j.envres.2017.06.036; California Department of Pesticide Regulation, "Pesticide Drift," accessed January 29, 2023.

94. US Environmental Protection Agency, How's My Waterway?, "Watsonville Slough Frontal," accessed January 29, 2023, https://mywaterway.epa.gov/community/watsonville%20slough%20frontal/overview.

95. LexisNexis Public Records, accessed December 29, 2021.

96. Mark Arax, *The Dreamt Land: Chasing Water and Dust across California* (New York: Vintage Books, 2019), 302, 300; Jonathan Griffin, "Stewart and Lynda Resnick," *Apollo*, March 2012.

97. Philpott, *Perilous Bounty*, 63, 66.

98. Philpott, *Perilous Bounty*, 21.

99. Babbitt, "How Driscoll's."

100. Richard Marosi, "Product of Mexico," *Los Angeles Times*, December 7, 2014, https://graphics.latimes.com/product-of-mexico-camps/; Kate Linthicum, "Inside the Bloody Cartel War for Mexico's Multibillion-Dollar Avocado Industry," *Los Angeles Times*, November 21, 2019, https://www.latimes.com/world-nation/story/2019-11-20/mexico-cartel-violence-avocados.

101. Dan Charles, "Why Ditching NAFTA Could Hurt America's Farmers More than Mexico's," *The Salt / All Things Considered*, NPR, February 16, 2017, https://www.npr.org/sections/thesalt/2017/02/16/515380213/why-ditching-nafta-could-hurt-americas-farmers-more-than-mexicos.

102. Felicity Barringer, "Strawberry Fields Forever? Baja Turning to Seawater to Grow Lucrative Crop," *Stanford Earth Matters*, July 13, 2018, https://earth.stanford.edu/news/strawberry-fields-forever-baja-turning-seawater-grow-lucrative-crop.

103. Olmo Bastida, "Mexican Berry Production in Recent Years," Produce Pay, December 17, 2021, https://producepay.com/blog/mexican-berry-production-analysis/.

104. Christian Zlolniski, *Made in Baja: The Lives of Farmworkers and Growers behind Mexico's Transnational Agricultural Boom* (Oakland: University of California Press, 2019), 52, 106.

105. Marco Campos, "Mexico Becomes World's Leading Strawberry Exporter," *Produce Reporter*, May 7, 2021, https://www.producebluebook.com/2021/05/07/mexico-becomes-worlds-leading-strawberry-exporter/.

106. Barringer, "Strawberry Fields Forever?; Matthew Cappucci, "Desert Downpours: Rare Summer Rains Soaked Death Valley and Parts of California on Monday," *Washington Post*, July 27, 2021, https://www.washingtonpost.com/weather/2021/07/27/rain-monsoon-death-valley-california/.

107. Barringer, "Strawberry Fields Forever?"

108. Zlolniski, *Made in Baja*, 192.

109. Barringer, "Strawberry Fields Forever?"

110. Luban, "Alleging Labor Abuses."

111. Richard Marosi, "Farmworkers Aim at Big Target; Baja Labor Leaders Criticize Global Berry Brand Driscoll's Despite Its Socially Responsible Image," *Los Angeles Times*, April 11, 2015.

112. Josh Rushing, "Strawberry Pickers Strain to See Fruits of Their Labor, Even after Strike," Al Jazeera America, June 21, 2015, http://america.aljazeera.com/articles/2015/6/21/strawberry-pickers-strain-to-see-fruits-of-their-labor.html.

113. Luban, "Alleging Labor Abuses."

114. "The Future of Food—Ceres Conference 2015," YouTube video, 51:00, June 23, 2015, https://www.youtube.com/watch?v=U0SexbAp2ZE.

115. Beatriz Ramalho da Silva and Corinne Redfern, "Workers Paid Less than Minimum Wage to Pick Berries Destined for UK Supermarkets," *Guardian*, January 25, 2022, https://www.theguardian.com/global-development/2022/jan/25/workers-paid-less-than-minimum-wage-to-pick-berries-allegedly-sold-in-uk-supermarkets.

116. Eduardo Porter, "Illegal Immigration Is Down, Changing the Face of California Farms," *New York Times*, May 28, 2022, https://www.nytimes.com/2022/05/28/business/economy/immigration-california-farm-labor.html.

117. Tim Johnson, "Mexico Becomes a Berry Powerhouse," *Mercury News* (San Jose, CA), March 13, 2015, https://www.mercurynews.com/2015/03/13/mexico-becomes-a-berry-powerhouse/; US Department of Agriculture, Economic Research Service, "Data by Commodity—Imports and Exports: Strawberries: U.S. Imports by Value ($1,000)," accessed February 21, 2023, https://data.ers.usda.gov/reports.aspx?programArea=fruit&top=5&HardCopy=True&RowsPerPage=25&groupName=Noncitrus&commodityName=Apples&ID=17851.

118. Renée Johnson, "Seasonal Fruit and Vegetable Competition in U.S.-Mexico Trade," Library of Congress, Congressional Research Service, February 22, 2023, https://crsreports.congress.gov/product/pdf/if/if11701.

119. Sophia Huang and Fred Gale, "China's Rising Profile in the Global Market for Fruits and Vegetables," *Amber Waves*, US Department of Agriculture, Economic Research Service, April 1, 2006, https://www.ers.usda.gov/amber-waves/2006/april/data-feature/; Kelsey Timmerman, "Follow Your Labels: Your Place in the Global Consumer Chain," *Christian Science Monitor*, July 21, 2013, https://www.csmonitor.com/World/Global-Issues/2013/0721/Follow-your-labels-Your-place-in-the-global-consumer-chain; Ephrat Livni, "The US War on Mexican Tomatoes Has Begun and Consumers Will Pay," Quartz, May 8, 2019, https://qz.com/1614050/the-us-war-on-mexican-tomatoes-has-begun-and-consumers-will-pay.

120. "The Fish on My Plate," *Frontline*, PBS, 2017, https://www.pbs.org/wgbh/frontline/documentary/the-fish-on-my-plate/; Craig A. Morris, "A Tale of a Fish from Two Countries," US Department of Agriculture, December 5, 2016, https://www.usda.gov/media/blog/2016/12/05/tale-fish-two-countries; Heather Haddon and Jesse Newman, "Fish Caught in America, Processed in China Get Trapped by Trade Dispute," *Wall Street Journal*, August 9, 2018, https://www.wsj.com/articles/u-s-seafood-industry-vulnerable-to-tariffs-aimed-at-china-1533812400.

121. Philpott, *Perilous Bounty*, 59; US Department of Agriculture, National Agricultural Statistics Service, "Census of Agriculture, 2017 Census Volume 1, Chapter 1: State Level Data, California, Table 36. Vegetables, Potatoes, and Melons Harvested for Sale: 2017 and 2012," https://www.nass.usda.gov/Publications/AgCensus/2017/Full_Report/Volume_1,_Chapter_1_State_Level/California/; US Department of Agriculture, National Agricultural Statistics Service, "Census of Agriculture, 2017 Census Volume 1, Chapter 1: State Level Data, California, Table 37. Specified Fruits and Nuts by Acres: 2017 and 2012," https://www.nass.usda.gov/Publications/AgCensus/2017/Full_Report/Volume_1,_Chapter_1_State_Level/California/.

122. Mengyu Li et al., "Global Food-Miles Account for Nearly 20% of Total Food-Systems Emissions," *Nature Food* 3 (2022): 445–53, https://www.nature.com/articles/s43016-022-00531-w.

123. Melissa Etehad, "Amid Thomas Fire, Farmworkers Weather Risks in Oxnard's Strawberry Fields," *Los Angeles Times*, December 23, 2017, https://www.latimes.com/business/la-me-fire-farmworkers-20171223-story.html; Liza Gross, "Fires Fuel New Risks to California Farmworkers," Inside Climate News, September 21, 2021, https://insideclimatenews.org/news/21092021/wildfires-california-farmworkers-smoke-health/.

124. "Driscoll's Acquires Berry Gardens Limited," Fresh Fruit Portal, June 27, 2022, https://www.freshfruitportal.com/news/2022/06/27/driscolls-acquires-berry-gardens-limited/; "Driscoll's Acquires Haygrove Africa," Fresh Fruit Portal, July 12, 2022, https://www.freshfruitportal.com/news/2022/07/12/driscolls-acquires-haygrove-africa/.

125. Zheng Yiran, "US Berry Giant Eyes Sweet Mkt Pickings," *China Daily*, May 12, 2023, https://www.chinadaily.com.cn/a/202305/12/WS645d77b2a310b6054fad2840.html.

126. Brian D. Sparks, "Virginia Will Soon Be Home to World's Largest Vertical Farm," *Greenhouse Grower*, September 14, 2022, https://www.greenhousegrower.com/crops/virginia-will-soon-be-home-to-worlds-largest-vertical-farm/.

Chapter 6: The Slaughter Barons

1. Chloe Sorvino, *Raw Deal: Hidden Corruption, Corporate Greed, and the Fight for the Future of Meat* (New York: Atria Books, 2022), 60–61.

2. Sorvino, *Raw Deal*.

3. Simon Romero, "Scandal in Brazil Raises Fear of Turmoil's Return," *New York Times*, May 19, 2017, https://www.nytimes.com/2017/05/19/world/americas/brazil-michel-temer.html.

4. Jenny Gonzales, "Brazil Agribusiness Company Accuses Ally Temer in Secret Bribe Taping," *Mongabay*, May 23, 2017, https://news.mongabay.com/2017/05/brazil-agribusiness-company-accuses-ally-temer-in-secret-bribe-taping/.

5. Dom Phillips, "Brazil President Endorsed Businessman's Bribes in Secret Tape, Newspaper Says," *New York Times*, May 17, 2017, https://www.nytimes.com/2017/05/17/world/americas/brazil-michel-temer-joesley-batista-corruption.html.

6. Gabriel Shinohara and Rachel Gamarski, "Ministry Torched as Brazil's Temer Faces Violence, Party Mutiny," Bloomberg, May 24, 2017, https://www.bloomberg.com/politics/articles/2017-05-24/ministry-torched-as-brazil-s-temer-faces-violence-party-mutiny#x j4y7vzkg; Natalia Cardenas, "Michel Temer," *Encyclopedia Britannica*, accessed April 14, 2023, https://www.britannica.com/biography/Michel-Temer.

7. Marina Lopes, "Former Brazil President Michel Temer Arrested on Corruption Charges," *Washington Post*, March 21, 2019, https://www.washingtonpost.com/world/the_americas/former-brazil-president-michel-temer-arrested-on-corruption-charges/2019/03/21/74e9 a92a-4be7-11e9-8cfc-2c5d0999c21e_story.html.

8. Tom Phillips and Dom Phillips, "Jair Bolsonaro Declared Brazil's Next President," *Guardian*, October 29, 2018, https://www.theguardian.com/world/2018/oct/28/jair-bolsonaro-wins-brazil-presidential-election.

9. Jessica Brice and Tatiana Freitas, "Brazil's Batista Clan: A Short Guide to an Empire Built on Beef," Bloomberg, May 18, 2017, https://www.bloomberg.com/news/articles/2017-05-18/brazil-s-batista-clan-a-short-guide-to-an-empire-built-on-beef#xj4y7vzkg; US Securities and Exchange Commission, "In the Matter of J&F Investimentos, S.A., JBS, S.A. Joesley Batista, Wesley Batista," Administrative Proceeding File No. 3-20124, October 14, 2020, https://www.sec.gov/whistleblower/award-claim/award-claim-2020-131.

10. "Brazil's Fabulous Batista Boys," *Economist*, May 25, 2017, https://www.economist.com/the-americas/2017/05/25/brazils-fabulous-batista-boys.

11. Dom Philips, "The Swashbuckling Meat Tycoons Who Nearly Brought Down a Government," *Guardian*, July 2, 2019, https://www.theguardian.com/environment/2019/jul/02/swashbuckling-meat-tycoons-nearly-brought-down-a-government-brazil; US Department of Justice, Office of Public Affairs, "J&F Investimentos S.A. Pleads Guilty and Agrees to Pay over $256 Million to Resolve Criminal Foreign Bribery Case," October 14, 2020, press release, https://www.justice.gov/opa/pr/jf-investimentos-sa-pleads-guilty-and-agrees-pay-over-256-million-resolve-criminal-foreign; Sorvino, *Raw Deal*, 73.

12. US Department of Justice, Office of Public Affairs, "J&F Investimentos S.A. Pleads Guilty."

13. Richard Vanderford, "Brazil's JBS Shakes Up Compliance Efforts," *Wall Street Journal*, August 16, 2022, https://www.wsj.com/articles/brazils-jbs-shakes-up-compliance-efforts-11660688586.

14. "Brazil Tycoon Wesley Batista Held for 'Insider Trading,'" BBC News, September 13, 2017, https://www.bbc.com/news/world-latin-america-41255817; Andres Schipani and Joe Leahy, "Brazil Prosecutors Charge JBS Owners with Insider Trading," *Financial Times*, October 10, 2017.

15. JBS Foods, "Investors," accessed March 14, 2023, https://jbsfoodsgroup.com/investors.

16. Felipe Marques and James Attwood, "Brazil's Batista Brothers Are out of Jail and Worth $6 Billion," Bloomberg News, July 15, 2021, https://www.bloomberg.com/news/articles/2021-07-15/brazil-s-batista-brothers-are-out-of-jail-and-worth-6-billion#xj4y7vzkg.

17. JBS Foods, "United States," accessed March 14, 2023, https://jbsfoodsgroup.com/locations/united-states; United Nations Population Fund, "World Population Dashboard: Total Population in Millions, 2022," accessed March 14, 2023.

18. "Can JBS Remain the World's Biggest Food Producer?," *Economist*, August 18, 2022,

https://www.economist.com/business/2022/08/18/can-jbs-remain-the-worlds-biggest
-food-producer; JBS, "Our History," accessed April 24, 2023, https://jbs.com.br/en/about
/our-history/.

19. JBS, "Our History."

20. Sorvino, *Raw Deal*, 63.

21. Jacob Bunge and David Kesmodel, "For Brazilian Beef Duo behind Pilgrim's Pride, a Swift Rise," *Wall Street Journal*, June 4, 2014, https://www.wsj.com/articles/DJFDBR002014 0604ea64djzba.

22. Raquel Landim, *Why Not* (Rio de Janeiro: Intrínseca, 2019).

23. Emilie Rusch, "Greeley Meatpacker JBS Eyes Bigger Role in Consumer Beef Markets," *Denver Post*, June 23, 2015, https://www.denverpost.com/2015/06/23/greeley-meatpacker -jbs-eyes-bigger-role-in-consumer-beef-markets/.

24. Peter S. Goodman, "Record Beef Prices, but Ranchers Aren't Cashing In," *New York Times*, December 27, 2021, https://www.nytimes.com/2021/12/27/business/beef-prices-cattle -ranchers.html.

25. Sorvino, *Raw Deal*, 62; US Department of Justice, Office of Public Affairs, "J&F Investimentos S.A. Pleads Guilty"; Luciana Magalhaes, Samantha Pearson, and Jacob Bunge, "Meat Giant JBS's Owner Settles U.S. Corruption Charges," *Wall Street Journal*, October 14, 2020, https://www.wsj.com/articles/meat-giant-jbss-owner-settles-u-s-corruption -charges-11602707950; "Brazil Court Suspends Part of Leniency Deal for JBS Holding Firm," Reuters, September 11, 2017 https://www.reuters.com/article/us-brazil-corruption -jbs-j-f-idUSKCN1BM2NL.

26. Philip H. Howard, "Corporate Concentration in Global Meat Processing: The Role of Feed and Finance Subsidies," in *Global Meat: Social and Environmental Consequences of the Expanding Meat Industry*, edited by Bill Winders and Elizabeth Ransom, 31–53 (Cambridge, MA: MIT Press, 2019); "Moy Park: JBS Buys NI-Based Poultry Company," BBC News, June 22, 2015, https://www.bbc.com/news/uk-northern-ireland-33223231.

27. David E. Bell, "JBS," Harvard Business School Case Study 515-066, December 12, 2014, https://store.hbr.org/product/jbs/515066?sku=515066-PDF-ENG.

28. JBS, "Institutional Presentation: Including 1Q21 Results," https://api.mziq.com/mzfile manager/v2/d/043a77e1-0127-4502-bc5b-21427b991b22/71ac5d61-306b-fe12-485e -7079041bb4ae?origin=1.

29. "Can JBS Remain the World's Biggest Food Producer?"

30. Sorvino, *Raw Deal*, 63.

31. "Brazil's Fabulous Batista Boys."

32. US Securities and Exchange Commission, "SEC Charges Brazilian Meat Producers with FCPA Violations," press release, October 14, 2020, https://www.sec.gov/news/press -release/2020-254; H. Claire Brown, "Pilgrim's Pride Agrees to $110 Million Settlement on Price-Fixing Charges after Executives Indicted," The Counter, October 14, 2020, https://thecounter.org/pilgrims-pride-settlement-price-fixing-department-of-justice/.

33. "Brazil's JBS Beefs Up with Swift Deal, Report Says," *New York Times*, May 29, 2007, https://archive.nytimes.com/dealbook.nytimes.com/2007/05/29/brazils-jbs-beefs-up-with -swift-deal-report-says/.

34. Keren Blankfeld Taqqu, "JBS: The Story behind the World's Biggest Meat Producer," *Forbes*, April 21, 2011, https://www.forbes.com/sites/kerenblankfeld/2011/04/21/jbs-the -story-behind-the-worlds-biggest-meat-producer/?sh=510b4d017e82.

35. "JBS Increasing Its Presence in Greeley with Campus Purchase, Expansion," *Greeley (CO) Tribune*, October 24, 2010, https://www.greeleytribune.com/2010/10/24/jbs-increasing -its-presence-in-greeley-with-campus-purchase-expansion/.

36. Perry Swanson, "The Company," *Greeley (CO) Tribune*, November 22, 2002, https://www
.greeleytribune.com/2002/11/22/the-company/.

37. "Company News: Conagra Deal for Monfort," *New York Times*, March 6, 1987, https://
nyti.ms/3Eg7DvO.

38. "Brazil's JBS to Buy U.S. Beef Company," Reuters, March 4, 2008, https://www.reuters
.com/article/us-brazil-jbs-idUSN0454263520080305; Inae Riveras and Bob Burgdorfer,
"JBS Says U.S. Justice Cleared Pilgrim's Takeover," Reuters, October 14, 2009, https://
www.reuters.com/article/us-jbs-pilgrims-idUSTRE59D5ZP20091014.

39. "Justice Department May Have Beef with JBS Deals," *New York Times*, March 7, 2008,
https://archive.nytimes.com/dealbook.nytimes.com/2008/03/07/justice-department-may
-have-beef-with-jbs-deals/.

40. Associated Press, "Regulators Challenge Merger of Beef Packers," *New York Times*, October
20, 2008, https://www.nytimes.com/2008/10/21/business/21beef.html.

41. "JBS-National Beef Merger Is Ended," *New York Times*, February 20, 2009, https://archive
.nytimes.com/dealbook.nytimes.com/2009/02/20/jbs-national-beef-merger-is-ended/;
Renée Johnson, "Recent Acquisitions of U.S. Meat Companies," Library of Congress,
Congressional Research Service, March 10, 2009, https://nationalaglawcenter.org/wp
-content/uploads/assets/crs/RS22980.pdf.

42. "JBS Seals Deal for XL's Two U.S. Beef Plants," AgCanada, April 5, 2013, https://www
.agcanada.com/daily/jbs-seals-deal-for-xls-two-u-s-beef-plants.

43. "JBS to Purchase U.S. Cargill Pork Assets for $1.45 Billion," Reuters, July 1, 2015, https://
www.reuters.com/article/us-jbs-m-a-cargill-idUKKCN0PB63720150701.

44. James M. MacDonald et al., "Consolidation in U.S. Meatpacking," US Department of
Agriculture, Economic Research Service, Report No. 785, February 2000, https://www.ers
.usda.gov/webdocs/publications/41108/18011_aer785_1_.pdf.

45. "Explainer: How Four Big Companies Control the U.S. Beef Industry," Reuters, June 17,
2021, https://www.reuters.com/business/how-four-big-companies-control-us-beef-industry
-2021-06-17/.

46. Grass Run Farms, "Grass Fed Beef for Retail," accessed March 14, 2023, https://grassrun
farms.com/grass-fed-beef-for-retail/.

47. Just Bare, "Our Promise," accessed March 14, 2023, https://www.justbarefoods.com
/about-us/.

48. Austin Frerick and Charlie Mitchell, "Multinational Meat Farms Could Be Making Us
Sick," *American Conservative*, April 21, 2020, https://www.theamericanconservative.com
/multinational-meat-companies-could-be-making-us-sick/.

49. Frerick and Mitchell, "Multinational Meat Farms."

50. Goodman, "Record Beef Prices."

51. Bill Bullard, "Chronically Besieged: The U.S. Live Cattle Industry," presentation delivered
at Yale Law School's Big Ag & Antitrust Conference, January 16, 2021, https://www.r
-calfusa.com/wp-content/uploads/2021/01/210116-Chronically-Beseiged-The-U.S.-Live
-Cattle-Industry-Final.pdf.

52. US Department of Agriculture, "2012 Annual Report: Packers and Stockyards Program,"
March 2013, https://ams.prod.usda.gov/sites/default/files/media/2012_psp_annual
_report.pdf.

53. Bullard, "Chronically Besieged," 20.

54. US Senate, "S.4647: Cattle Market Transparency Act of 2020," introduced September 22,
2020, https://www.congress.gov/bill/116th-congress/senate-bill/4647; US Senate, "S.543:
Cattle Market Transparency Act of 2021," introduced March 2, 2021, https://www

.congress.gov/bill/117th-congress/senate-bill/543; US Senate, "S.228: Cattle Price Discovery and Transparency Act of 2023," introduced February 2, 2023, https://www.congress.gov/bill/118th-congress/senate-bill/228; Senator Chuck Grassley, "Grassley, Colleagues Introduce Bipartisan Bill to Increase Transparency in Cattle Pricing," press release, May 12, 2020, https://www.grassley.senate.gov/news/news-releases/grassley-colleagues-introduce-bipartisan-bill-increase-transparency-cattle.

55. Goodman, "Record Beef Prices."

56. US Department of Justice, Office of Public Affairs, "One of the Nation's Largest Chicken Producers Pleads Guilty to Price Fixing and Is Sentenced to a $107 Million Criminal Fine," press release, February 23, 2021, https://www.justice.gov/opa/pr/one-nation-s-largest-chicken-producers-pleads-guilty-price-fixing-and-sentenced-107-million.

57. Eshe Nelson and Carlos Tejada, "Pilgrim's Pride to Pay $110 Million to Settle Charges of Fixing Chicken Prices," *New York Times*, October 14, 2020, https://www.nytimes.com/2020/10/14/business/pilgrims-pride-price-fixing.html.

58. Jacob Bunge and Brent Kendall, "Pilgrim's Pride Reaches Plea Deal with Justice Department on Chicken Price-Fixing Allegations," *Wall Street Journal*, October 14, 2020, https://www.wsj.com/articles/pilgrim-s-pride-reaches-plea-agreement-with-justice-department-on-chicken-price-fixing-allegations-11602649655.

59. Matthew Sedacca, "JBS Agrees to Pay Beef Wholesalers $52.5 Million in Latest Price-Fixing Settlement," *The Counter*, February 4, 2022, https://thecounter.org/jbs-price-fixing-settlement-meatpackers-52-million-antitrust/.

60. Austin Frerick, "Rise of Majority-Minority Districts in Rural Iowa: How Changes in Meatpacking Impacted Rural Schooling" (thesis, Grinnell College, August 2011).

61. Grant Gerlock, "We Don't Know How Many Workers Are Injured at Slaughterhouses. Here's Why," *The Salt*, NPR, May 25, 2016, https://www.npr.org/sections/thesalt/2016/05/25/479509221/we-dont-know-how-many-workers-are-injured-at-slaughterhouses-heres-why.

62. Austin Frerick, "Big Meat, Small Towns: The Meatpacking Industry's Shift to Rural America and the Reemergence of Company Towns" (thesis, Grinnell College, May 2012).

63. Upton Sinclair, *The Jungle* (New York: Doubleday, 1906).

64. Deborah Blum, *The Poison Squad: One Chemist's Single-Minded Crusade for Food Safety at the Turn of the Twentieth Century* (New York: Penguin Books, 2019), 143; Edwin McDowell, "Sinclair's Jungle with All Muck Restored," *New York Times*, August 22, 1988, https://nyti.ms/3qVOSuz.

65. Daniel E. Slotnik, "Upton Sinclair, Whose Muckraking Changed the Meat Industry," *New York Times*, June 30, 2016, https://www.nytimes.com/interactive/projects/cp/obituaries/archives/upton-sinclair-meat-industry.

66. Slotnik, "Upton Sinclair."

67. Swift & Co. v. United States, 196 U.S. 375 (1905).

68. Eric Schlosser, "Hog Hell," *Nation*, August 28, 2006, https://www.thenation.com/article/archive/hog-hell/; Rick Halpern, "Packinghouse Unions," Electronic Encyclopedia of Chicago, accessed April 24, 2023, http://www.encyclopedia.chicagohistory.org/pages/943.html.

69. "The Union Stockyards: 'A Story of American Capitalism,'" WTTW-PBS Chicago, accessed March 14, 2023, https://interactive.wttw.com/chicago-stories/union-stockyards/the-union-stockyards-a-story-of-american-capitalism.

70. Schlosser, "Hog Hell."

71. US Department of Labor, Bureau of Labor Statistics, "Collective Bargaining: Meat-

Packing Industry," Bulletin No. 1063, 1952, https://fraser.stlouisfed.org/files/docs
/publications/bls/bls_1063_1952.pdf.

72. Wilson J. Warren, *Tied to the Great Packing Machine: The Midwest and Meatpacking* (Iowa City: University of Iowa Press, 2006), 17–28.

73. James Cook, "Those Simple Barefoot Boys from Iowa Beef," *Forbes*, June 22, 1981.

74. Michael J. Broadway, "From City to Countryside: Recent Changes in the Structure and Location of the Meat- and Fish-Processing Industries" in *Any Way You Cut It: Meat Processing and Small-Town America*, edited by Donald D. Stull, Michael J. Broadway, and David Griffith, 18, 26 (Lawrence: University Press of Kansas, 1995).

75. Julie Young, "Monopsony: Definition, Causes, Objections, and Example," Investopedia, February 3, 2020.

76. "Monuments to Power: The Politics and Culture of Urban Development," *Economist*, October 14, 2010, https://www.economist.com/books-and-arts/2010/10/14/monuments -to-power.

77. Hardy Green, *The Company Town: The Industrial Edens and Satanic Mills That Shaped the American Economy* (New York: Basic Books, 2010).

78. Broadway, "From City to Countryside," 23.

79. Schlosser, "Hog Hell."

80. Josh Bivens, Lawrence Mishel, and John Schmitt, "It's Not Just Monopoly and Monopsony: How Market Power Has Affected American Wages," Economic Policy Institute, April 25, 2018, https://www.epi.org/publication/its-not-just-monopoly-and-monopsony-how -market-power-has-affected-american-wages/.

81. Bryant Simon, *The Hamlet Fire: A Tragic Story of Cheap Food, Cheap Government, and Cheap Lives* (New York: New Press, 2017), 35; Lynn Waltz, *Hog Wild: The Battle for Workers' Rights at the World's Largest Slaughterhouse* (Iowa City: University of Iowa Press, 2018), 15.

82. Warren, *Tied to the Great Packing Machine*, 67.

83. Janet Maslin, "Review/Film Festival: A Tragedy at a Plant as Lived by Strikers," *New York Times*, October 6, 1990, https://nyti.ms/3qV9Xp1; Hardy Green, *On Strike at Hormel: The Struggle for a Democratic Labor Movement* (Philadelphia, PA: Temple University Press, 2018); US Bureau of Labor Statistics, "CPI Inflation Calculator," accessed March 14, 2023, https://www.bls.gov/data/inflation_calculator.htm.

84. US Bureau of Labor Statistics, Occupational Employment and Wage Statistics, "Occupational Employment and Wages, May 2021: 51-3023 Slaughterers and Meat Packers," May 2021, https://www.bls.gov/oes/2021/may/oes513023.htm.

85. Simon, *The Hamlet Fire*, 44.

86. William Kandel and Emilio A. Parrado, "Restructuring of the US Meat Processing Industry and New Hispanic Migrant Destinations," *Population and Development Review* 31, no. 3 (September 2005): 447–71, http://www.jstor.org/stable/3401474.

87. Lourdes Gouveia and Donald D. Stull, "Dances with Cows: Beefpacking's Impact on Garden City, Kansas, and Lexington, Nebraska," in *Any Way You Cut It: Meat Processing and Small-Town America*, edited by Donald D. Stull, Michael J. Broadway, and David Griffith, 100 (Lawrence: University Press of Kansas, 1995).

88. Esther Honig and Ted Genoways, "'The Workers Are Being Sacrificed': As Cases Mounted, Meatpacker JBS Kept People on Crowded Factory Floors," *Mother Jones*, May 1, 2020, https://www.motherjones.com/food/2020/05/meatpacking-coronavirus-workers-factory -jbs-tyson-smithfield-covid-crisis-sacrifice-outbreaks-beef/.

89. Lionel Cantú, "The Peripheralization of Rural America: A Case Study of Latino Migrants

in America's Heartland," *Sociological Perspectives* 38, no. 3 (1995): 402, https://doi.org/10.2307/1389434.

90. Michael Grabell, "Tyson Foods' Secret Recipe for Carving Up Workers' Comp," ProPublica, December 11, 2015, https://www.propublica.org/article/tyson-foods-secret-recipe-for-carving-up-workers-comp; Dani Replogle and Delcianna J. Winders, "Accelerating Catastrophe: Slaughter Line Speeds and the Environment," *Environmental Law* 51, no. 4 (2021): 1277–99, https://www.jstor.org/stable/48647573.

91. Ted Genoways, *The Chain: Farm, Factory, and the Fate of Our Food* (New York: Harper, 2014), 50–51.

92. Denise Grady, "A Medical Mystery Unfolds in Minnesota," *New York Times*, February 5, 2008, https://www.nytimes.com/2008/02/05/health/05pork.html.

93. Genoways, *The Chain*, 51.

94. Julie Creswell, "How Many Hogs Can Be Slaughtered per Hour? Pork Industry Wants More," *New York Times*, August 9, 2019, https://www.nytimes.com/2019/08/09/business/pork-factory-regulations.html; David Shepardson, "U.S. Judge: Passengers in Fatal Boeing 737 MAX Crashes Are 'Crime Victims,'" Reuters, October 21, 2022, https://www.reuters.com/world/us/us-judge-passengers-fatal-boeing-737-max-crashes-crime-victims-2022-10-21/; Ben Kesslen, "737 Max Crashes That Killed 346 Were 'Horrific Culmination' of Failures by Boeing and FAA, House Report Says," NBC News, September 16, 2020, https://www.nbcnews.com/news/us-news/737-max-crashes-killed-346-were-horrific-culmination-failures-boeing-n1240192.

95. Kimberly Kindy, "Biden Administration to Allow Reversal of Trump Program to Accelerate Pork Plant Line Speeds," *Washington Post*, May 27, 2021, https://www.washingtonpost.com/politics/pork-plants-speed/2021/05/27/fed67152-bef1-11eb-83e3-0ca705a96ba4_story.html.

96. Tom Polansek, "U.S. Approves Faster Processing Speeds at Three Pork Plants," Reuters, March 14, 2022, https://www.reuters.com/legal/transactional/us-approves-faster-processing-speeds-three-pork-plants-2022-03-14/; US Department of Agriculture, Food Safety and Inspection Service, "Constituent Update—March 3, 2023," March 3, 2023, https://www.fsis.usda.gov/news-events/news-press-releases/constituent-update-march-3-2023.

97. Michael Corkery and David Yaffe-Bellany, "The Food Chain's Weakest Link: Slaughterhouses," *New York Times*, April 18, 2020, https://www.nytimes.com/2020/04/18/business/coronavirus-meat-slaughterhouses.html; United Food and Commercial Workers International Union, "UFCW Calls on USDA and White House to Protect Meatpacking Workers and America's Food Supply" (blog post), April 30, 2020, updated September 4, 2020, https://www.ufcw.org/covidpacking/.

98. Ana Swanson and David Yaffe-Bellany, "Trump Declares Meat Supply 'Critical,' Aiming to Reopen Plants," *New York Times*, April 28, 2020, https://www.nytimes.com/2020/04/28/business/economy/coronavirus-trump-meat-food-supply.html.

99. Zack Budryk, "Tyson Foods Takes Out Full-Page Ad: 'The Food Supply Chain Is Breaking,'" The Hill, April 27, 2020, https://thehill.com/policy/healthcare/494772-tyson-foods-takes-out-full-page-ad-the-food-supply-chain-is-breaking/.

100. Michael Grabell and Bernice Yeung, "Emails Show the Meatpacking Industry Drafted an Executive Order to Keep Plants Open," ProPublica, September 14, 2020, https://www.propublica.org/article/emails-show-the-meatpacking-industry-drafted-an-executive-order-to-keep-plants-open.

101. Rollo Ross, "Los Angeles Union, Joined by 'Pandemic Pig,' Demands Meatpacking Plant Closure," Reuters, May 28, 2020, https://www.reuters.com/article/us-health-coronavirus-usa-meat-plant-idUSKBN23504T; Jessica Miller, Nate Carlisle, and Norma Gonzalez, "Workers Protest against Utah Meatpacking Plant amid Outbreak—'It's Not Safe,' Says

One," *Salt Lake (UT) Tribune*, June 9, 2020, https://www.sltrib.com/news/politics/2020 /06/09/meatpacking-workers/; "JBS Meat Processing Workers Stage Wildcat Strike," Democracy Now!, July 13, 2020, https://www.democracynow.org/2020/7/13/headlines /jbs_meat_processing_workers_stage_wildcat_strike.

102. Leah Douglas, "Nearly 90% of Big US Meat Plants Had COVID-19 Cases in Pandemic's First Year—Data," Reuters, January 14, 2022, https://www.reuters.com/business/nearly -90-big-us-meat-plants-had-covid-19-cases-pandemics-first-year-data-2022-01-14/.

103. Adeel Hassan, "Coronavirus Cases and Deaths Were Vastly Underestimated in U.S. Meat-packing Plants, a House Report Says," *New York Times*, October 28, 2021, https://www .nytimes.com/2021/10/28/world/meatpacking-workers-covid-cases-deaths.html.

104. Sorvino, *Raw Deal*, 6.

105. Andrea Shalal, "Meat Packers' Profit Margins Jumped 300% during Pandemic—White House Economics Team," Reuters, December 10, 2021, https://www.reuters.com/business /meat-packers-profit-margins-jumped-300-during-pandemic-white-house-economics-2021 -12-10/.

106. Waltz, *Hog Wild*, 3.

107. Christopher Drew, "Regulators Slow Down as Packers Speed," *Chicago Tribune*, October 26, 1988.

108. Simon, *The Hamlet Fire*, 174.

109. Editorial Board, "Why Is OSHA AWOL?," *New York Times*, June 21, 2020, https://www .nytimes.com/2020/06/21/opinion/coronavirus-osha-work-safety.html; Deborah Berkow-itz, "Worker Safety in Crisis: The Cost of a Weakened OSHA," National Employment Law Project, Policy & Data Brief, April 28, 2020, https://www.nelp.org/publication/ worker-safety-crisis-cost-weakened-osha/.

110. Simon, *The Hamlet Fire*, 12.

111. Simon, *The Hamlet Fire*, 64.

112. Schlosser, "Hog Hell"; Michael Grabell and Bernice Yeung, "The Battle for Waterloo," ProPublica, December 21, 2020, https://features.propublica.org/waterloo-meatpacking /as-covid-19-ravaged-this-iowa-city-officials-discovered-meatpacking-executives-were-the -ones-in-charge/.

113. David Barboza and Andrew Ross Sorkin, "Tyson to Acquire IBP in $3.2 Billion Deal," *New York Times*, January 2, 2001, https://nyti.ms/3sDtWZD.

114. US Department of Labor, Wage and Hour Division, "More than 100 Children Illegally Employed in Hazardous Jobs, Federal Investigation Finds; Food Sanitation Contractor Pays $1.5M in Penalties," press release 23-325-NAT, February 17, 2023, https://www.dol .gov/newsroom/releases/whd/whd20230217-1.

115. Lauren Kaori Gurley, "U.S. Fines Firm $1.5 Million for Hiring Kids to Clean Meatpack-ing Plants," *Washington Post*, February 17, 2023, https://www.washingtonpost.com/busi ness/2023/02/17/child-labor-meatpacking-department-of-labor/.

116. Remy Tumin, "Labor Department Finds 31 Children Cleaning Meatpacking Plants," *New York Times*, November 11, 2022, https://www.nytimes.com/2022/11/11/business/child -labor-meatpacking-plants.html.

117. Simon Romero, "Brazil's Largest Food Companies Raided in Tainted Meat Scandal," *New York Times*, March 17, 2017, https://www.nytimes.com/2017/03/17/world/americas /brazil-food-companies-bribe-scandal-salmonella.html.

118. Tatiana Freitas and Mike Dorning, "Congresswoman Urges USDA to Investigate Payments to JBS USA," Bloomberg, November 21, 2019, https://www.bloomberg.com/news/articles /2019-11-21/congresswoman-urges-usda-to-investigate-payments-to-jbs#xj4y7vzkg.

119. ABC Australia, *Four Corners*, "The World's Biggest Meat Company Is Built on Corruption and It's Growing in Australia," YouTube video, 16:00, April 25, 2022, https://www.you tube.com/watch?v=NYfIXLkoB68.

120. Xiaoming Xu et al., "Global Greenhouse Gas Emissions from Animal-Based Foods Are Twice Those of Plant-Based Foods," *Nature Food* 2 (September 2021): 724–32, https://doi .org/10.1038/s43016-021-00358-x.

121. Bryan Harris, "Meatpacker JBS Comes under Fire over 50% Emissions Rise," *Financial Times*, April 21, 2022, https://www.ft.com/content/92904829-3a28-4d6e-aab7-467c625 497c7.

122. Stefano Menegat, Alicia Ledo, and Reyes Tirado, "Greenhouse Gas Emissions from Global Production and Use of Nitrogen Synthetic Fertilisers in Agriculture," *Scientific Reports* 12, article 14490 (2022), https://doi.org/10.1038/s41598-022-18773-w.

123. Joanna Foster, "Farmers, Scientists Seek Solutions to Global Warming Caused by Cows," Environmental Defense Fund, accessed January 17, 2023, https://vitalsigns.edf.org/story /farmers-scientists-seek-solutions-global-warming-caused-cows.

124. Matthew Cimitile, "Amazon Deforestation: Earth's Heart and Lungs Dismembered," National Science Foundation, January 23, 2009, https://new.nsf.gov/news/amazon -deforestation-earths-heart-lungs; "How Big Beef and Soya Firms Can Stop Deforestation," *Economist*, June 11, 2020, https://www.economist.com/the-americas/2020/06/11/how -big-beef-and-soya-firms-can-stop-deforestation; Marin Elisabete Skidmore et al., "Cattle Ranchers and Deforestation in the Brazilian Amazon: Production, Location, and Policies," *Global Environmental Change* 68 (May 2021): 102280, https://doi.org/10.1016/j.gloen vcha.2021.102280.

125. Kate Silver, "Sponsored Content [by JBS]: Feeding Our Future," *Politico*, February 22, 2022, https://www.politico.com/sponsored-content/2022/02/feeding-our-future.

126. Harris, "Meatpacker JBS Comes under Fire."

127. Manuela Andreoni, Hiroko Tabuchi, and Albert Sun, "How Americans' Appetite for Leather in Luxury SUVs Worsens Amazon Deforestation," *New York Times*, November 17, 2021, https://www.nytimes.com/2021/11/17/climate/leather-seats-cars-rainforest.html.

128. Anthony Boadle, "Brazil's JBS Accused of Violating Amazon Rainforest Protection Laws," Reuters, March 31, 2017, https://www.reuters.com/article/us-brazil-environment-cattle -idUKKBN1722O1.

129. Clifford Krauss, David Yaffe-Bellany, and Mariana Simões, "Why Amazon Fires Keep Raging 10 Years after a Deal to End Them," *New York Times*, October 10, 2019, https:// www.nytimes.com/2019/10/10/world/americas/amazon-fires-brazil-cattle.html.

130. Andrew Wasley and Alexandra Heal, "Walmart Selling Beef from Firm Linked to Amazon Deforestation," *Guardian*, February 13, 2021, https://www.theguardian.com/environ ment/2021/feb/13/walmart-selling-beef-from-firm-linked-to-amazon-deforestation.

131. Kimberly Kindy, "This Foreign Meat Company Got U.S. Tax Money. Now It Wants to Conquer America," *Washington Post*, November 7, 2019, https://www.washingtonpost .com/politics/this-foreign-meat-company-got-us-tax-money-now-it-wants-to-conquer -america/2019/11/04/854836ae-eae5-11e9-9306-47cb0324fd44_story.html.

132. Maggie Haberman and Alan Rappeport, "Farm Bailout Paid to Brazilian Meat Processor Angers Lawmakers," *New York Times*, February 7, 2020, https://www.nytimes.com/2020 /02/07/us/politics/farm-bailout-jbs.html.

133. Marcia Brown, "Federal Government Won't Stop Buying Food from Meatpacker Tied to Bribery Case," *Politico*, January 10, 2023, https://www.politico.com/news/2023/01/10 /usda-meatpacker-bribery-case-00077093.

134. "The Biden Plan for Rural America," Biden President, December 6, 2019, https://web

.archive.org/web/20191206205542/https://joebiden.com/rural/; White House, "Remarks by President Biden at Signing of an Executive Order Promoting Competition in the American Economy," July 9, 2021, https://www.whitehouse.gov/briefing-room/speeches-remarks/2021/07/09/remarks-by-president-biden-at-signing-of-an-executive-order-promoting-competition-in-the-american-economy/.

135. Will Feuer, "White House Blames Big Meat for Rising Prices, Alleges 'Profiteering,'" *New York Post*, September 9, 2021, https://nypost.com/2021/09/09/white-house-blames-big-meat-for-rising-prices-alleges-profiteering/; Brian Deese, Sameera Fazili, and Bharat Ramamurti, "Addressing Concentration in the Meat-Processing Industry to Lower Food Prices for American Families," White House, September 8, 2021, https://www.whitehouse.gov/briefing-room/blog/2021/09/08/addressing-concentration-in-the-meat-processing-industry-to-lower-food-prices-for-american-families/.

136. Saul Elbein, "Small Ranchers Say Biden Letting Them Get Squeezed," The Hill, January 23, 2022, https://thehill.com/policy/equilibrium-sustainability/590941-small-ranchers-say-biden-letting-them-get-squeezed/.

137. Jessica Fu, "Can $1 Billion Really Fix a Meat Industry Dominated by Just Four Companies?," The Counter, January 5, 2022, https://thecounter.org/big-four-meatpackers-antitrust-consolidation/.

138. Saul Elbein, "Biden Meatpacking Reforms Lack Punch, Say Critics," The Hill, January 4, 2022, https://thehill.com/policy/equilibrium-sustainability/588267-biden-meatpacking-reforms-lack-punch-say-critics/.

139. Fu, "Can $1 Billion Really Fix?"

140. Marco Rubio, U.S. Senator for Florida, "Rubio, Menendez Urge CFIUS to Review Brazilian Meat-Processing Conglomerate in Interest of Safeguarding U.S. Economic, National Security Interests," press release, August 13, 2021, https://www.rubio.senate.gov/rubio-menendez-urge-cfius-to-review-brazilian-meat-processing-conglomerate-in-interest-of-safeguarding-u-s-economic-national-security-interests/.

Chapter 7: The Grocery Barons

1. Lindsay Whipp, "Walmart Suffers Worst Sales Performance in 35 Years," *Financial Times*, February 18, 2016.

2. Elizabeth A. Harris, "A Succession at Walmart Puts an Insider at the Helm," *New York Times*, November 25, 2013, https://www.nytimes.com/2013/11/26/business/walmart-names-chief-of-international-unit-as-new-ceo.html; Jason Del Rey, *Winner Sells All: Amazon, Walmart, and the Battle for Our Wallets* (New York: Harper Business, 2023), 60.

3. US Securities and Exchange Commission, "Schedule 14A: Walmart Inc." June 3, 2020; Amazon, "Notice of 2023 Annual Meeting of Shareholders & Proxy Statement," May 24, 2023, https://s2.q4cdn.com/299287126/files/doc_downloads/governance/2023/07/Amazon-2023-Proxy-Statement.pdf; Olivia Munson, "Who Owns Walmart? It's Not China. History and Look at the Top Shareholders in the Company," *USA Today*, February 24, 2023.

4. Shelly Banjo, "Wal-Mart Looks to Grow by Embracing Smaller Stores," *Wall Street Journal*, July 8, 2014, https://www.wsj.com/articles/wal-mart-looks-to-grow-by-embracing-smaller-stores-1404787817.

5. James B. Stewart, "Walmart Plays Catch-Up with Amazon," *New York Times*, October 22, 2015, https://www.nytimes.com/2015/10/23/business/walmart-plays-catch-up-with-amazon.html.

6. "Walmart: Lower Price Every Day," *Financial Times*, October 14, 2015.

7. Julie Creswell and Hiroko Tabuchi, "Walmart Chief Defends Investments in Labor, Stores

and the Web," *New York Times*, October 18, 2015, https://www.nytimes.com/2015/10/19/business/walmart-chief-defends-investments-in-labor-stores-and-the-web.html.

8. "Here Is the Full Transcript of Billionaire Investor Warren Buffett's Interview with CNBC," CNBC, February 27, 2017, https://www.cnbc.com/2017/02/27/billionaire-investor-warren-buffett-speaks-with-cnbcs-becky-quick-on-squawk-box.html; John Szramiak, "Amazon Is the Reason Warren Buffett Sold Walmart," Insider, March 13, 2017, https://www.businessinsider.com/why-warren-buffett-sold-walmart-2017-3.

9. Natalie Gagliordi, "Walmart CEO Outlines Omnichannel Retail Strategy to Shareholders, Associates," ZDNET, June 5, 2015, https://www.zdnet.com/article/walmart-ceo-outlines-omnichannel-retail-strategy-to-shareholders-associates/.

10. Gagliordi, "Walmart CEO."

11. Walmart, "Walmart Changes Its Legal Name to Reflect How Customers Want to Shop," press release, December 5, 2017, https://corporate.walmart.com/news/2017/12/05/walmart-changes-its-legal-name-to-reflect-how-customers-want-to-shop.

12. Karen Webster, "Why the Amazon-Walmart Retail Battle Won't Be Fought in the Grocery Aisle," PYMNTS, February 27, 2023, https://www.pymnts.com/news/retail/2023/why-the-amazon-walmart-retail-battle-wont-be-fought-in-the-grocery-aisle/; Statista, "Net Sales Share of Walmart U.S. in the United States in Fiscal Year 2023, by Merchandise Category," March 2023, https://www.statista.com/statistics/252678/walmarts-net-sales-in-the-us-by-merchandise-unit/.

13. Alex Fitzpatrick and Erin Davis, "The Most Popular Grocery Stores in the U.S." Axios, April 20, 2023, https://www.axios.com/2023/04/20/most-popular-grocery-stores.

14. Sarah Nassauer, "Walmart's Food-Delivery Challenges: Patchwork of Drivers, Tolls, Crowded Aisles," *Wall Street Journal*, March 14, 2019, https://www.wsj.com/articles/walmart-turns-to-food-delivery-to-fend-off-amazon-11552555801.

15. Sarah Nassauer, "Walmart's Secret Weapon to Fight Off Amazon: The Supercenter," *Wall Street Journal*, December 21, 2019, https://www.wsj.com/articles/walmarts-secret-weapon-to-fight-off-amazon-the-supercenter-11576904460.

16. Kim Souza, "Walmart Pushing Food Sales Improvements as a Catalyst for Revenue Growth," *Talk Business & Politics*, March 7, 2016, https://talkbusiness.net/2016/03/walmart-pushing-food-sales-improvements-as-a-catalyst-for-revenue-growth/.

17. Sarah Nassauer and Imani Moise, "Wal-Mart in the Crosshairs of Amazon's Takeover of Whole Foods," *Wall Street Journal*, June 16, 2017, https://www.wsj.com/articles/wal-mart-buys-online-retailer-bonobos-for-310-million-1497621286; Walmart, "Automation Is Reshaping Work across America. A New Report Explores the Impact—and How Communities Might Respond," press release, February 13, 2019, https://corporate.walmart.com/news/2019/02/13/automation-is-reshaping-work-across-america-a-new-report-explores-the-impact-and-how-communities-might-respond; Kim Souza, "Exec Says Walmart Supercenters Are an Opportunity, Not a Drag," *Talk Business & Politics*, March 28, 2019, https://talkbusiness.net/2019/03/exec-says-walmart-supercenters-are-an-opportunity-not-a-drag/.

18. Karen Weise, "Amazon Wants to Rule the Grocery Aisles, and Not Just at Whole Foods," *New York Times*, July 28, 2019, https://www.nytimes.com/2019/07/28/technology/whole-foods-amazon-grocery.html.

19. Rachel Abrams and Julie Creswell, "Amazon Deal for Whole Foods Starts a Supermarket War," *New York Times*, June 16, 2017, https://www.nytimes.com/2017/06/16/business/whole-foods-walmart-amazon-grocery-stores.html.

20. Lauren Silva Laughlin, "Walmart Will Struggle to Top Amazon's Offer for Whole Foods," *New York Times*, June 19, 2017, https://www.nytimes.com/2017/06/19/business/dealbook/walmart-will-struggle-to-top-amazons-offer-for-whole-foods.html.

21. "Sam Walton," *Encyclopedia Britannica*, https://www.britannica.com/biography/Sam -Walton, accessed April 24, 2023.

22. Nelson Lichtenstein, *The Retail Revolution: How Wal-Mart Created a Brave New World of Business* (New York: Metropolitan Books, 2009), 25.

23. Sam Walton and John Huey, *Sam Walton: Made in America; My Story* (New York: Double-day, 1992), 46.

24. Stephan Meier and Felix Oberholzer-Gee, "Walmart: In Search of Renewed Growth," Columbia Business School, Columbia CaseWorks, Fall 2020, https://www8.gsb.columbia .edu/caseworks/node/303.

25. Andrea Lillo, "Wal-Mart Gains Strength from Distribution Chain," *Home Textiles Today*, March 24, 2003.

26. Lichtenstein, *Retail Revolution*, 41.

27. Walton and Huey, *Sam Walton*, 256.

28. Walton and Huey, *Sam Walton*, 254; Kim Souza, "On Its 30th Anniversary, the Super-center Format Remains a Key Sales Driver for Walmart," *Talk Business & Politics*, May 31, 2018, https://talkbusiness.net/2018/05/on-its-30th-anniversary-the-supercenter-format -remains-a-key-sales-driver-for-walmart/.

29. Thomas C. Hayes, "The Hypermarket: 5 Acres of Store," *New York Times*, February 4, 1988, https://nyti.ms/45vTE11.

30. Joyce M. Rosenberg, "European Retailing Concept Spreading," Associated Press, Decem-ber 26, 1987.

31. Hayes, "Hypermarket."

32. Walton and Huey, *Sam Walton*, 254; Walmart, "The Beginning of Big: Walmart 60th," Walmart World Newsletter, accessed June 8, 2023, https://one.walmart.com/content /walmart-world/en_us/articles/2022/07/the-beginning-of-big.html.

33. Judith VandeWater, "Wal-Mart Takes Washington by Store," *St. Louis Post-Dispatch*, March 2, 1988, https://www.newspapers.com/article/71834958/st-louis-post-dispatch/.

34. Meier and Oberholzer-Gee, "Walmart."

35. Misha Petrovic and Gary G. Hamilton, "Making Global Markets: Wal-Mart and Its Suppliers," in *Wal-Mart: The Face of Twenty-First-Century Capitalism*, edited by Nelson Lichtenstein, 123 (New York: New Press, 2006).

36. Bobby J. Martens, "The Effect of Entry by Wal-Mart Supercenters on Retail Grocery Concentration," *Journal of Food Distribution Research* 39, no. 3 (November 2008): 13–28, http://dx.doi.org/10.22004/ag.econ.55981.

37. US Securities and Exchange Commission, "Form 10-K: Walmart Inc.," January 31, 2023.

38. Meier and Oberholzer-Gee, "Walmart."

39. Robert Berner and Stephanie Anderson Forest, "Wal-Mart Is Eating Everybody's Lunch," Bloomberg, April 15, 2002, https://www.bloomberg.com/news/articles/2002-04-14/wal -mart-is-eating-everybodys-lunch.

40. US Securities and Exchange Commission, "Form 10-K: Walmart Inc."

41. "Grocery Goliaths: How Food Monopolies Impact Consumers," Food & Water Watch, December 2013, https://foodandwaterwatch.org/wp-content/uploads/2021/03/Grocery -Goliaths-Report-Dec-2013.pdf.

42. Fitzpatrick and Davis, "Most Popular Grocery Stores in the U.S."

43. Julie Morris, "Store Shuts Doors on Texas Town; Economic Blow for Community," *USA Today*, October 11, 1990.

44. Stacy Mitchell, *Big-Box Swindle: The True Cost of Mega-Retailers and the Fight for America's Independent Businesses* (Boston: Beacon Press, 2006), 135.

45. Walton and Huey, *Sam Walton*, 177.

46. David Karjanen, "The Wal-Mart Effect and the New Face of Capitalism: Labor Market and Community Impacts of the Megaretailer," in *Wal-Mart: The Face of Twenty-First-Century Capitalism*, edited by Nelson Lichtenstein, 151 (New York: New Press, 2006); Kenneth E. Stone, "Impact of Wal-Mart Stores on Iowa Communities: 1983–93," *Economic Development Review* 13, no. 2 (Spring 1995): 60.

47. George Ford, "Walmart Unveiling Remodeled Southwest Cedar Rapids Store," *Cedar Rapids (IA) Gazette*, June 14, 2011, https://www.thegazette.com/business/walmart -unveiling-remodeled-southwest-cedar-rapids-store/.

48. Anthony Bianco and Wendy Zellner, "Is Wal-Mart Too Powerful?," Bloomberg, October 6, 2003, https://www.bloomberg.com/news/articles/2003-10-05/is-wal-mart-too-powerful #xj4y7vzkg.

49. David Merriman et al., "The Impact of an Urban WalMart Store on Area Businesses: The Chicago Case," *Economic Development Quarterly* 26, no. 4 (2012): 321–33, https://doi .org/10.1177/0891242412457985.

50. Joe Fassler, "The Man Who's Going to Save Your Neighborhood Grocery Store," The Counter and Longreads, April 23, 2019, https://longreads.com/2019/04/23/the-man-whos -going-to-save-your-grocery-store/.

51. Lichtenstein, *Retail Revolution*, 135.

52. Stacy Mitchell, "Walmart's Monopolization of Local Grocery Markets," Institute for Local Self-Reliance, June 26, 2019, https://ilsr.org/walmarts-monopolization-of-local-grocery -markets/.

53. Eliana Zeballos, Xiao Dong, and Ergys Islamaj, "A Disaggregated View of Market Concentration in the Food Retail Industry," US Department of Agriculture, Economic Research Service, Economic Research Report No. ERR-314, January 2023, https://www.ers.usda .gov/publications/pub-details?pubid=105557.

54. Daniel Hosken, Luke M. Olson, and Loren K. Smith, "Do Retail Mergers Affect Competition? Evidence from Grocery Retailing," Working Paper No. 313, Federal Trade Commission, Bureau of Economics, December 2012, https://purl.fdlp.gov/GPO/gpo64516.

55. Martens, "Effect of Entry by Wal-Mart Supercenters"; "Kroger / Harris Teeter: Last Man Standing," *Financial Times*, July 10, 2013, https://www.ft.com/content/ffe55ac8-e979 -11e2-9f11-00144feabdc0; Arriana McLymore and Siddharth Cavale, "Analysis: Kroger Looks to Fight Both Inflation and Walmart with New Merger," Reuters, October 14, 2022, https://www.reuters.com/markets/deals/kroger-looks-fight-both-inflation-walmart -with-new-merger-2022-10-14/.

56. Fitzpatrick and Davis, "Most Popular Grocery Stores in the U.S."

57. The Kroger Company, "Grocery Retail," accessed June 8, 2023, https://www.thekrogerco .com/about-kroger/our-business/grocery-retail/.

58. Rachel Lerman, "Kroger Says It Will Buy Albertsons, Creating Grocery Empire," *Washington Post*, October 14, 2022, https://www.washingtonpost.com/business/2022/10/14 /kroger-albertsons-grocery-merger/; Albertsons Companies, "About ACI," accessed June 8, 2023, https://www.albertsonscompanies.com/about-aci/overview/default.aspx.

59. David Dayen, "Antitrust Incompetence from the FTC, as Albertson's/Safeway Divestiture Goes Awry," Naked Capitalism, November 17, 2015, https://www.nakedcapitalism.com /2015/11/antitrust-incompetence-from-the-ftc-as-albertsonssafeway-divestiture-goes-awry .html.

60. Brendan Case, "Kroger Bets $25 Billion on Bulking Up to Be More Like Walmart,"

Bloomberg, October 16, 2022, https://www.bloomberg.com/news/articles/2022-10-16
/kroger-bets-25-billion-on-bulking-up-to-be-more-like-walmart#xj4y7vzkg.

61. Jaewon Kang, "A Supermarket Megamerger Will Redefine What You Buy at the Grocery
Store," *Wall Street Journal*, March 11, 2023, https://www.wsj.com/articles/supermarket
-future-kroger-albertsons-234bbb0d.

62. "Statement of Vivek Sankaran, Chief Executive Officer, Albertsons Companies, Inc.,
before the U.S. Senate Judiciary Committee Subcommittee on Competition Policy, Antitrust, and Consumer Rights, November 29, 2022," https://www.judiciary.senate.gov/imo
/media/doc/Testimony%20-%20Sankaran%20-%202022-11-28.pdf.

63. Kim Souza, "Real Estate Exec Says Planned New Wal-Mart HQ Could Hit $1 Billion,"
Talk Business & Politics, October 9, 2017, https://talkbusiness.net/2017/10/real-estate
-exec-says-planned-new-wal-mart-hq-could-hit-1-billion/; Patrick Sisson, "Why Walmart
Is Turning Its New Headquarters into a Walkable Town Square," Curbed, November 19,
2019, https://archive.curbed.com/2019/11/19/20970158/walmart-home-office
-urbanism-corporate-hq-retail; Kathryn Gilker, "Construction of Walmart Home Office in
Bentonville Moving Along," KFSM-TV, June 2, 2022, https://www.5newsonline.com
/article/money/business/construction-walmart-home-office-bentonville/527-5b7eb96d
-3fe4-4abb-82b5-9db1276744fa.

64. Mark Carter, "Bentonville's Transformation Subject of Ad Age Spotlight," *Arkansas Business*, October 28, 2014, https://www.arkansasbusiness.com/post/101596/bentonvilles
-transformation-subject-of-ad-age-spotlight.

65. Don Warden and Monte Harris, "Bentonville (Benton County)," Encyclopedia of Arkansas, December 15, 2022, https://encyclopediaofarkansas.net/entries/bentonville-828/.

66. Rhett Brinkley, "Three Bentonville Restaurants Represented among Semi-finalists for the
2022 James Beard Awards," *Arkansas Times*, March 4, 2022, https://arktimes.com/eat
-arkansas/2022/03/04/three-bentonville-restaurants-represented-among-semi-finalists-for
-the-2022-james-beard-awards.

67. Dayana Mustak, "The Waltons: World's Richest Family Trims Exposure to Emerging
Markets," Bloomberg, November 14, 2022, https://www.bloomberg.com/news/articles
/2022-11-14/walton-family-investment-firm-trims-exposure-to-emerging-markets#xj
4y7vzkg.

68. Ken Belson, "Rams Moving to Los Angeles Area, and Chargers Could Join Them," *New
York Times*, January 12, 2016, https://www.nytimes.com/2016/01/13/sports/football
/rams-moving-to-los-angeles-area-and-chargers-could-join-later.html; Samuel Agini,
"Walmart Heir Agrees to Buy Denver Broncos," *Financial Times*, June 8, 2022, https://
www.ft.com/content/fad8da8b-96ab-47cb-8087-560d211761ae.

69. Paul Gatling, "Bentonville Medical School Site Revealed; New Name is Alice L. Walton
School of Medicine," *Talk Business & Politics*, June 30, 2022, https://talkbusiness.net/2022
/06/bentonville-medical-school-site-revealed-new-name-is-alice-l-walton-school-of
-medicine/; Northwest Arkansas National Airport, "XNA History," accessed June 8, 2023,
https://www.flyxna.com/xna-history; Alice L. Walton School of Medicine, "Education,"
accessed June 27, 2023, https://www.alwmedschool.org/education.

70. Jonathan Birchall, "Observer from Bentonville," *Financial Times*, April 10, 2005, https://
www.ft.com/content/01b3f26e-a9f1-11d9-aa38-00000e2511c8; Kastalia Medrano, "The
Curious Cultural Rise of the Town That Gave Us Walmart," Thrillist, January 9, 2020,
https://www.thrillist.com/travel/nation/bentonville-arkansas-revival-walmart.

71. Rebecca Mead, "Alice's Wonderland," *New Yorker*, June 20, 2011, https://www.newyorker
.com/magazine/2011/06/27/alices-wonderland; Caroline Eubanks, "Visiting Crystal
Bridges Museum of Art," This Is My South, June 29, 2015, https://www.thisismysouth
.com/visiting-crystal-bridges-museum-of-art/.

72. Suzi Parker, "U.S. Heiress Brings Art to Middle America," Reuters, November 9, 2011, https://www.reuters.com/article/us-finearts-middleamerica-idUSTRE7A84S120111109; Melissa Smith, "Crystal Bridges Made Arkansas a Hub for American Art. Can a New Offshoot Make It a Destination for Contemporary Work, Too?," Artnet News, February 13, 2020, https://news.artnet.com/art-world/the-momentary-crystal-bridges-1776441; Crystal Bridges Museum of American Art, "Crystal Bridges Museum of American Art Reveals Plans for Major Expansion Designed by Safdie Architects," April 7, 2021, https://crystal bridges.org/news-room/crystal-bridges-museum-of-american-art-reveals-plans-for-major -expansion-designed-by-safdie-architects/; Derek Blasberg, "How Alice Walton Is Doubling Down on Her Mega-Museum in Arkansas," *Wall Street Journal*, September 11, 2021, https://www.wsj.com/articles/alice-walton-interview-crystal-bridges-11631104447.

73. Kelly Crow, "Walmart Heirs Launching Their Own Woodstock with an Art and Music Festival," *Wall Street Journal*, April 19, 2022, https://www.wsj.com/articles/walmart-heirs -walton-art-music-festival-format-bentonville-11650322568.

74. Andrew Tilin, "The Walmart Heirs Putting Arkansas on the Fat-Tire Map," Outside, May 2, 2018, https://www.outsideonline.com/outdoor-adventure/biking/single-track-minds/.

75. Devon Pendleton, "These Are the World's Richest Families," Bloomberg, October 30, 2022, https://www.tbsnews.net/bloomberg-special/these-are-worlds-richest-families -522826.

76. "International Cycling Race in Fayetteville Adds Walmart as Lead Sponsor," *Talk Business & Politics*, October 8, 2022, https://talkbusiness.net/2022/10/international-cycling-race -in-fayetteville-adds-walmart-as-lead-sponsor/; Paul Gatling, "With Walton Backing, USA Cycling Announces Bentonville Satellite Office," *Talk Business & Politics*, December 15, 2022, https://talkbusiness.net/2022/12/with-walton-backing-usa-cycling-announces -bentonville-satellite-office/; Libertina Brandt, "Walmart Helped Put Northwest Arkansas on the Map. Now Everybody Wants a Piece of It," *Wall Street Journal*, March 15, 2023, https://www.wsj.com/articles/northwest-arkansas-real-estate-market-180f9a15; "Bicycling Industry a Boon for Northwest Arkansas," *Arkansas Democrat Gazette*, June 26, 2023, https://www.arkansasonline.com/news/2023/jun/26/bicycling-industry-a-boon-for -northwest-arkansas/.

77. Kim Souza, "Income Inequality in NWA Widens, Child Poverty Rates Remain High," *Talk Business & Politics*, September 13, 2018, https://talkbusiness.net/2018/09/income -inequality-in-nwa-widens-child-poverty-rates-remain-high/; Laura Kellams, "Child Poverty in Northwest Arkansas: Policy Solutions to Build a Stronger Community," Arkansas Advocates for Children and Families, September 2018, https://www.aradvocates.org/wp -content/uploads/AACF-NWA-pov.webfinal.9.7.18.pdf.

78. Bingbing Wang, "Is Walmart the Same as Ten Years Ago? A Non-Parametric Difference-in -Differences Analysis of Walmart Development," *Regional Science and Urban Economics* 99, article 103863 (March 2023), https://doi.org/10.1016/j.regsciurbeco.2022.103863.

79. Jeremy Bowman, "Where Have All the Inner-City Grocery Stores Gone?," Insider, April 4, 2012; Michael Corkery, "Walmart 'Surprised' Old Store Is a Migrant Shelter. Records Hinted at the Possibility," *New York Times*, June 20, 2018, https://www.nytimes.com/2018 /06/20/business/walmart-migrant-children-shelter.html.

80. Lela Nargi, "How Some Big Grocery Chains Help Ensure That Food Deserts Stay Barren," The Counter, May 3, 2022, https://thecounter.org/supermarket-chains-poor-communities -lease-agreements-food-insecurity/.

81. Corkery, "Walmart 'Surprised' Old Store Is a Migrant Shelter."

82. Sam Bloch, "How the 'Dark Stores' Loophole Helps Big-Box Retailers Evade Millions in Property Taxes," The Counter, November 23, 2018, https://thecounter.org/how-dark -stores-loophole-helps-retailers-evade-taxes-walmart/.

83. Philip Mattera and Anna Purinton, "Shopping for Subsidies: How Wal-Mart Uses Tax-payer Money to Finance Its Never-Ending Growth," Good Jobs First, May 2004, https://goodjobsfirst.org/wp-content/uploads/docs/pdf/wmtstudy.pdf; Barnaby J. Feder, "Wal-Mart's Expansion Aided by Many Taxpayer Subsidies," *New York Times*, May 24, 2004, https://www.nytimes.com/2004/05/24/business/wal-mart-s-expansion-aided-by-many-taxpayer-subsidies.html.

84. Zachary R. Mider, "How Wal-Mart's Waltons Maintain Their Billionaire Fortune: Taxes," Bloomberg, September 12, 2013, https://www.bloomberg.com/news/articles/2013-09-12/how-wal-mart-s-waltons-maintain-their-billionaire-fortune-taxes#xj4y7vzkg.

85. Nelson Lichtenstein, "Walmart: A Template for Twenty-First-Century Capitalism," in *Wal-Mart: The Face of Twenty-First-Century Capitalism*, edited by Nelson Lichtenstein, 13 (New York: New Press, 2006).

86. Nathaniel Meyersohn, "America's Largest Private Employer Just Hiked Wages," CNN, January 24, 2023, https://www.cnn.com/2023/01/24/business/walmart-raising-wages/index.html; Walmart, "About," accessed June 8, 2023, https://corporate.walmart.com/about.

87. US Census Bureau, "State Population Totals and Components of Change: 2020–2022," accessed June 8, 2023, https://www.census.gov/data/tables/time-series/demo/popest/2020s-state-total.html.

88. Justin Wiltshire, "Walmart Supercenters and Monopsony Power: How a Large, Low-Wage Employer Impacts Local Labor Markets," Washington Center for Equitable Growth, Working Paper Series, January 2022, https://equitablegrowth.org/working-papers/walmart-supercenters-and-monopsony-power-how-a-large-low-wage-employer-impacts-local-labor-markets/.

89. Lichtenstein, "Walmart: A Template," 4.

90. Michael Corkery, "Walmart Raises Starting Wages for Store Workers," *New York Times*, January 24, 2023, https://www.nytimes.com/2023/01/24/business/walmart-minimum-wage.html.

91. Mitchell, *Big-Box Swindle*, 7.

92. Thomas Jessen Adams, "Making the New Shop Floor: Wal-Mart, Labor Control, and the History of the Postwar Discount Retail Industry in America," in *Wal-Mart: The Face of Twenty-First-Century Capitalism*, edited by Nelson Lichtenstein, 218 (New York: New Press, 2006).

93. Walmart, "Notice of 2022 Annual Shareholders' Meeting," June 1, 2022.

94. Walton and Huey, *Sam Walton*, 129.

95. Emek Basker, "The Causes and Consequences of Wal-Mart's Growth," *Journal of Economic Perspectives* 21, no. 3 (Summer 2007): 177–98, http://doi.org/10.1257/jep.21.3.177.

96. Katie Lobosco, "Walmart Fired 2,200 to Fix the Plumbing," CNN, April 17, 2015, https://money.cnn.com/2015/04/16/news/companies/walmart-closing-plumbing/index.html; Hiroko Tabuchi, "Laid-Off Walmart Workers Head to Labor Board," *New York Times*, April 19, 2015, https://www.nytimes.com/2015/04/20/business/laid-off-walmart-workers-head-to-labor-board.html; Laura Rice, "Texas Walmart Stores Close Suddenly for 'Plumbing Problems'?," *Texas Standard*, April 21, 2015, https://www.texasstandard.org/stories/texas-walmart-stores-close-suddenly-for-plumbing-problems/.

97. Rachel Abrams, "Walmart Is Accused of Punishing Workers for Sick Days," *New York Times*, June 1, 2017, https://www.nytimes.com/2017/06/01/business/walmart-workers-sick-days.html.

98. Hiroko Tabuchi, "Next Goal for Walmart Workers: More Hours," *New York Times*, February 25, 2015, https://www.nytimes.com/2015/02/26/business/next-goal-for-walmart-workers-more-hours.html.

99. Mara Leighton, "A TikToker Raised Nearly $170,000 for an Older Walmart Worker So She Could Pay Off Her Mortgage and Retire," Insider, November 9, 2022, https://www .insider.com/tiktoker-gofundme-older-walmart-worker-retirement-2022-11; Andrew Lloyd, "Yet Another Elderly Walmart Employee Has Gone Viral on Tiktok and Raised Thousands of Dollars from Viewers as Part of an Emerging Trend," Insider, December 20, 2022, https://news.yahoo.com/yet-another-elderly-walmart-employee-184415457.html; Andrew Lloyd, "A TikToker Helped Raise over $129,000 for an 82-Year-Old Walmart Worker Who Said She Had to Work to Pay Her Medical Bills," Insider, December 20, 2022, https://www.yahoo.com/entertainment/tiktoker-helped-raise-over-129-173737051 .html.

100. Edna Bonacich with Khaleelah Hardie, "Walmart and the Logistics Revolution," in *Wal-Mart: The Face of Twenty-First-Century Capitalism*, edited by Nelson Lichtenstein, 181 (New York: New Press, 2006).

101. Timothy Egan, "The Corporate Daddy," *New York Times*, June 19, 2014, https://www. nytimes.com/2014/06/20/opinion/timothy-egan-walmart-starbucks-and-the-fight-against -inequality.html.

102. Jason Furman, "Wal-Mart: A Progressive Success Story," Mackinac Center for Public Policy, November 28, 2005, https://www.mackinac.org/archives/2006/walmart.pdf.

103. Lichtenstein, "Walmart: A Template," 23–24.

104. Walmart, "Wal-Mart Announces Sale of German Business," press release, July 28, 2006.

105. US Department of Agriculture, Food and Nutrition Service, "A Short History of SNAP," September 11, 2018, https://www.fns.usda.gov/snap/short-history-snap.

106. Renée Johnson and Jim Monke, "Farm Bill Primer: What Is the Farm Bill?," Library of Congress, Congressional Research Service, February 17, 2023, https://crsreports.congress .gov/product/pdf/IF/IF12047/1.

107. US Department of Agriculture, Food and Nutrition Service, "Supplemental Nutrition Assistance Program Participation and Cost," May 12, 2023.

108. Krissy Clark, "The Secret Life of a Food Stamp Might Become a Little Less Secret," Slate, August 5, 2014, https://slate.com/business/2014/08/how-much-walmart-gets-in-food -stamp-dollars-the-answer-may-be-forthcoming.html.

109. US Department of Agriculture, Office of Inspector General, "Food and Nutrition Service's Financial Statements for Fiscal Years 2016 and 2015," Audit Report 27401-0001-11, November 2016, https://usdaoig.oversight.gov/sites/default/files/reports/2023-07/27401 -0001-11.pdf.

110. Walmart's SNAP market share was 25.5 percent from April 1, 2022, to March 31, 2023, according to Numerator, "SNAP Shopper Scorecard: Which Retailers Win with SNAP Shoppers?," accessed June 9, 2023, https://www.numerator.com/snap/shopper-scorecard. Between October 1, 2020, and September 30, 2021, the government spent $105 billion on SNAP benefits, according to the Center on Budget and Policy Priorities, "Policy Basics: The Supplemental Nutrition Assistance Program (SNAP)," June 9, 2022, https://www .cbpp.org/research/food-assistance/the-supplemental-nutrition-assistance-program-snap.

111. H. Claire Brown, "Which Retailers Profit from Food Stamps? Journalists Have Been Asking for Years—and We May Never Know," The Counter, August 9, 2018, https://the counter.org/argus-leader-usda-snap-retail-lawsuit-farm-bill/.

112. H. Claire Brown, "Supreme Court Sides with Retailers in SNAP Data Case," The Counter, June 24, 2019, https://thecounter.org/supreme-court-snap-usda-data-argus-leader/.

113. "The Supply Side: Nestle Studies SNAP Impact on Product Sales," *Talk Business & Politics*, April 28, 2014, https://talkbusiness.net/2014/04/the-supply-side-nestle-studies-snap -impact-on-product-sales/.

114. Walmart, "Customers Paying with SNAP Can Now Use Pickup at Nearly 3,000 Stores," press release, July 13, 2020, https://corporate.walmart.com/news/2020/07/13/customers -paying-with-snap-can-now-use-pickup-at-nearly-3-000-stores.

115. H. Claire Brown, "Covid-19 Has Increased Online SNAP Purchases Twentyfold—and Amazon, Walmart Have a Lock on Virtually All Those Sales," The Counter, July 9, 2020, https://thecounter.org/amazon-walmart-online-snap-sales-explode-instacart/.

116. Jeffrey Goldberg, "At Wal-Mart a Microcosm of U.S. Inequalities: Jeffrey Goldberg," Bloomberg, December 19, 2011, https://www.bloomberg.com/view/articles/2011-12-20 /at-wal-mart-a-microcosm-of-u-s-inequalities-jeffrey-goldberg#xj4y7vzkg.

117. Mead, "Alice's Wonderland."

118. Paul Gatling, "Philanthropist Alice Walton Discusses Her Interest in Healthcare Reform," *Talk Business & Politics*, November 9, 2021, https://talkbusiness.net/2021/11 /philanthropist-alice-walton-discusses-her-interest-in-healthcare-reform/.

119. Kim Souza, "Walmart Shareholders Approve Directors, Discuss Worker Safety amid Rising Gun Violence," *Talk Business & Politics*, May 31, 2023, https://talkbusiness.net/2023/05 /walmart-shareholders-approve-directors-discuss-worker-safety-amid-rising-gun-violence/.

120. Jan Hoffman, "Walmart Agrees to Pay $3.1 Billion to Settle Opioid Lawsuits," *New York Times*, November 15, 2022, https://www.nytimes.com/2022/11/15/health/walmart -opioids-settlement.html.

121. Heartland Forward, "About," accessed June 9, 2023, https://heartlandforward.org/about/.

122. Heartland Forward, "Heartland Summit," accessed June 9, 2023, https://heartlandforward .org/heartland-summit/.

123. Paul Gatling, "Walton-Backed Heartland Summit Convenes before 'Powerful Room' in Bentonville," *Talk Business & Politics*, May 11, 2022, https://talkbusiness.net/2022/05 /walton-backed-heartland-summit-convenes-before-powerful-room-in-bentonville/.

124. Motoko Rich, "A Walmart Fortune, Spreading Charter Schools," *New York Times*, April 25, 2014, https://www.nytimes.com/2014/04/26/us/a-walmart-fortune-spreading-charter -schools.html.

125. Lauren Hirsch, "Walmart Joins Companies Suspending Donations to Lawmakers Who Voted against Certifying the Election," *New York Times*, January 12, 2021, https://www .nytimes.com/2021/01/12/business/walmart-political-donations-Republicans.html; Frank E. Lockwood, "Walmart Pauses Giving to Electoral-Vote Deniers," *Arkansas Democrat Gazette*, January 13, 2021, https://www.arkansasonline.com/news/2021/jan/13/walmart -pauses-giving-to-electoral-vote-deniers/.

126. "Fortune 500 Companies Have Given Millions to Election Deniers Since Jan. 6: Walmart," ProPublica, November 1, 2022.

127. Mitchell, *Big-Box Swindle*, 40.

128. Ronak Patel, "Walton, Dillard, Stephens Discuss Third Generation Arkansas at LR Rotary," *Talk Business & Politics*, February 21, 2023, https://talkbusiness.net/2023/02 /walton-dillard-stephens-discuss-third-generation-arkansas-at-lr-rotary/.

129. Walton and Huey, *Sam Walton*, 199.

130. Fitzpatrick and Davis, "Most Popular Grocery Stores in the U.S."

131. Mitchell, "Walmart's Monopolization of Local Grocery Markets."

132. Robert LaValva, "Public Markets, Antitrust, & Food Systems," in *Reforming America's Food Retail Markets*, Yale University conference compendium edited by Austin Frerick, 226–41, June 2022, https://law.yale.edu/sites/default/files/area/center/isp/documents/grocery -compendium_may2023.pdf.

133. Benjamin Lorr, *The Secret Life of Groceries: The Dark Miracle of the American Supermarket* (New York: Avery, 2021), 136–37.

134. Bethany E. Moreton, "It Came from Bentonville: The Agrarian Origins of Wal-Mart Culture," in *Wal-Mart: The Face of Twenty-First-Century Capitalism*, edited by Nelson Lichtenstein, 68 (New York: New Press, 2006).

135. Leah Nylen and Brendan Case, "Small Retailers Finally Get a Fighting Chance Thanks to a Roosevelt-Era Antitrust Law," Bloomberg, January 17, 2023, https://www.bloomberg.com /news/articles/2023-01-17/roosevelt-era-law-gets-revival-as-ftc-targets-consumer-behe moths-on-pricing#xj4y7vzkg.

136. Josh Sisco, "Pepsi, Coke Soda Pricing Targeted in New Federal Probe," *Politico*, January 9, 2023, https://www.politico.com/news/2023/01/09/pepsi-coke-soda-federal-probe-0007 7126.

137. Christopher R. Leslie, "Predatory Pricing and Recoupment," *Columbia Law Review* 113, no. 7 (November 2013): 1695–1771, https://papers.ssrn.com/sol3/papers.cfm?abstract _id=2363725; Del Rey, *Winner Sells All*, 37.

138. Brooke Group Ltd. v. Brown & Williamson Tobacco Corp., 509 U.S. 209 (1993); Kenneth L. Glazer, "Predatory Pricing and Beyond: Life after Brooke Group," *Antitrust Law Journal* 62, no. 3 (Spring 1994): 605–33, https://www.jstor.org/stable/40843253; Mitchell, *Big-Box Swindle*, 179–80.

139. David W. Boyd, "From 'Mom and Pop' to Wal-Mart: The Impact of the Consumer Goods Pricing Act of 1975 on the Retail Sector in the United States," *Journal of Economic Issues* 31, no. 1 (March 1997): 223–32, https://www.jstor.org/stable/4227158.

140. Lichtenstein, *Retail Revolution*, 25–26.

141. Kim Souza, "The Supply Side: Walmart's Supplier Contract Changes Force Hard Decisions," *Talk Business & Politics*, June 1, 2016, https://talkbusiness.net/2016/06/the-supply -side-walmarts-supplier-contract-changes-force-hard-decisions/.

142. Souza, "Supply Side: Walmart's Supplier Contract Changes Force Hard Decisions"; Boyd Evert, "The Squeeze Continues for Retail Suppliers," *Talk Business & Politics*, October 1, 2017, https://talkbusiness.net/2017/10/the-squeeze-continues-for-retail-suppliers/.

143. Jennifer Smith and Sarah Nassauer, "Walmart Toughens Delivery Demands for Suppliers," *Wall Street Journal*, March 6, 2019, https://www.wsj.com/articles/walmart-toughens -delivery-demands-for-suppliers-11551914501; Kim Souza, "Walmart Demands All Suppliers Comply with 98% On-Time In-Full Shipment Rule," *Talk Business & Politics*, September 3, 2020, https://talkbusiness.net/2020/09/walmart-demands-all-suppliers -comply-with-98-on-time-in-full-shipment-rule/; "Prepared Testimony and Statement for the Record of David Smith, President & CEO, Associated Wholesale Grocers, on Behalf of the National Grocers Association, Hearing on 'Beefing up Competition: Examining America's Food Supply Chain' before the Senate Judiciary Committee, July 28, 2021," https://www.judiciary.senate.gov/imo/media/doc/Smith%20-%20Testimony.pdf.

144. National Grocers Association, "NGA Member Testifies to Congress on Grocery Market Consolidation," *Supermarket News*, January 25, 2022, https://www.supermarketnews.com /issues-trends/nga-member-testifies-congress-grocery-market-consolidation.

145. City Wire Staff, "The Supply Side: Suppliers near Wal-Mart 30% Rule to See More Pressure," *Talk Business & Politics*, April 20, 2015, https://talkbusiness.net/2015/04/the -supply-side-suppliers-near-wal-mart-30-rule-to-see-more-pressure/.

146. Lichtenstein, *Retail Revolution*, 52.

147. Mitchell, *Big-Box Swindle*, 20.

148. Petrovic and Hamilton, "Making Global Markets," 131.

149. Mitchell, *Big-Box Swindle*, 138.

150. Stacy Mitchell, "Is Your Stuff Falling Apart? Thank Walmart," Grist, November 11, 2011, https://grist.org/business-technology/2011-11-11-is-your-stuff-falling-apart-thank-walmart/.

151. Stacy Mitchell, "Walmart's New Green Product Label Is the Most Misleading Yet," Grist, March 5, 2015, https://grist.org/business-technology/walmarts-new-green-product-label -is-the-most-misleading-yet/.

152. Sabrina Tavernise (host), "Why 'Made in China' Is Becoming 'Made in Mexico,'" *The Daily* (podcast), *New York Times*, February 21, 2023, https://www.nytimes.com/2023/02/21 /podcasts/the-daily/us-mexico-trade-china.html.

153. Hiroko Tabuchi, "Walmart's Imports from China Displaced 400,000 Jobs, a Study Says," *New York Times*, December 9, 2015, https://www.nytimes.com/2015/12/09/business /economy/walmart-china-imports-job-losses.html.

154. Charles Fishman, *The Wal-Mart Effect: How the World's Most Powerful Company Really Works—and How It's Transforming the American Economy* (New York: Penguin, 2006), 183.

155. Steven Greenhouse, "Documents Indicate Walmart Blocked Safety Push in Bangladesh," *New York Times*, December 5, 2012, https://www.nytimes.com/2012/12/06/world/asia/3 -walmart-suppliers-made-goods-in-bangladeshi-factory-where-112-died-in-fire.html.

156. Steven Greenhouse, "As Firms Line Up on Factories, Wal-Mart Plans Solo Effort," *New York Times*, May 14, 2013, https://www.nytimes.com/2013/05/15/business/six-retailers -join-bangladesh-factory-pact.html.

157. Elizabeth Paton, "International Brands Sign a New Accord to Protect Garment Workers in Bangladesh," *New York Times*, August 25, 2021, https://www.nytimes.com/2021/08/25 /business/garment-worker-safety-accord.html.

158. Claire Kelloway and Matthew Jinoo Buck, "Kickbacks and Corporate Concentration: How Exclusionary Discounts Limit Market Access for Community-Based Food Businesses," in *Reforming America's Food Retail Markets*, Yale University conference compendium edited by Austin Frerick, 90–104, June 2022, https://law.yale.edu/sites/default/files /area/center/isp/documents/grocery-compendium_may2023.pdf.

159. Emily Sundberg, "Welcome to the Shoppy Shop: Why Does Every Store Suddenly Look the Same?," *Grub Street*, January 25, 2023, https://www.grubstreet.com/2023/01/why -every-shoppy-shop-looks-exactly-the-same.html.

160. Charles Courtemanche and Art Carden, "Supersizing Supercenters? The Impact of Walmart Supercenters on Body Mass Index and Obesity," *Journal of Urban Economics* 69, no. 2 (March 2011): 165–81, https://doi.org/10.1016/j.jue.2010.09.005.

161. "Walmart: Retail Resurrection," *Financial Times*, November 14, 2019, https://www.ft.com /content/9a90d04c-48a6-4abf-85f0-fcb8a8aa1e00.

162. Alistair Gray and Dave Lee, "Walmart vs Amazon: The Battle to Dominate Grocery," *Financial Times*, May 10, 2021, https://www.ft.com/content/9ab41b9e-a294-430f-951d -49cfc3415460.

163. Melissa Repko, "As Retail Gets Choppy, Walmart Flexes Its Grocery Muscle, Deep Pockets and Huge Reach," CNBC, April 4, 2023, https://www.cnbc.com/2023/04/04/walmart -grocery-core-strengths.html.

164. Alistair Gray, "Walmart Plays Catch-up in Amazon Ecommerce Battle," *Financial Times*, November 18, 2019, https://www.ft.com/content/b4134d6e-08ab-11ea-bb52-34c8d9 dc6d84.

165. Kim Souza, "Report: Walmart Focuses on Millennials, Multichannel While Facing a 'Perfect Storm,'" *Talk Business & Politics*, March 10, 2016, https://talkbusiness.net/2016/03 /report-walmart-focuses-on-millennials-multichannel-while-facing-a-perfect-storm/.

166. Russell Redman, "Walmart Sees Stores as Linchpin of Last-Mile Strategy," *Supermarket News*, March 2, 2022, https://www.supermarketnews.com/online-retail/walmart-sees-stores

-linchpin-last-mile-strategy; Walmart, "InHome Delivery Basics," accessed May 16, 2023, https://inhome.walmart.com/fyi/inhome-delivery-basics.

167. Walmart, "A New Era of Fulfillment: Introducing Walmart's Next Generation Fulfillment Centers," press release, June 3, 2022, https://corporate.walmart.com/news/2022/06/03/a -new-era-of-fulfillment-introducing-walmarts-next-generation-fulfillment-centers; Russell Redman, "Walmart to Automate All Regional Distribution Centers," *Supermarket News,* May 23, 2022, https://www.supermarketnews.com/retail-financial/walmart-automate-all -regional-distribution-centers.

168. Suman Bhattacharyya, "Walmart Bets on Digital Retail Future, CFO Says," CFO Dive, March 9, 2023, https://www.cfodive.com/news/walmart-bets-digital-retail-future-cfo-says /644651/.

169. Sarah Nassauer, "Walmart Pushes New Delivery Services for a Post-pandemic World," *Wall Street Journal,* February 27, 2022, https://www.wsj.com/articles/walmart-pushes-new- delivery-services-for-a-post-pandemic-world-11645971260.

170. Sarah Nassauer, "Welcome to Walmart. The Robot Will Grab Your Groceries," *Wall Street Journal,* January 8, 2020, https://www.wsj.com/articles/welcome-to-walmart-the-robot -will-grab-your-groceries-11578499200.

171. "Big-Box Retailers: Winner Takes All," *Financial Times,* November 24, 2020.

172. "Grocery Shoppers Take the Omnichannel Route," *Supermarket News,* September 9, 2022, https://www.supermarketnews.com/consumer-trends/grocery-shoppers-take-omnichannel -route.

173. US Securities and Exchange Commission, "Form 10-K: Walmart Inc."

174. Walmart, "Walmart Media Group Expands Sponsored Search Offering through Walmart Advertising Partners Program," press release, January 3, 2020, https://corporate.walmart .com/news/2020/01/03/walmart-media-group-expands-sponsored-search-offering-through -walmart-advertising-partners-program; Walmart, "Walmart Announces Expanded Vision and New Name for Its Media Business," press release, January 28, 2021, https://corporate .walmart.com/news/2021/01/28/walmart-announces-expanded-vision-and-new-name-for -its-media-business.

175. Alexandra Bruell, "Walmart Revamps Ad-Sales Business to Expand Its Reach," *Wall Street Journal,* January 28, 2021, https://www.wsj.com/articles/walmart-revamps-ad-sales -business-to-expand-its-reach-11611838810.

176. Walmart, "Walmart Media Group Expands Sponsored Search Offering"; Sahil Patel and Alexandra Bruell, "Walmart Buys Ad Tech to Chase Small-Business Advertisers," *Wall Street Journal,* February 4, 2021, https://www.wsj.com/articles/walmart-buys-ad-tech-to -chase-small-business-advertisers-11612438200.

177. Peter Adams, "Walmart Ramps Up Connected TV Ambitions," Grocery Dive, March 21, 2023, https://www.grocerydive.com/news/walmart-innovid-retail-media-networks-CTV -ads/645583/.

178. "Walmart to Open Milk Processing Plant in Indiana," *Supermarket News,* March 18, 2016, https://www.supermarketnews.com/dairy/walmart-open-milk-processing-plant-indiana; Walmart, "Walmart Selects Indiana for New Milk Processing Plant, 200+ Hoosier Jobs," press release, March 18, 2016; "Walmart to Bring Milk Processing In-House with Indiana Plant," *Talk Business & Politics,* March 21, 2016, https://talkbusiness.net/2016/03/wal mart-to-bring-milk-processing-in-house-with-indiana-plant/.

179. Walmart, "Walmart and Plenty Partner to Lead the Future of Fresh Produce," press release, January 25, 2022, https://corporate.walmart.com/news/2022/01/25/walmart-and-plenty -partner-to-lead-the-future-of-fresh-produce.

180. Walmart, "Walmart to Create Angus Beef Supply Chain," press release, April 24, 2019,

https://corporate.walmart.com/news/2019/04/24/walmart-to-create-angus-beef-supply
-chain.

181. Matthew Boyle and Lydia Mulvany, "Walmart Creates an Angus Beef Supply Chain,
     Bypassing Tyson," Bloomberg, April 24, 2019, https://www.bloomberg.com/news/articles
     /2019-04-24/walmart-creates-its-own-angus-beef-supply-chain-bypassing-tyson#xj4y7vzkg.

182. Nathaniel Meyersohn, "Why Walmart Wants to Sell Its Own Line of Steaks," CNN Busi-
     ness, June 15, 2019, https://www.cnn.com/2019/06/15/business/walmart-angus-beef
     -steaks-meat/index.html.

183. Matthew Boyle, "Checkup for $30, Teeth Cleaning $25: Walmart Gets into Health Care,"
     Bloomberg, February 25, 2020, https://www.bloomberg.com/news/articles/2020-02-25
     /walmart-takes-on-cvs-amazon-with-low-price-health-care-clinics#xj4y7vzkg.

184. Charley Grant, "Amazon and Walmart Have an Rx for Healthcare. The Cure Won't Be
     Easy," *Wall Street Journal*, May 28, 2021, https://www.wsj.com/articles/amazon-and
     -walmart-have-an-rx-for-healthcare-the-cure-wont-be-easy-11622194240.

185. Russell Redman, "Walmart Health Center Makes Debut in Georgia," *Supermarket News*,
     September 16, 2019, https://www.supermarketnews.com/health-wellness/walmart-health
     -center-makes-debut-georgia; Walmart, "Walmart Health Expands to Florida with Five
     New Health Centers," press release, April 5, 2022, https://corporate.walmart.com/news
     /2022/04/05/walmart-health-expands-to-florida-with-five-new-health-centers; Walmart
     Health, "Behavioral Health," accessed June 29, 2023, https://www.walmarthealth.com
     /schedule/behavioralhealth.

186. "Walmart to Open 4,000 Healthcare 'Supercenters' by 2029 That Include 'Comprehen-
     sive' Clinical Laboratory Services," Dark Daily, May 3, 2021, https://www.darkdaily.com
     /2021/05/03/walmart-to-open-4000-healthcare-supercenters-by-2029-that-include
     -comprehensive-clinical-laboratory-services/.

187. Walmart, "Our Goal of Becoming America's Neighborhood Health Destination: Introduc-
     ing the Walmart Health Center," press release, September 13, 2019, https://corporate
     .walmart.com/news/2019/09/13/our-goal-of-becoming-americas-neighborhood-health
     -destination-introducing-the-walmart-health-center.

188. Melissa Repko, "Walmart Quietly Registers Insurance Business in Its Latest Move into
     Health Care," CNBC, July 8, 2020, https://www.cnbc.com/2020/07/08/walmart-quietly
     -registers-insurance-business-in-its-latest-move-into-health-care.html; Sarah Nassauer
     and Rolfe Winkler, "Walmart Deal Shows Expansion in Telehealth, New Front with Ama-
     zon," *Wall Street Journal*, May 6, 2021, https://www.wsj.com/articles/walmart-deal-shows
     -expansion-in-telehealth-new-front-with-amazon-11620340379.

189. Alarice Rajagopal, "Why Walmart Has Added Pet Services," *Supermarket News*, September
     22, 2023, https://www.supermarketnews.com/center-store/why-walmart-has-added-pet
     -services.

190. Barney Jopson and Tom Braithwaite, "Amex and Walmart Challenge Retail Banks," *Finan-
     cial Times*, October 8, 2012, https://www.ft.com/content/ebd6d6e0-1154-11e2-8d5f-001
     44feabdc0; Vivianne Rodrigues and Barney Jopson, "Insurance Green Light for Amex-
     Walmart Card," *Financial Times*, March 26, 2013, https://www.ft.com/content/47b5cfe4
     -958e-11e2-a4fa-00144feabdc0.

191. Sarah Nassauer, "Walmart-Backed Fintech Startup Is Acquiring Two Firms and a New
     Name," *Wall Street Journal*, January 26, 2022, https://www.wsj.com/articles/walmart
     -backed-fintech-startup-is-acquiring-two-firms-and-a-new-name-11643199601.

192. Michael Corkery, "F.T.C. Accuses Walmart of Facilitating Consumer Fraud through Its
     Money Transfer Business." *New York Times*, June 28, 2022, https://www.nytimes.com/2022
     /06/28/business/ftc-walmart-money-transfer-fraud.html.

193. National Retail Federation, "Top 100 Retailers 2022 List," accessed June 10, 2023, https://nrf.com/resources/top-retailers/top-100-retailers/top-100-retailers-2022-list.

194. Dave Lee, "Walmart Turns to Robot-Staffed Warehouses to Handle Online Orders," *Financial Times*, January 27, 2021, https://www.ft.com/content/1b1b11c8-200c-4f7c-a431-6460f90bb95d.

195. "Development of Amazon Fresh Stores on 'Pause.' Will Possible Staten Island Location Ever Open?," SI Live, April 5, 2023, https://www.silive.com/business/2023/04/development-of-amazon-fresh-stores-on-pause-will-possible-staten-island-location-ever-open.html; Peyton Bigora, "Amazon Fresh Reportedly Exiting Twin Cities Stores as It Reworks Strategy," Grocery Dive, May 10, 2023, https://www.grocerydive.com/news/amazon-fresh-twin-cities-grocery-stores/649909/.

196. Matt Day, "Amazon Quietly Began Building a Grocery Chain during Pandemic," Bloomberg, March 11, 2021, https://www.bloomberg.com/news/articles/2021-03-11/amazon-quietly-began-building-a-grocery-chain-during-pandemic#xj4y7vzkg.

197. Kim Souza, "Walmart Hires New Chief Antitrust Counsel," *Talk Business & Politics*, March 4, 2019, https://talkbusiness.net/2019/03/walmart-hires-new-chief-antitrust-counsel/.

198. James V. Grimaldi, "A 'Grass Roots' Campaign to Take Down Amazon Is Funded by Amazon's Biggest Rivals," *Wall Street Journal*, September 20, 2019, https://www.wsj.com/articles/a-grassroots-campaign-to-take-down-amazon-is-funded-by-amazons-biggest-rivals-11568989838.

199. Stephen Foley, "Wal-Mart President Tells UK to Investigate the Power of Tesco," *Independent*, August 29, 2005, https://www.independent.co.uk/news/business/news/walmart-president-tells-uk-to-investigate-the-power-of-tesco-504692.html; Kellie Ell, "Former Walmart US CEO Says Congress Should Consider Splitting Up Amazon," CNBC, April 2, 2018, https://www.cnbc.com/2018/03/29/former-walmart-us-ceo-congress-consider-splitting-up-amazon.html.

Conclusion

1. Gracy Olmstead, "Seeding Control to Big Ag," *American Conservative*, February 27, 2019, https://www.theamericanconservative.com/seeding-control-to-big-ag/; Open Markets Institute, "Baby Formula," accessed July 1, 2020, http://concentrationcrisis.openmarketsinstitute.org/industry/baby-formula/.

2. Caroline Daniel, "Château Cargill Throws Open Its Halls," *Financial Times*, February 26, 2004; Tarso Veloso Ribeiro, "Cargill's Annual Revenue Surges 23% to Record $165 Billion," Bloomberg, August 10, 2022, https://www.bloomberg.com/news/articles/2022-08-10/cargill-posts-record-revenue-of-165-billion-for-fiscal-2022#xj4y7vzkg.

3. Marion Nestle, "Today's 'Eat More' Environment: The Role of the Food Industry," in *A Place at the Table: The Crisis of 49 Million Hungry Americans and How to Solve It*, edited by Peter Pringle, 95 (New York: PublicAffairs, 2013).

4. Zachary J. Ward et al., "Projected U.S. State-Level Prevalence of Adult Obesity and Severe Obesity," *New England Journal of Medicine* 381, no. 25 (December 19, 2019): 2440–50, https://doi.org/10.1056/nejmsa1909301.

5. Wisconsin Farmers Union, "2022 Policy," January 29, 2022.

6. Monica Watrous, "Lactalis to Acquire Siggi's," *Food Business News*, January 5, 2018.

7. Melvin Backman, "General Mills Buys Annie's for $820 million," CNN Business, September 8, 2014, https://money.cnn.com/2014/09/08/news/companies/general-mills-annies/index.html.

8. Julie Guthman, *Weighing In: Obesity, Food Justice, and the Limits of Capitalism* (Oakland: University of California Press, 2011), 139.

9. Iowa Department of Education, "2017–18 Iowa Public School K–12 Students Eligible for Free and Reduced-Price Lunch by District," February 12, 2018, https://educateiowa.gov /documents/district-frl/2021/05/2017-18-iowa-public-school-k-12-students-eligible-free -and-reduced; Betsy Freese, "Pork Powerhouses 2019: Expansion Continues," *Successful Farming*, October 1, 2019, https://www.agriculture.com/livestock/pork-powerhouses/pork -powerhouses-2019-expansion-continues; Christopher Ingraham, "Why Many 'Essential' Workers Get Paid So Little, according to Experts," *Washington Post*, April 6, 2020, https:// www.washingtonpost.com/business/2020/04/06/why-do-so-many-essential-workers-get -paid-so-little-heres-what-economists-have-say/.

10. David Dayen, "Attacking Monopoly Power Can Be Stunningly Good Politics, Survey Finds," The Intercept, November 28, 2018, https://theintercept.com/2018/11/28 /monopoly-power-corporate-concentration/.

Index

About the Author

Austin Frerick is an expert on agricultural and antitrust policy and a Fellow at Yale University. He previously
worked at the Open Markets Institute, the US Department of the Treasury, and the Congressional Research
Service. He is a seventh-generation
Iowan and first-generation college
graduate. He received degrees from
Grinnell College and the University
of Wisconsin–Madison. This is his
first book.